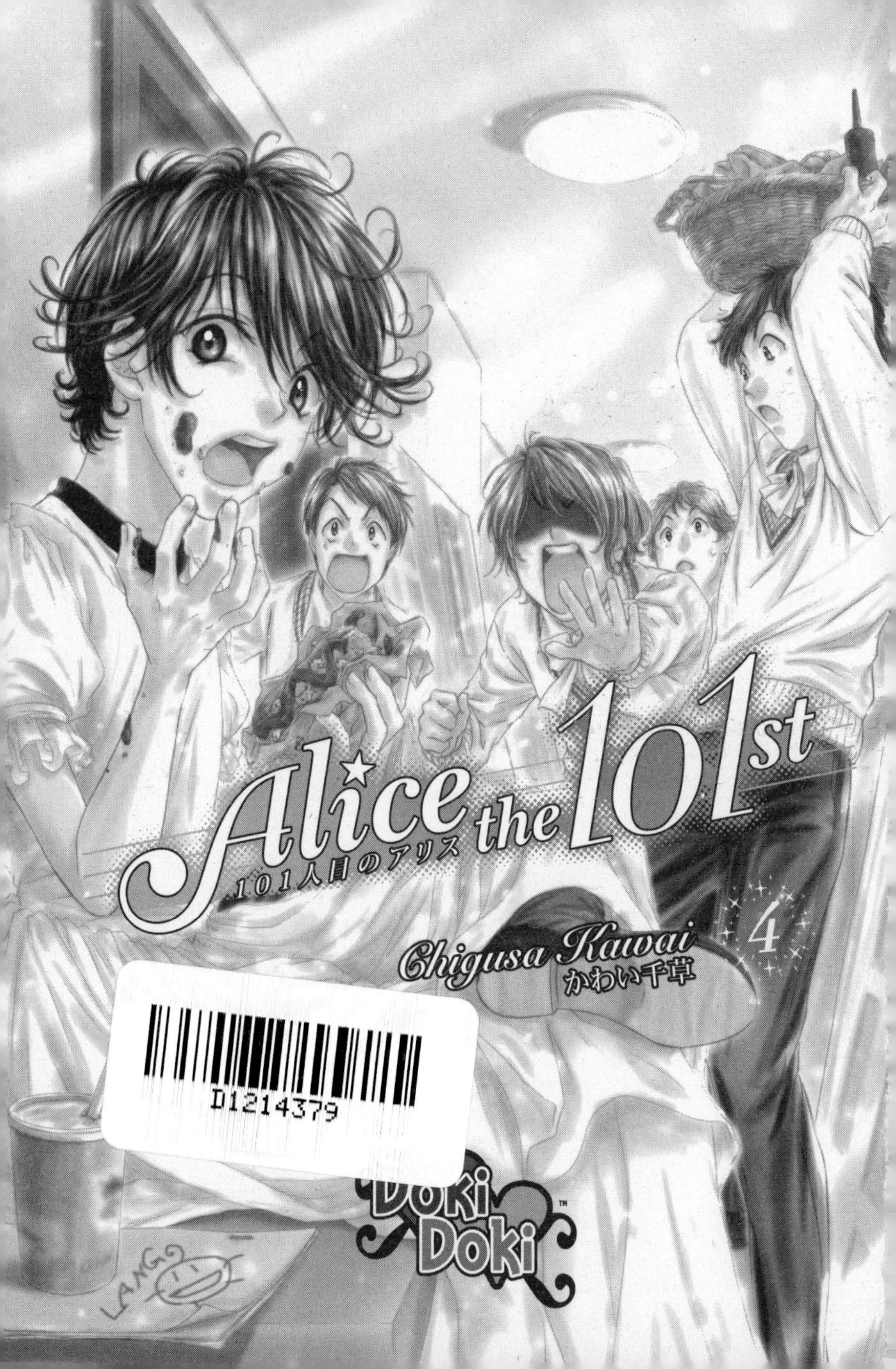
Alice the 101st
101人目のアリス
4
Chigusa Kawai
かわい千草
Doki Doki™
LANG

Alice the 101st

101人目のアリス

Chigusa Kawai
かわい千草

4

Contents

Translation	Ben Sabin
Lettering	April Brown
Graphic Design	Stephanie Han
Editing	Stephanie Donnelly
Editor in Chief	Fred Lui
Publisher	Hikaru Sasahara

English Edition Published by
DIGITAL MANGA PUBLISHING
A division of DIGITAL MANGA, Inc.
1487 W 178th Street, Suite 300
Gardena, CA 90248

www.dmpbooks.com

First Edition: June 2014
ISBN-10: 1-56970-291-8
ISBN-13: 978-1-56970-291-8

1 3 5 7 9 10 8 6 4 2

Printed in Canada

ALICE THE 101ST
101人目のアリス
4
かわい千草
Chigusa Kawai presents

Contents & Story

Alice the 101st

101人目のアリス

4

THE STORY SO FAR

ARISTIDE (AKA ALICE) SUCCESSFULLY ENROLLS IN THE ELITE MONDONVEILLE SCHOOL OF MUSIC AS THE 101ST MEMBER OF HIS CLASS...DESPITE NOT BEING ABLE TO READ MUSICAL NOTATION. ALICE'S INEPTITUDE IS QUICKLY DISCOVERED AND HE BECOMES THE BUTT OF THE CLASS'S JOKES...THAT IS, UNTIL HE BURSTS INTO A RENDITION OF A SONG HIS VIOLINIST FATHER CREATED. SINCE THE INCIDENT, THE STUDENT BODY HAS COME TO REGARD HIM AS SOMEWHAT OF A MYSTERY.

AMIDST IT ALL, VICTOR (VIC)—WHO'S BEEN HANGING AROUND ALICE EVER SINCE HE CAME TO THE ACADEMY—AGREES TO HELP HIM SEARCH FOR HIS FATHER'S VIOLIN, BUT ONLY UNDER THE CONDITION THAT HE BE RIVALS WITH MAXIMILLIEN, THE ACADEMY'S NUMBER-ONE VIOLINIST.

NOW THAT WINTER VACATION IS OVER, PREPARATIONS FOR THE SCHOOL FESTIVAL ARE IN FULL SWING. ALICE'S CLASS DECIDED NOT ONLY TO PERFORM "CINDERELLA," BUT ALSO TO CAST HIM AS THE LEADING LADY!

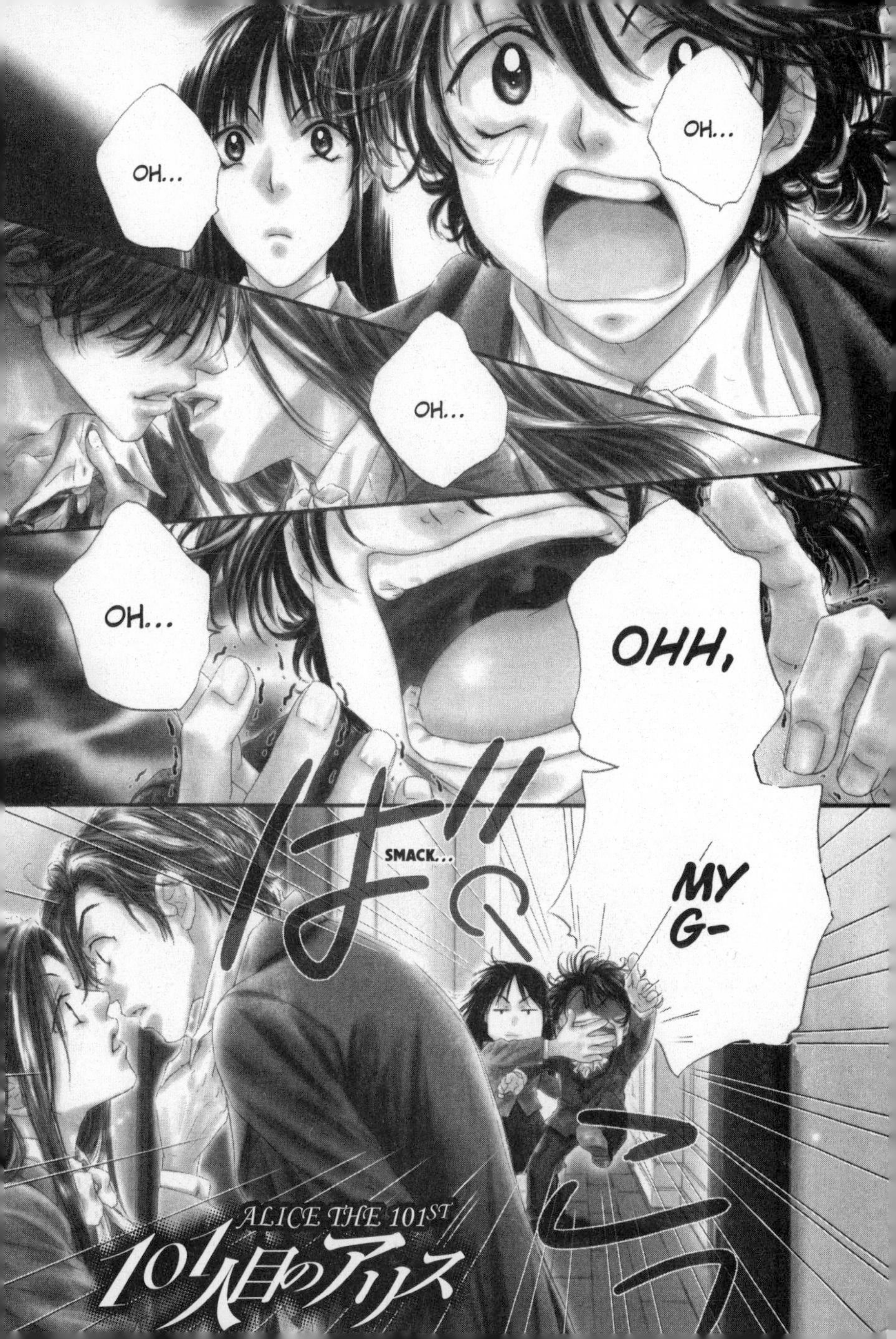

OH...
OH...
OH...
OH...
OHH,
MY G-
SMACK...
ALICE THE 101ST
101人目のアリス

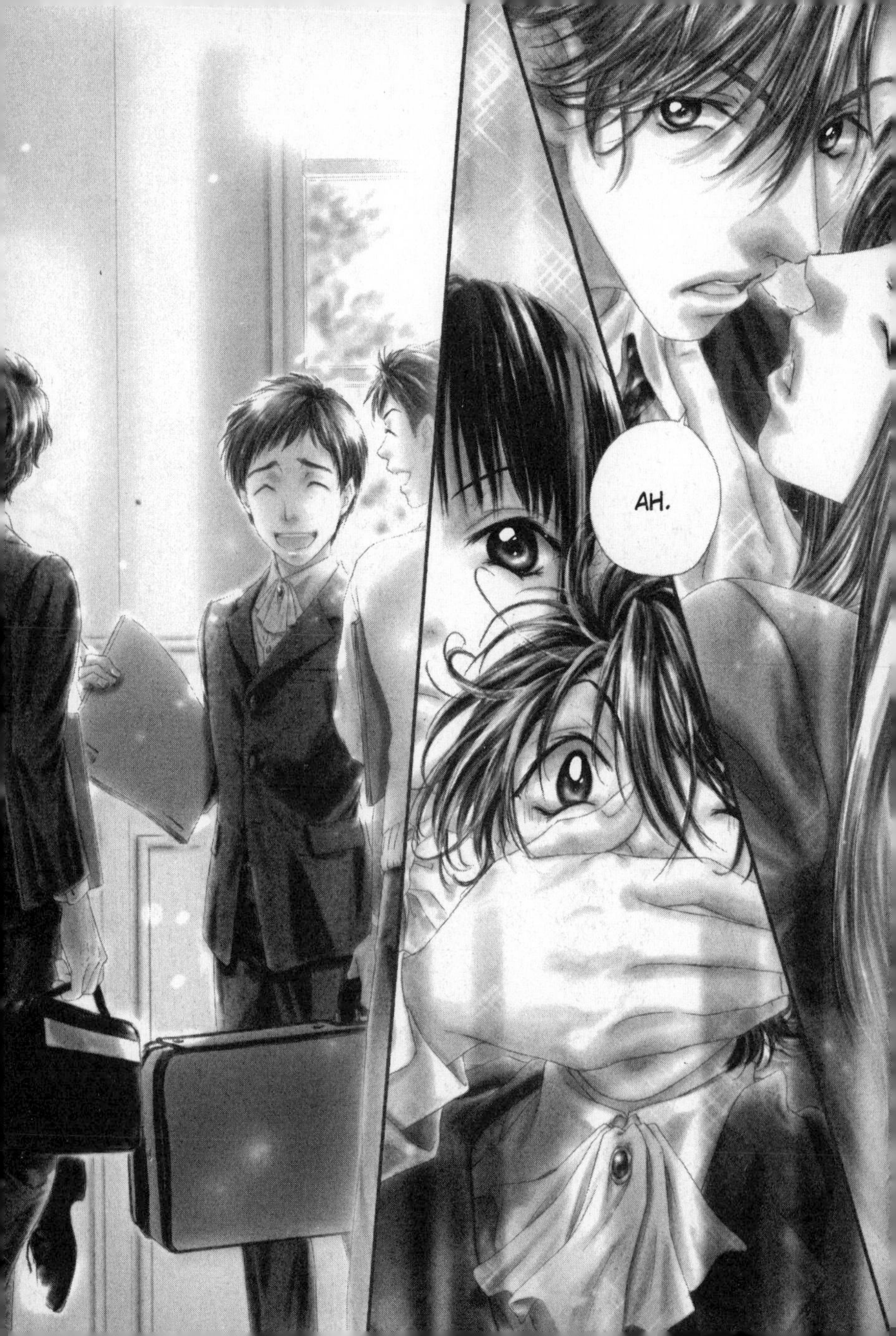
AH.

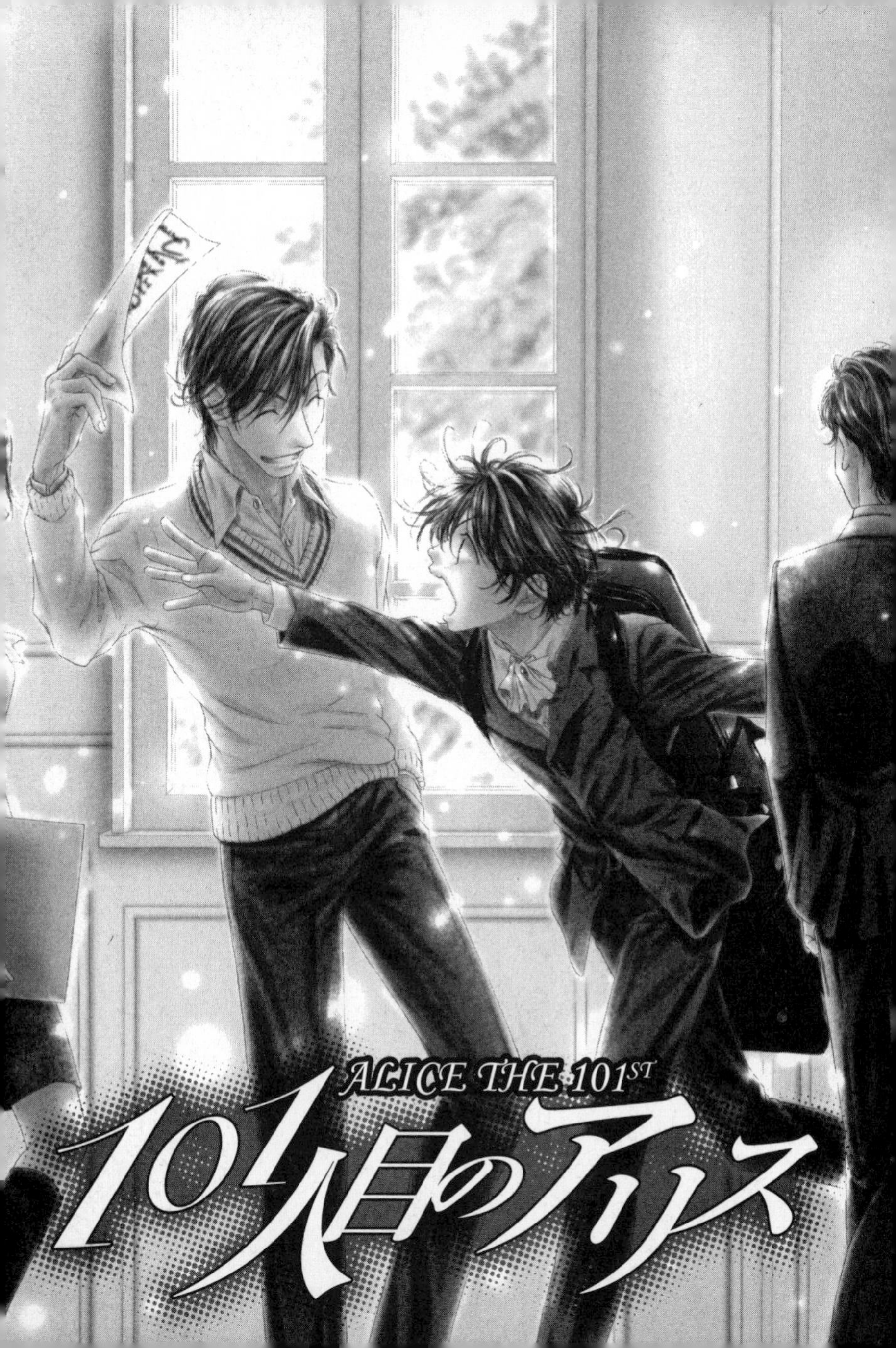
ALICE THE 101ST
101人目のアリス

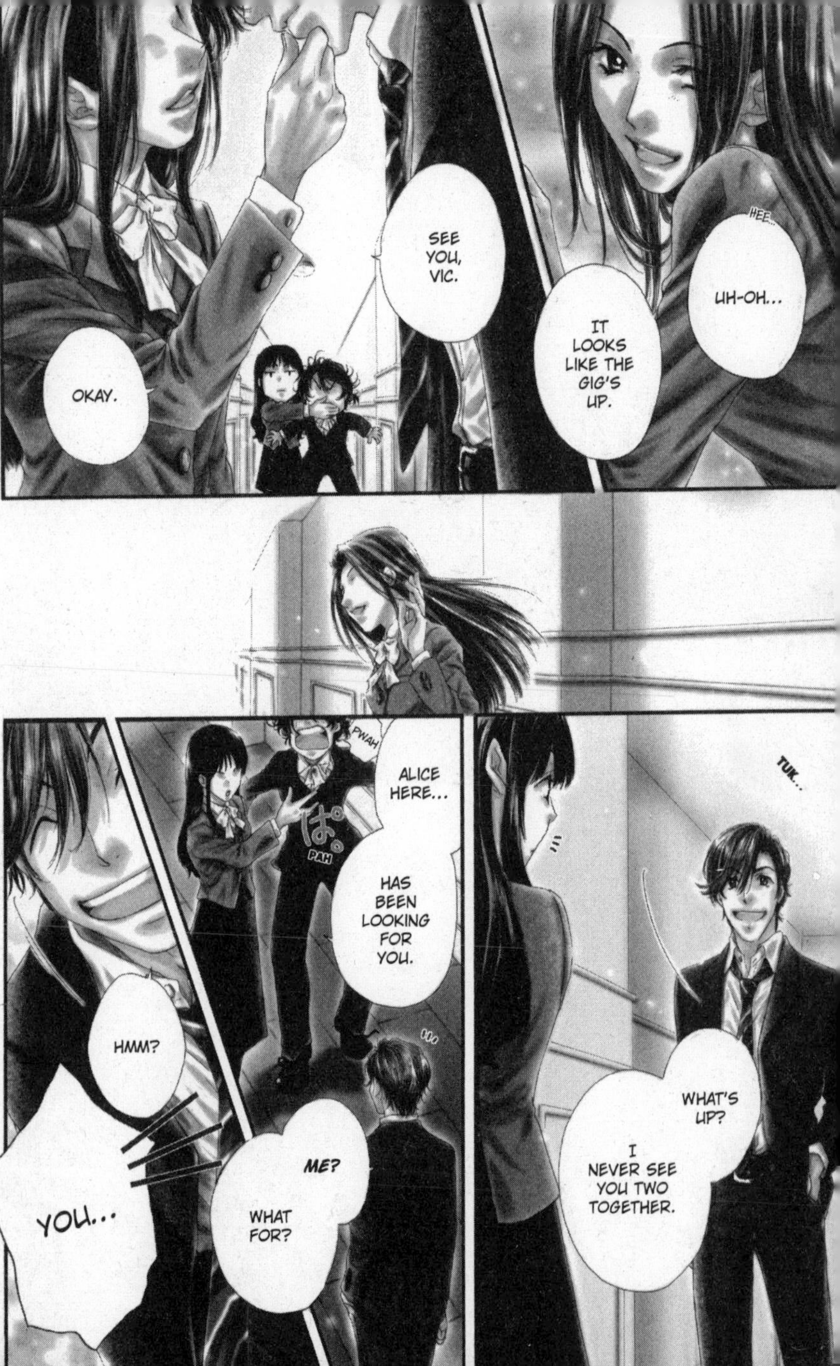
HEE...
UH-OH...
IT LOOKS LIKE THE GIG'S UP.
SEE YOU, VIC.
OKAY.
TUK...
WHAT'S UP?
I NEVER SEE YOU TWO TOGETHER.
PWAH
ALICE HERE...
HAS BEEN LOOKING FOR YOU.
ぱ。
PAH
ME?
WHAT FOR?
HMM?
YOU...

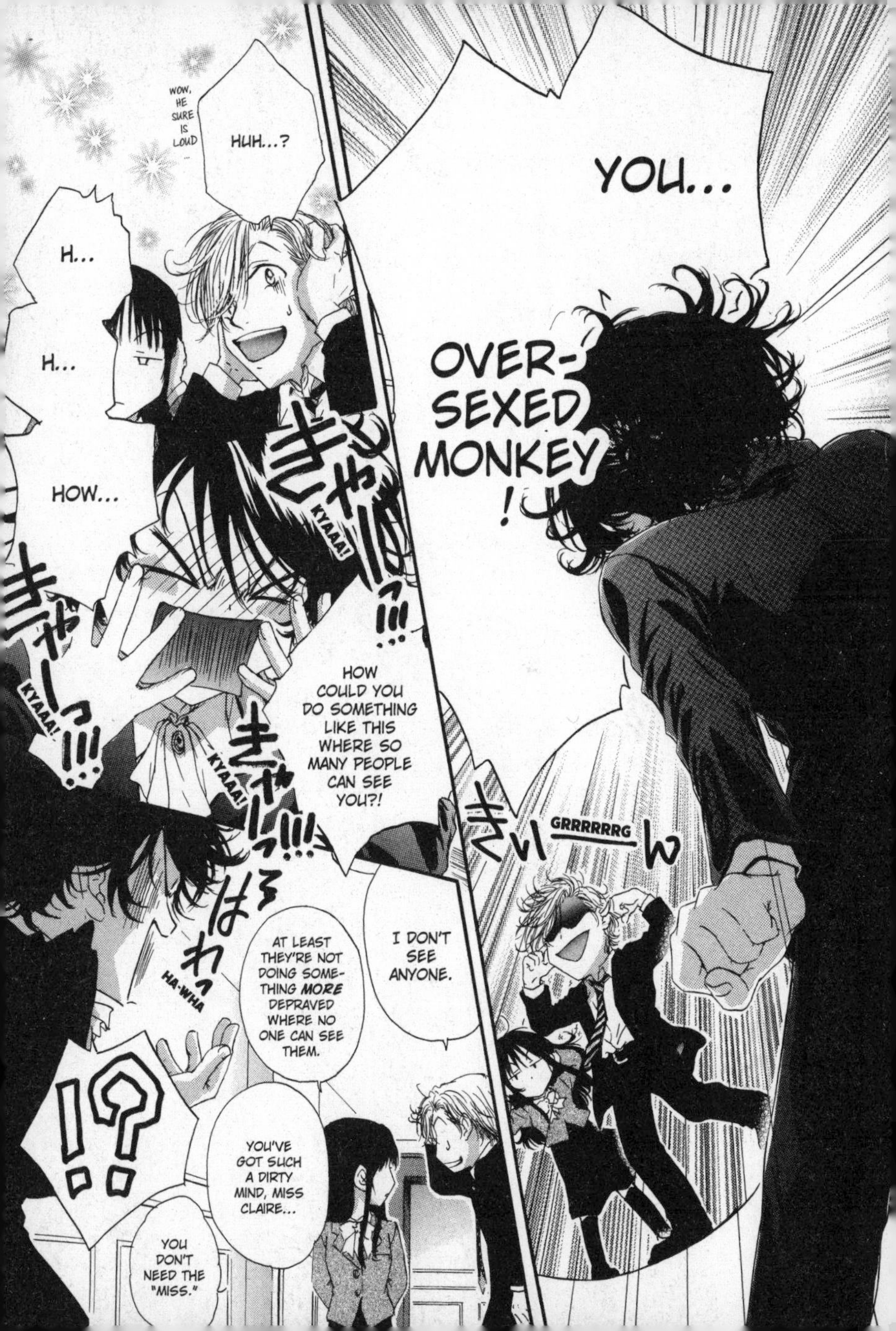
YOU...
OVER-SEXED MONKEY!
きぃーん GRRRRRRG
HUH...?
WOW, HE SURE IS LOUD...
H...
H...
HOW...
HOW COULD YOU DO SOMETHING LIKE THIS WHERE SO MANY PEOPLE CAN SEE YOU?!
きゃーっ!!! KYAAA!
きゃーっ!!! KYAAA!
きゃーっ!!! KYAAA!
I DON'T SEE ANYONE.
AT LEAST THEY'RE NOT DOING SOME-THING MORE DEPRAVED WHERE NO ONE CAN SEE THEM.
はわっ HA-WHA
!?
YOU'VE GOT SUCH A DIRTY MIND, MISS CLAIRE...
YOU DON'T NEED THE "MISS."

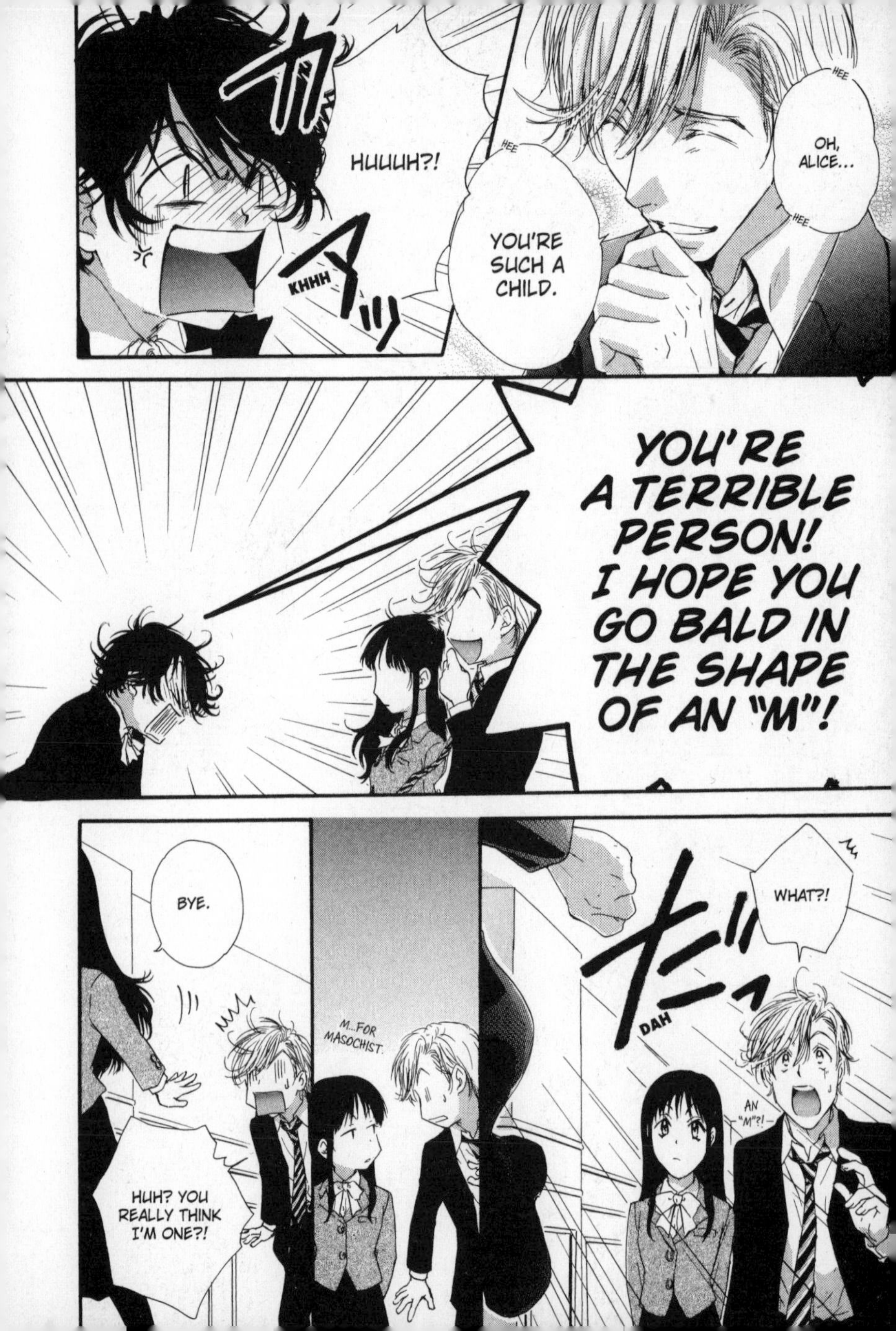
HEE
OH, ALICE...
HEE
HEE
YOU'RE SUCH A CHILD.
HUUUH?!
KHHH
YOU'RE A TERRIBLE PERSON! I HOPE YOU GO BALD IN THE SHAPE OF AN "M"!
WHAT?!
DAH
AN "M"?!
M...FOR MASOCHIST.
BYE.
HUH? YOU REALLY THINK I'M ONE?!

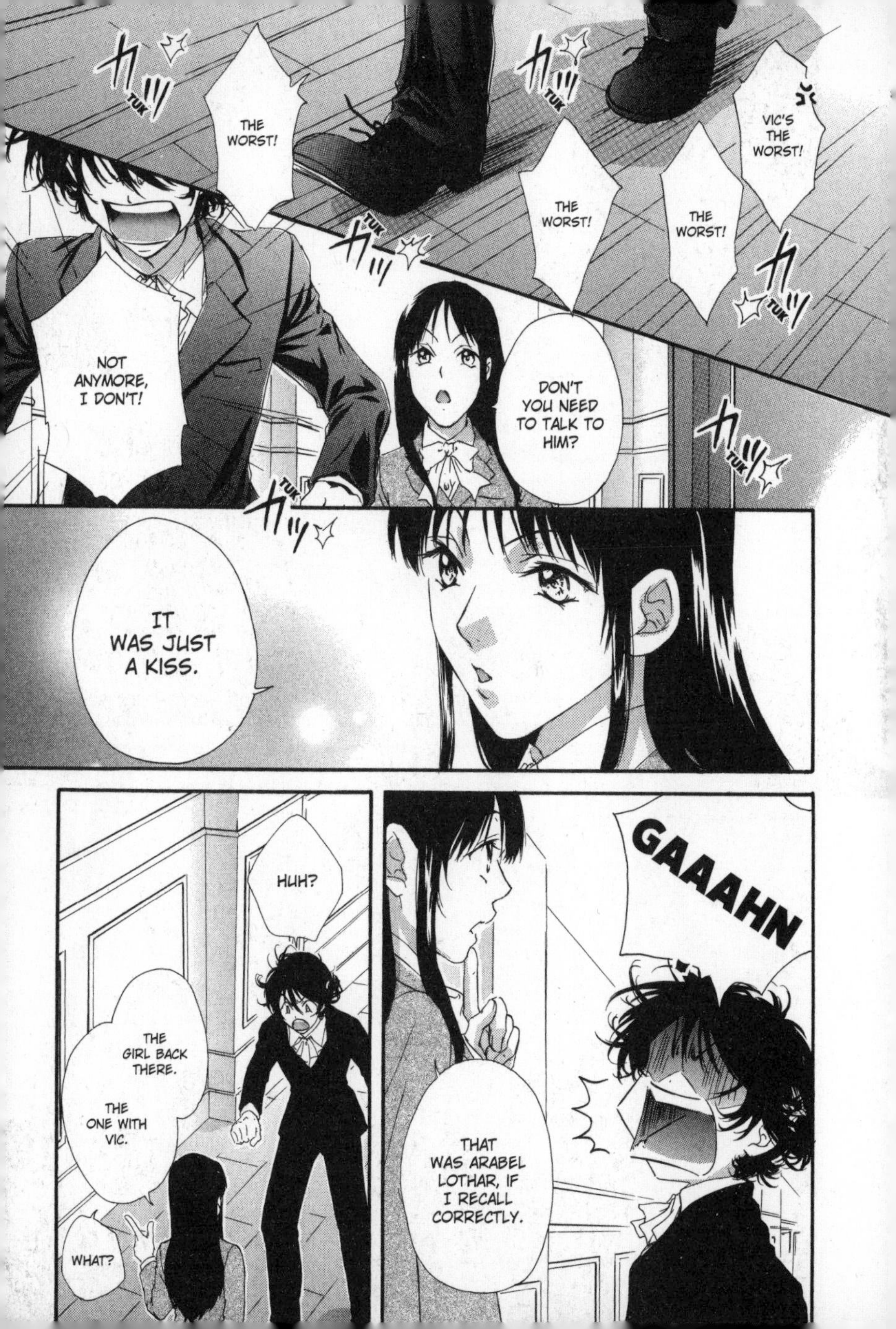
TUK
VIC'S THE WORST!
THE WORST!
TUK
THE WORST!
TUK
THE WORST!
TUK
DON'T YOU NEED TO TALK TO HIM?
NOT ANYMORE, I DON'T!
TUK
TUK
IT WAS JUST A KISS.
GAAAHN
THAT WAS ARABEL LOTHAR, IF I RECALL CORRECTLY.
HUH?
THE GIRL BACK THERE.
THE ONE WITH VIC.
WHAT?

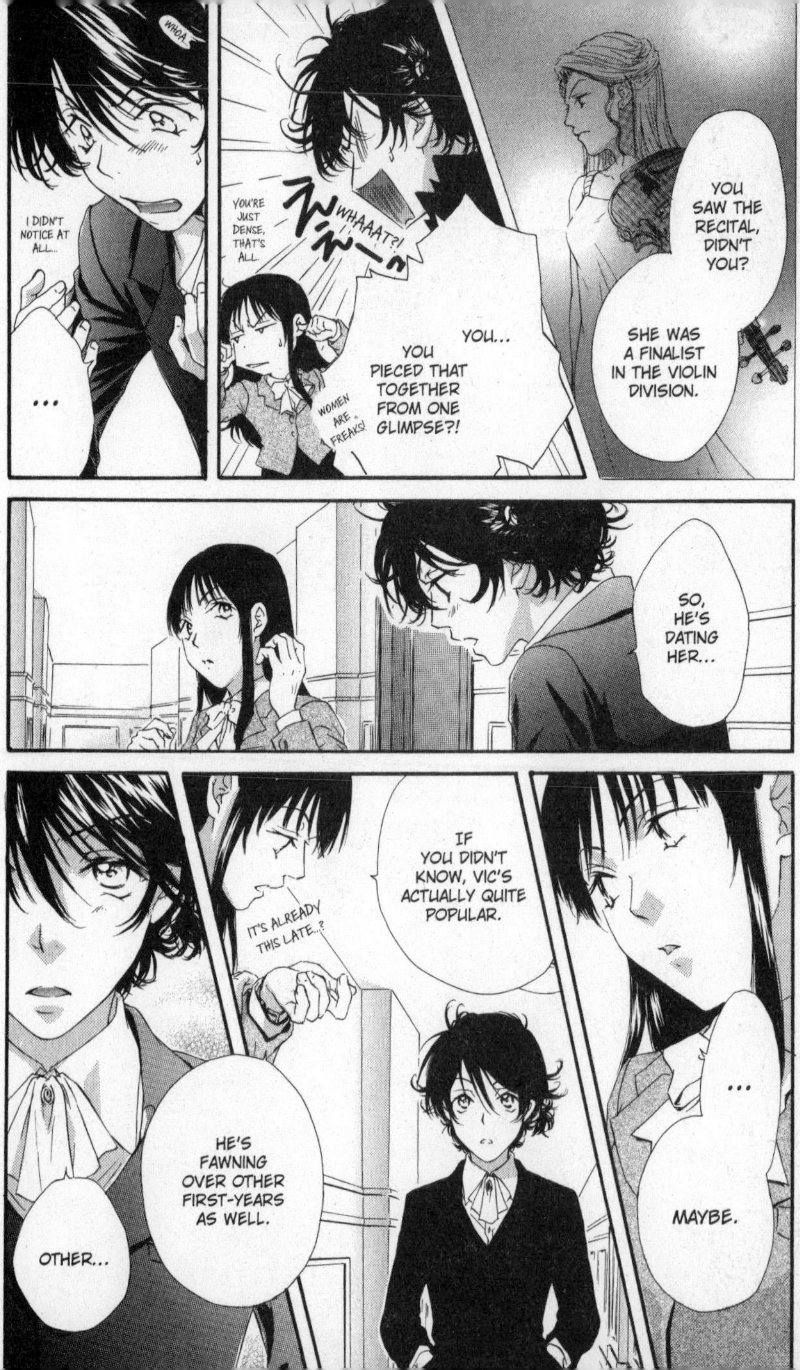
YOU SAW THE RECITAL, DIDN'T YOU?
SHE WAS A FINALIST IN THE VIOLIN DIVISION.
WHAAAT?!
YOU... YOU PIECED THAT TOGETHER FROM ONE GLIMPSE?!
YOU'RE JUST DENSE, THAT'S ALL.
WOMEN ARE FREAKS!
WHOA...
I DIDN'T NOTICE AT ALL...
...
SO, HE'S DATING HER...
...
MAYBE.
IF YOU DIDN'T KNOW, VIC'S ACTUALLY QUITE POPULAR.
IT'S ALREADY THIS LATE...?
HE'S FAWNING OVER OTHER FIRST-YEARS AS WELL.
OTHER...

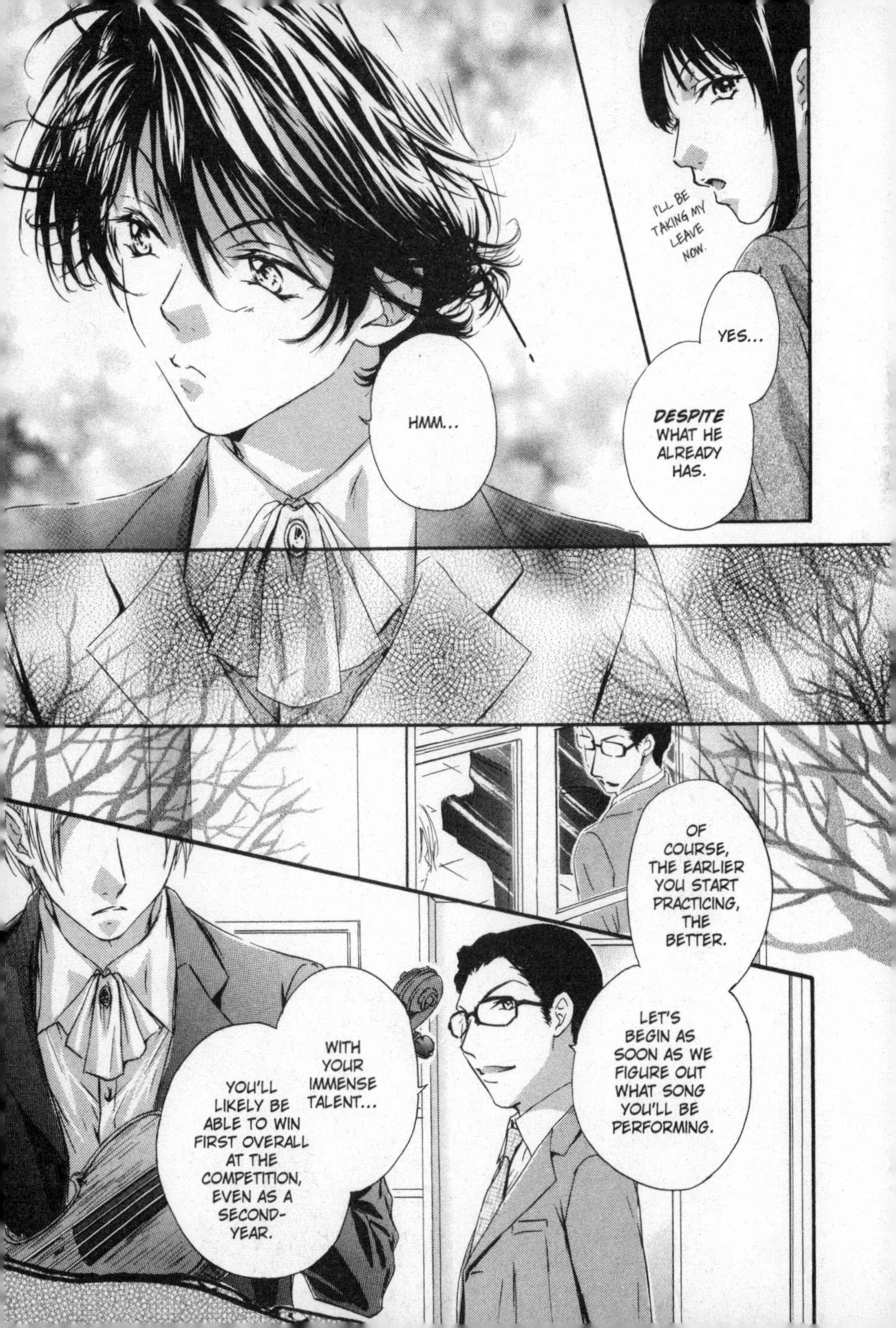
I'LL BE TAKING MY LEAVE NOW.
YES...
DESPITE WHAT HE ALREADY HAS.
HMM...
OF COURSE, THE EARLIER YOU START PRACTICING, THE BETTER.
LET'S BEGIN AS SOON AS WE FIGURE OUT WHAT SONG YOU'LL BE PERFORMING.
WITH YOUR IMMENSE TALENT...
YOU'LL LIKELY BE ABLE TO WIN FIRST OVERALL AT THE COMPETITION, EVEN AS A SECOND-YEAR.

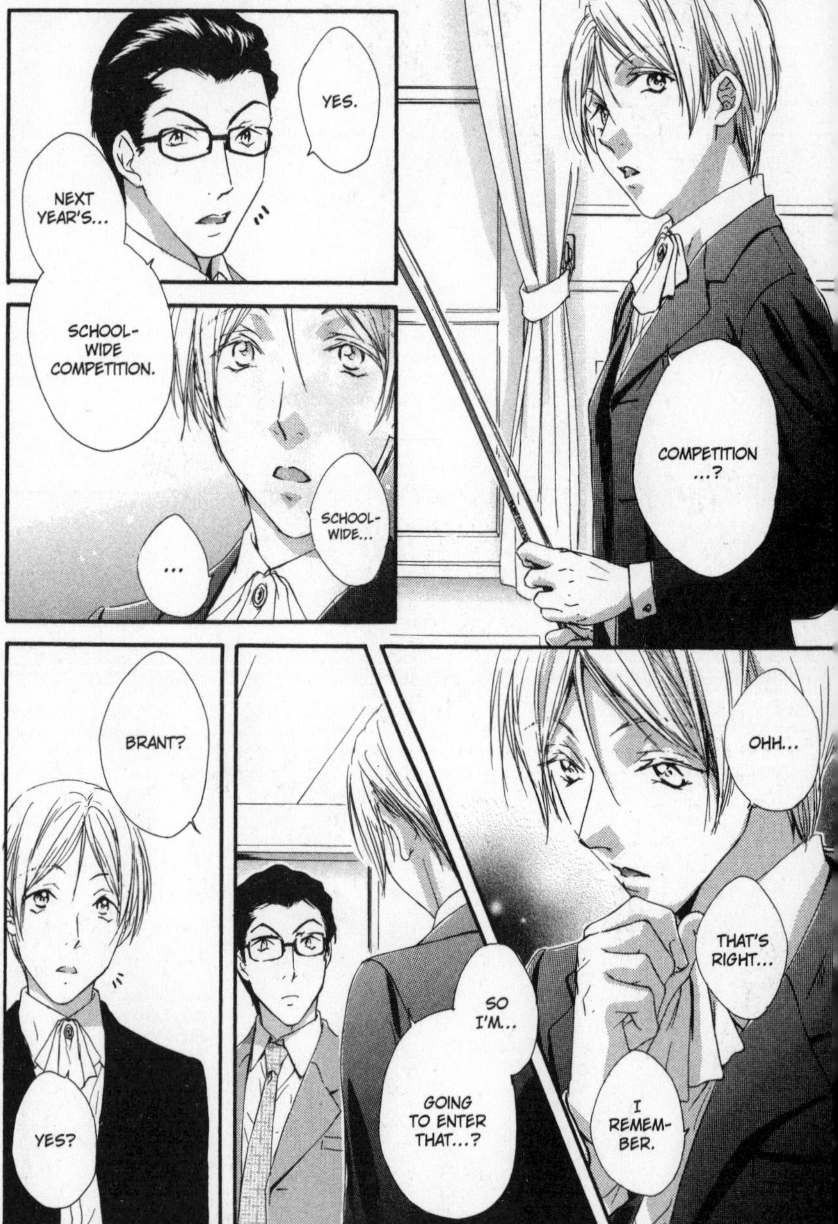
COMPETITION ...?
YES.
NEXT YEAR'S...
SCHOOL-WIDE COMPETITION.
SCHOOL-WIDE...
...
OHH...
THAT'S RIGHT...
I REMEMBER.
SO I'M...
GOING TO ENTER THAT...?
BRANT?
YES?

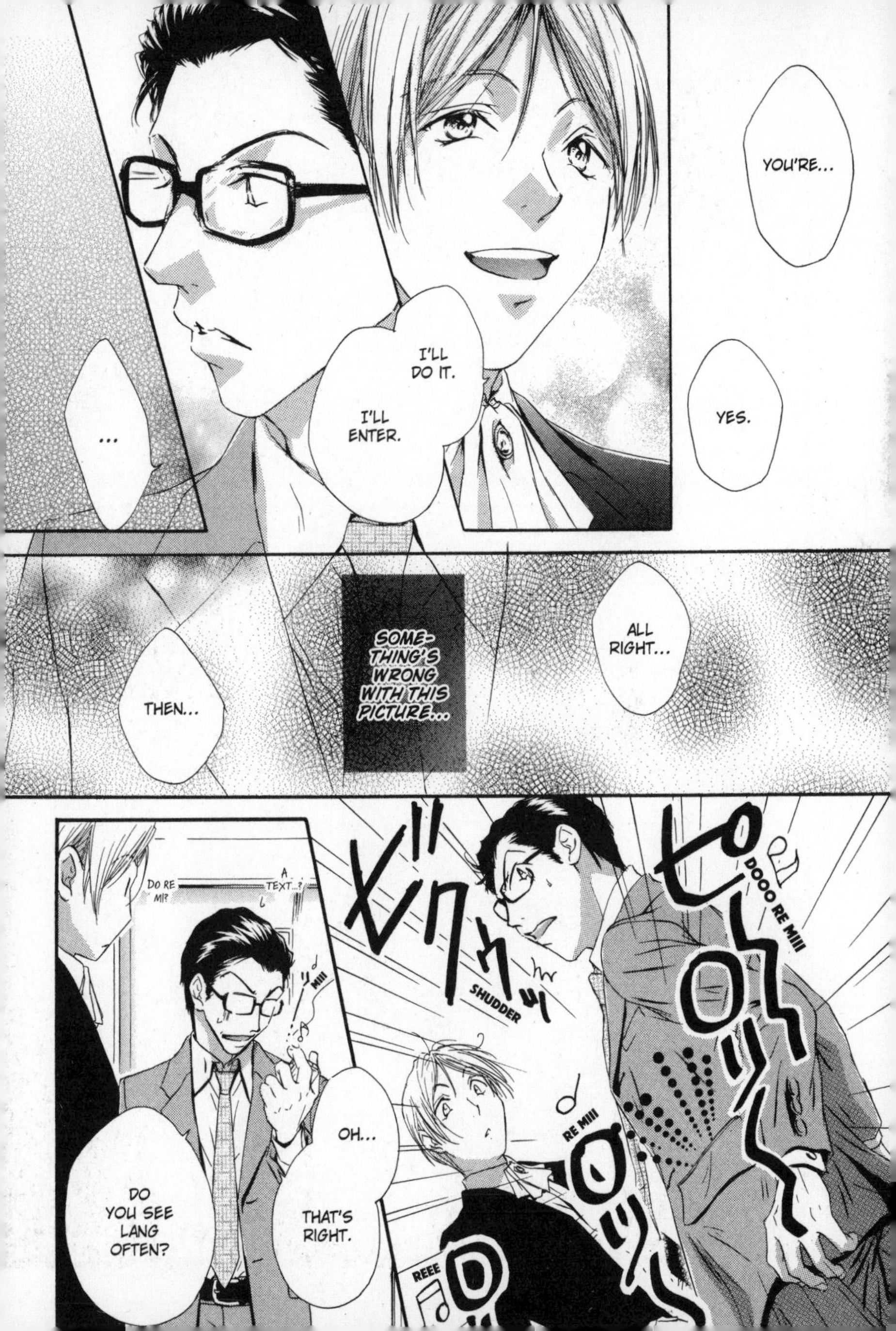

YOU'RE...
YES.
I'LL DO IT.
I'LL ENTER.
...
ALL RIGHT...
SOMETHING'S WRONG WITH THIS PICTURE...
THEN...
DOOOO RE MIII
SHUDDER
RE MIII
REEE
A TEXT...?
DO RE MI?
MIII
OH...
THAT'S RIGHT.
DO YOU SEE LANG OFTEN?

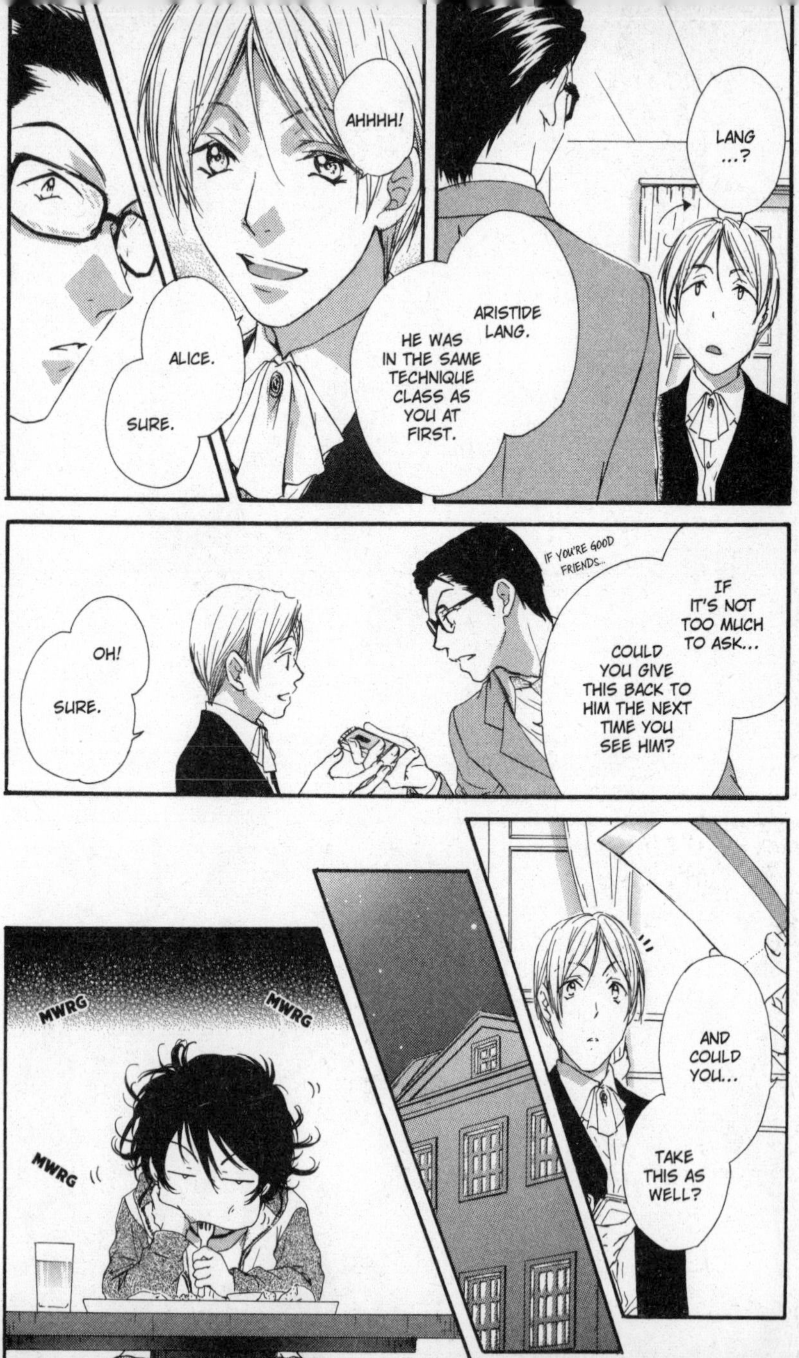
LANG ...?
ARISTIDE LANG.
HE WAS IN THE SAME TECHNIQUE CLASS AS YOU AT FIRST.
AHHHH!
ALICE.
SURE.
IF YOU'RE GOOD FRIENDS...
IF IT'S NOT TOO MUCH TO ASK...
COULD YOU GIVE THIS BACK TO HIM THE NEXT TIME YOU SEE HIM?
OH!
SURE.
AND COULD YOU...
TAKE THIS AS WELL?
MWRG
MWRG
MWRG

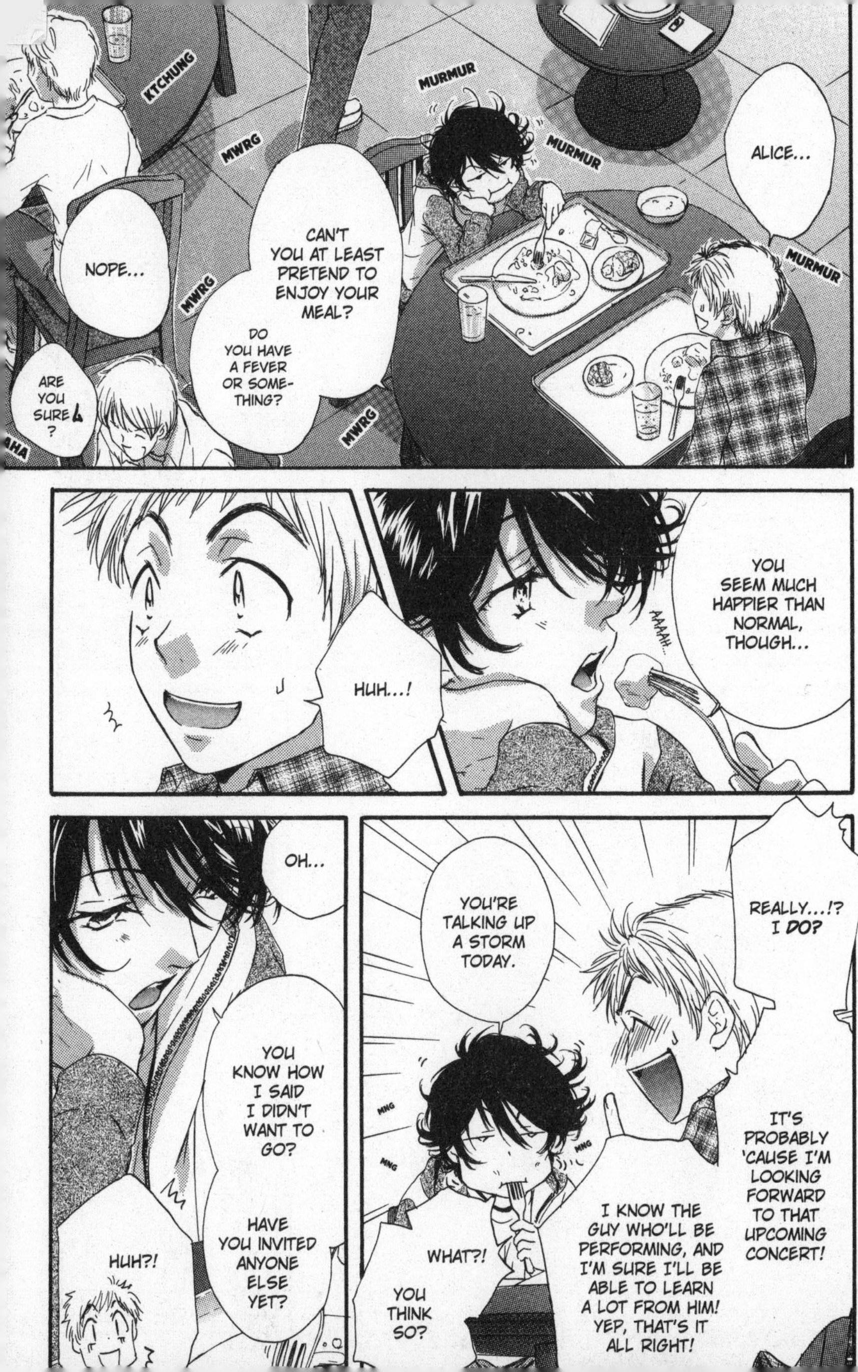
ALICE...
MURMUR
MURMUR
MURMUR
CAN'T YOU AT LEAST PRETEND TO ENJOY YOUR MEAL?
DO YOU HAVE A FEVER OR SOMETHING?
MWRG
MWRG
MWRG
KTCHUNG
NOPE...
ARE YOU SURE ?
HAHA
YOU SEEM MUCH HAPPIER THAN NORMAL, THOUGH...
AAAAAH...
HUH...!
REALLY...!? I DO?
YOU'RE TALKING UP A STORM TODAY.
IT'S PROBABLY 'CAUSE I'M LOOKING FORWARD TO THAT UPCOMING CONCERT!
I KNOW THE GUY WHO'LL BE PERFORMING, AND I'M SURE I'LL BE ABLE TO LEARN A LOT FROM HIM! YEP, THAT'S IT ALL RIGHT!
WHAT?!
YOU THINK SO?
OH...
YOU KNOW HOW I SAID I DIDN'T WANT TO GO?
HAVE YOU INVITED ANYONE ELSE YET?
HUH?!

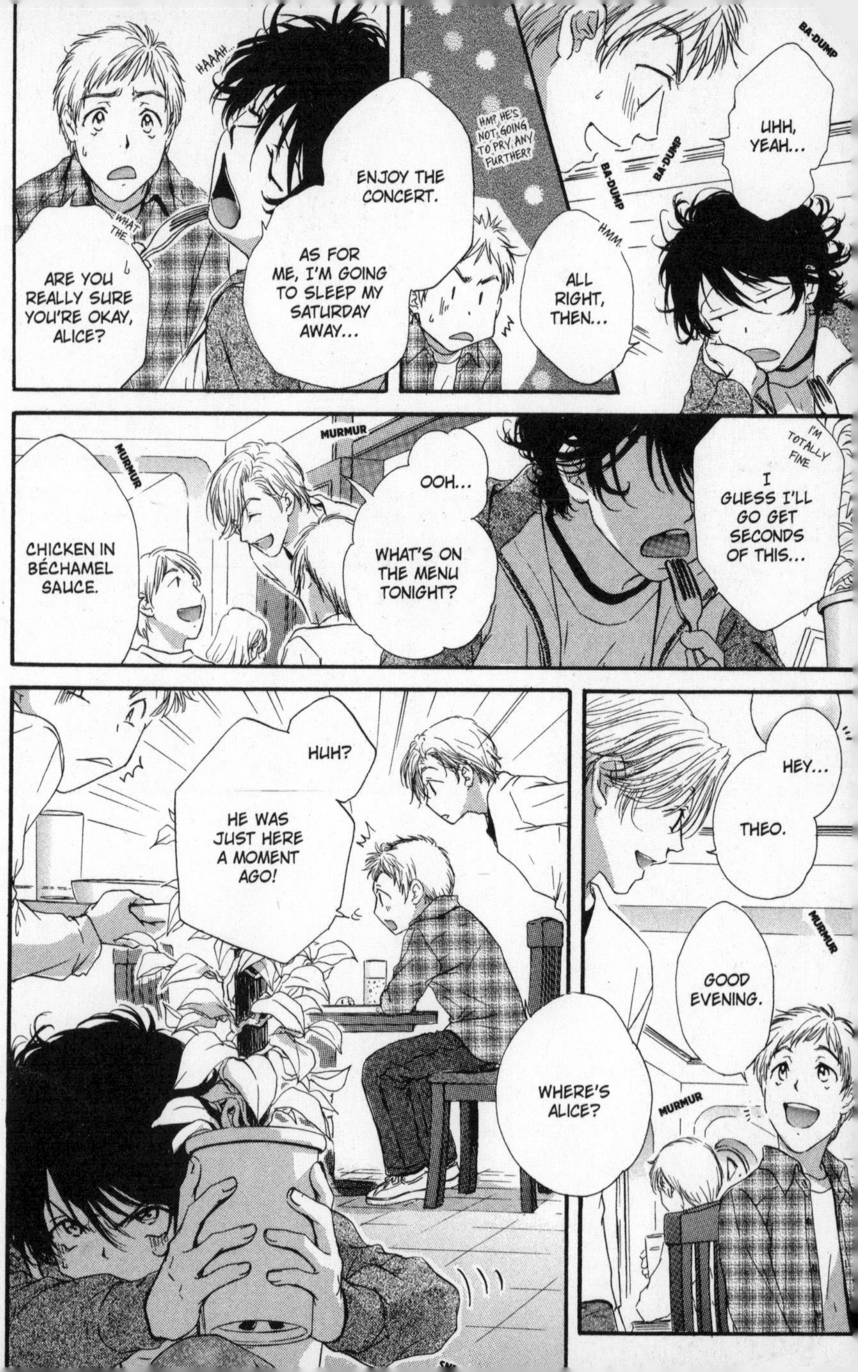
BA-DUMP
UHH, YEAH...
BA-DUMP
BA-DUMP
BA-DUMP
HM? HE'S NOT GOING TO PRY ANY FURTHER?
HMM.
ALL RIGHT, THEN...
HAAAH...
ENJOY THE CONCERT.
AS FOR ME, I'M GOING TO SLEEP MY SATURDAY AWAY...
WHAT THE...
ARE YOU REALLY SURE YOU'RE OKAY, ALICE?
I'M TOTALLY FINE
I GUESS I'LL GO GET SECONDS OF THIS...
OOH...
WHAT'S ON THE MENU TONIGHT?
MURMUR
MURMUR
CHICKEN IN BÉCHAMEL SAUCE.
HEY...
THEO.
MURMUR
GOOD EVENING.
WHERE'S ALICE?
MURMUR
HUH?
HE WAS JUST HERE A MOMENT AGO!

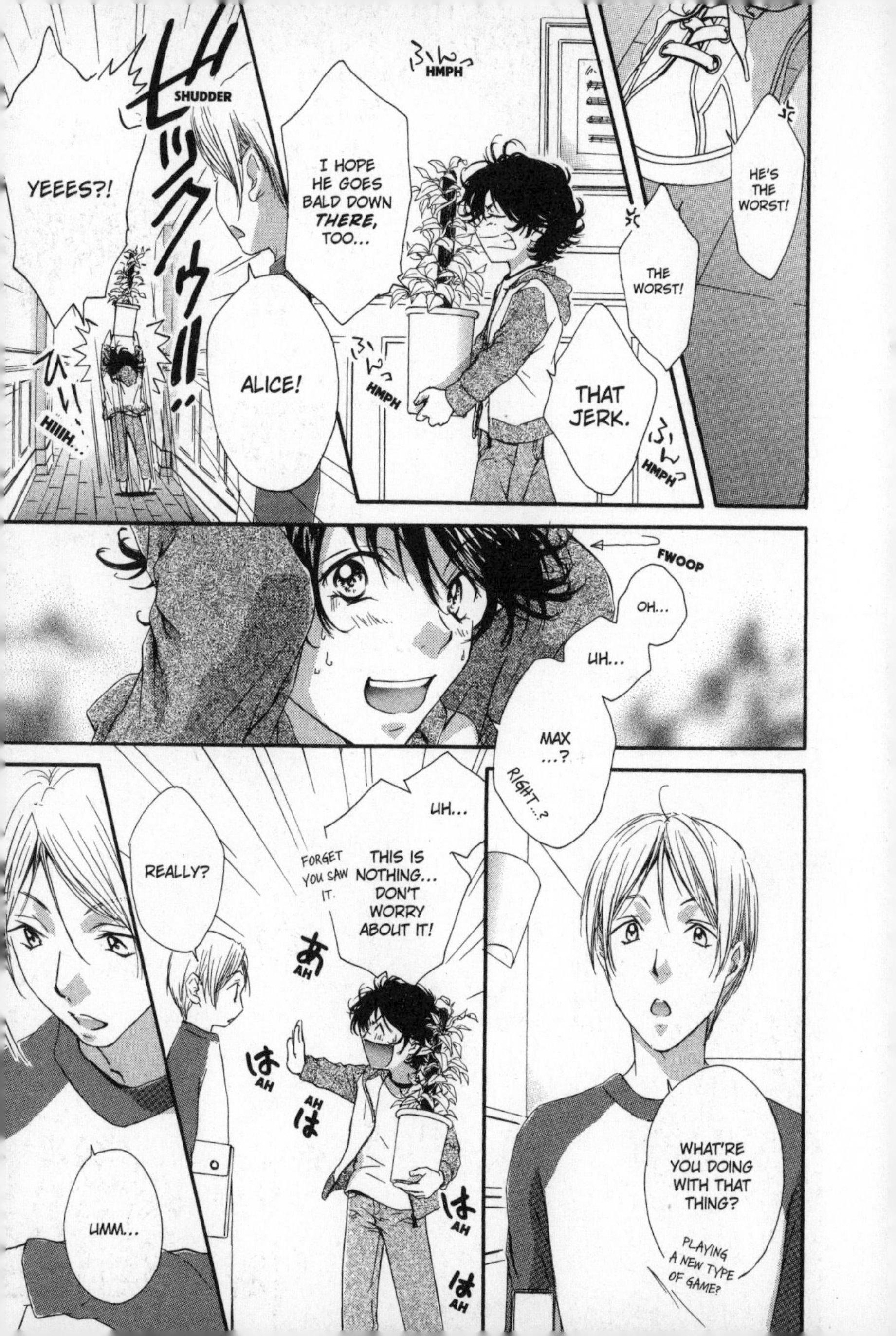
HE'S THE WORST!
THE WORST!
THAT JERK.
ふんっ HMPH
ふんっ HMPH
I HOPE HE GOES BALD DOWN THERE, TOO...
ふんっ HMPH
ALICE!
ビックウゥ!! SHUDDER
YEEES?!
ひぃぃ… HIIIH...
FWOOP
OH...
UH...
MAX ...?
RIGHT...?
WHAT'RE YOU DOING WITH THAT THING?
PLAYING A NEW TYPE OF GAME?
UH...
THIS IS NOTHING... DON'T WORRY ABOUT IT!
FORGET YOU SAW IT.
あ AH
は AH
は AH
は AH
は AH
REALLY?
UMM...

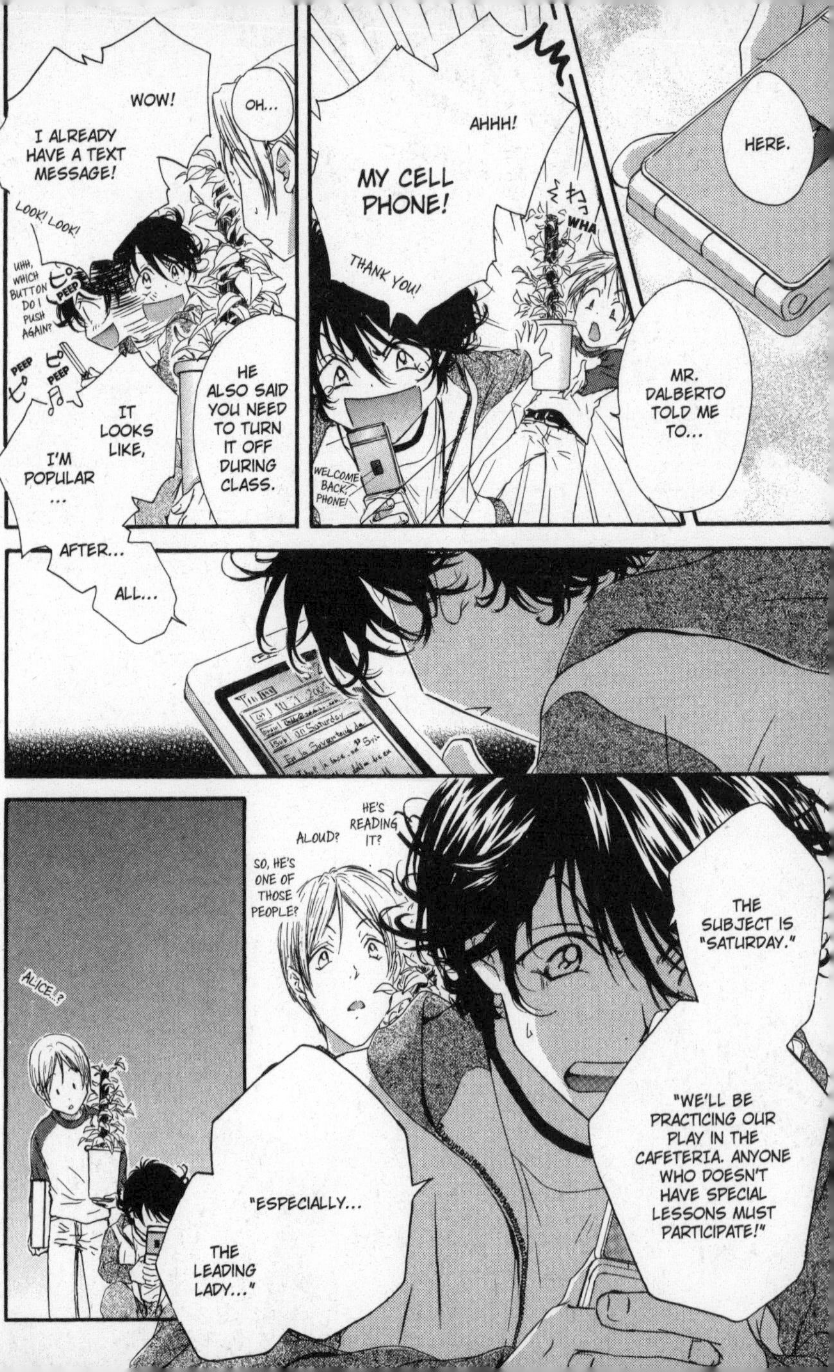
HERE.
MR. DALBERTO TOLD ME TO...
AHHH!
MY CELL PHONE!
WHA
THANK YOU!
WELCOME BACK, PHONE!
OH...
WOW!
I ALREADY HAVE A TEXT MESSAGE!
LOOK! LOOK!
UHH, WHICH BUTTON DO I PUSH AGAIN?
PEEP
PEEP
PEEP
HE ALSO SAID YOU NEED TO TURN IT OFF DURING CLASS.
IT LOOKS LIKE,
I'M POPULAR ...
AFTER...
ALL...
THE SUBJECT IS "SATURDAY."
HE'S READING IT?
ALOUD?
SO, HE'S ONE OF THOSE PEOPLE?
"WE'LL BE PRACTICING OUR PLAY IN THE CAFETERIA. ANYONE WHO DOESN'T HAVE SPECIAL LESSONS MUST PARTICIPATE!"
"ESPECIALLY...
THE LEADING LADY..."
ALICE..?

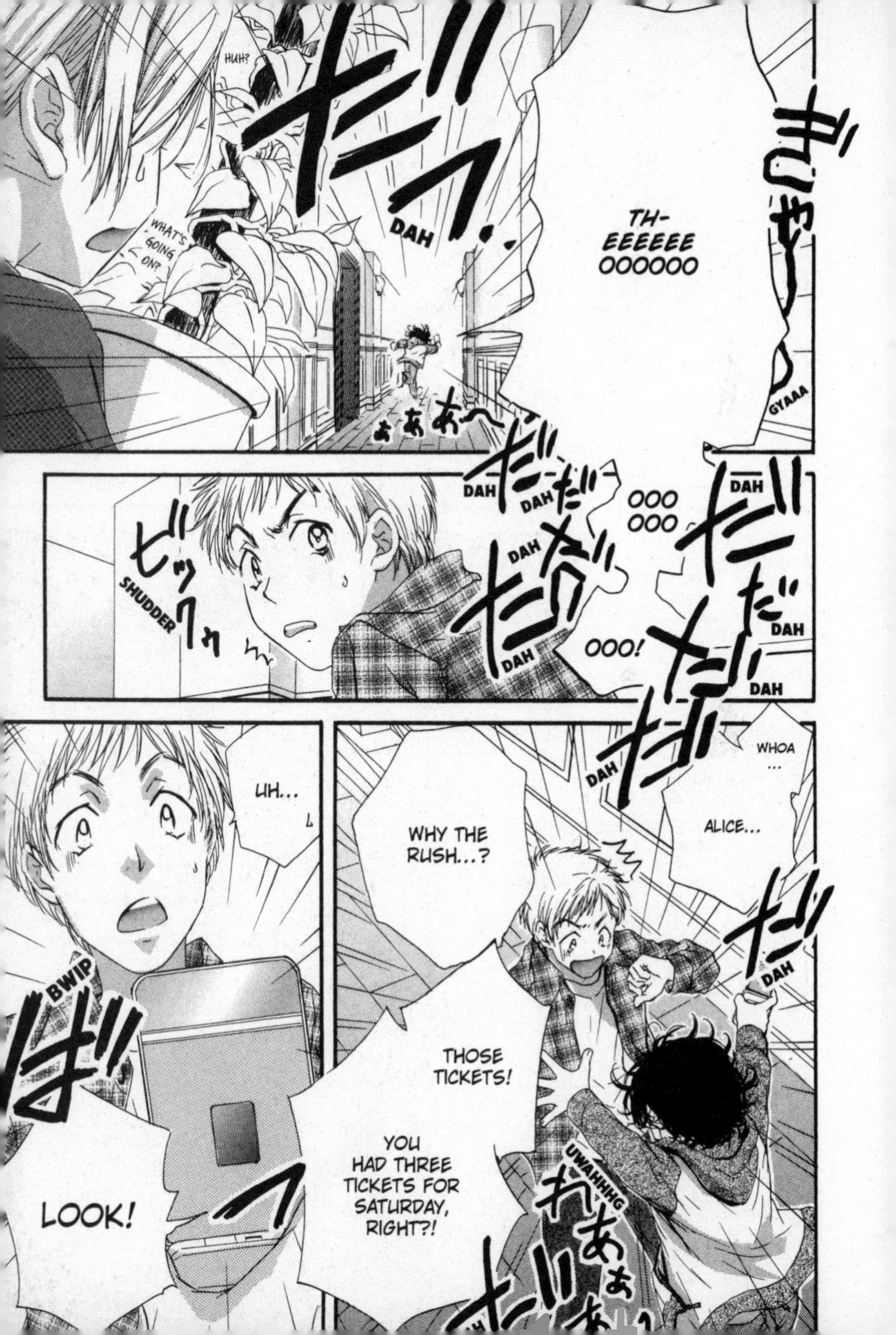
GYAAA
TH-
EEEEEE
OOOOOO
DAH
HUH?
WHAT'S GOING ON?
DAH
DAH
OOO
OOO
DAH
DAH
DAH
DAH
DAH
OOO!
SHUDDER
WHOA
...
ALICE...
DAH
DAH
WHY THE RUSH...?
THOSE TICKETS!
YOU HAD THREE TICKETS FOR SATURDAY, RIGHT?!
UWAHHHG
UH...
BWIP
LOOK!

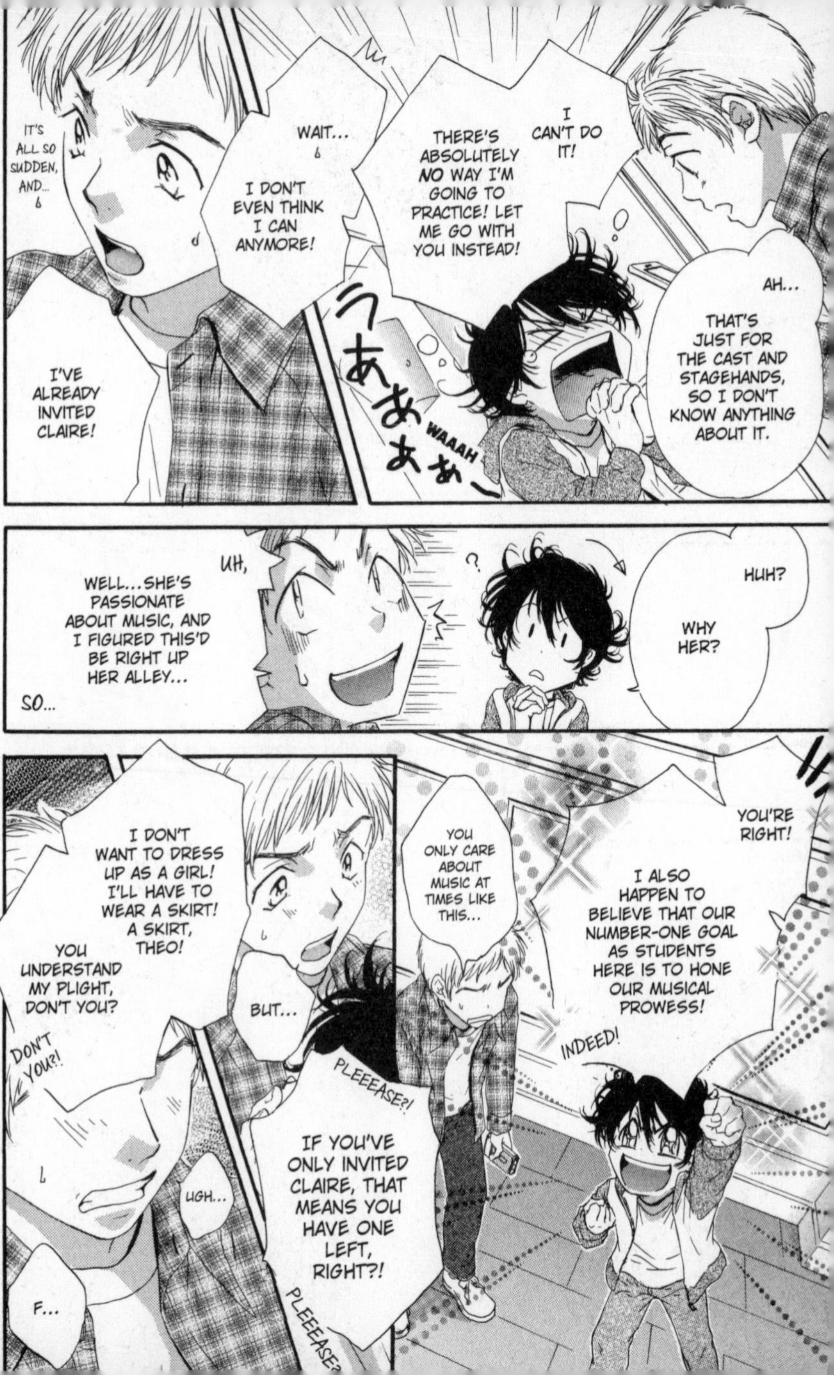
I CAN'T DO IT!
THERE'S ABSOLUTELY NO WAY I'M GOING TO PRACTICE! LET ME GO WITH YOU INSTEAD!
AH...
THAT'S JUST FOR THE CAST AND STAGEHANDS, SO I DON'T KNOW ANYTHING ABOUT IT.
うあああ
WAAAH
WAIT...
I DON'T EVEN THINK I CAN ANYMORE!
IT'S ALL SO SUDDEN, AND...
I'VE ALREADY INVITED CLAIRE!
HUH?
WHY HER?
UH,
WELL...SHE'S PASSIONATE ABOUT MUSIC, AND I FIGURED THIS'D BE RIGHT UP HER ALLEY...
SO...
YOU'RE RIGHT!
I ALSO HAPPEN TO BELIEVE THAT OUR NUMBER-ONE GOAL AS STUDENTS HERE IS TO HONE OUR MUSICAL PROWESS!
INDEED!
YOU ONLY CARE ABOUT MUSIC AT TIMES LIKE THIS...
I DON'T WANT TO DRESS UP AS A GIRL! I'LL HAVE TO WEAR A SKIRT! A SKIRT, THEO!
YOU UNDERSTAND MY PLIGHT, DON'T YOU?
DON'T YOU?!
BUT...
PLEEEASE?!
IF YOU'VE ONLY INVITED CLAIRE, THAT MEANS YOU HAVE ONE LEFT, RIGHT?!
PLEEEASE?!
UGH...
F...

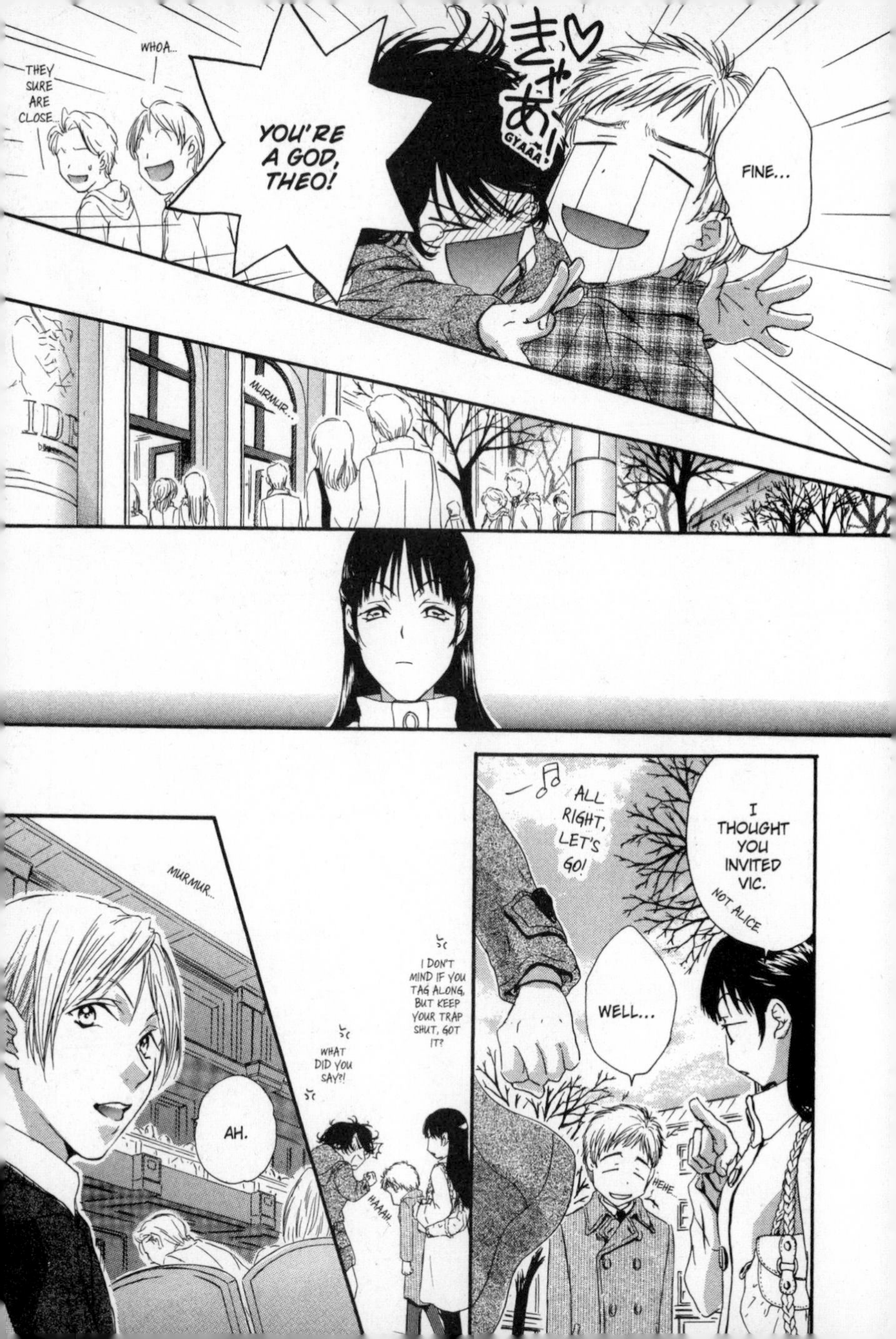
FINE...
GYAAA!
YOU'RE A GOD, THEO!
WHOA...
THEY SURE ARE CLOSE...
MURMUR...
I THOUGHT YOU INVITED VIC.
NOT ALICE
ALL RIGHT, LET'S GO!
WELL...
HEHE...
I DON'T MIND IF YOU TAG ALONG, BUT KEEP YOUR TRAP SHUT, GOT IT?
WHAT DID YOU SAY?!
HAAAH...
MURMUR...
AH.

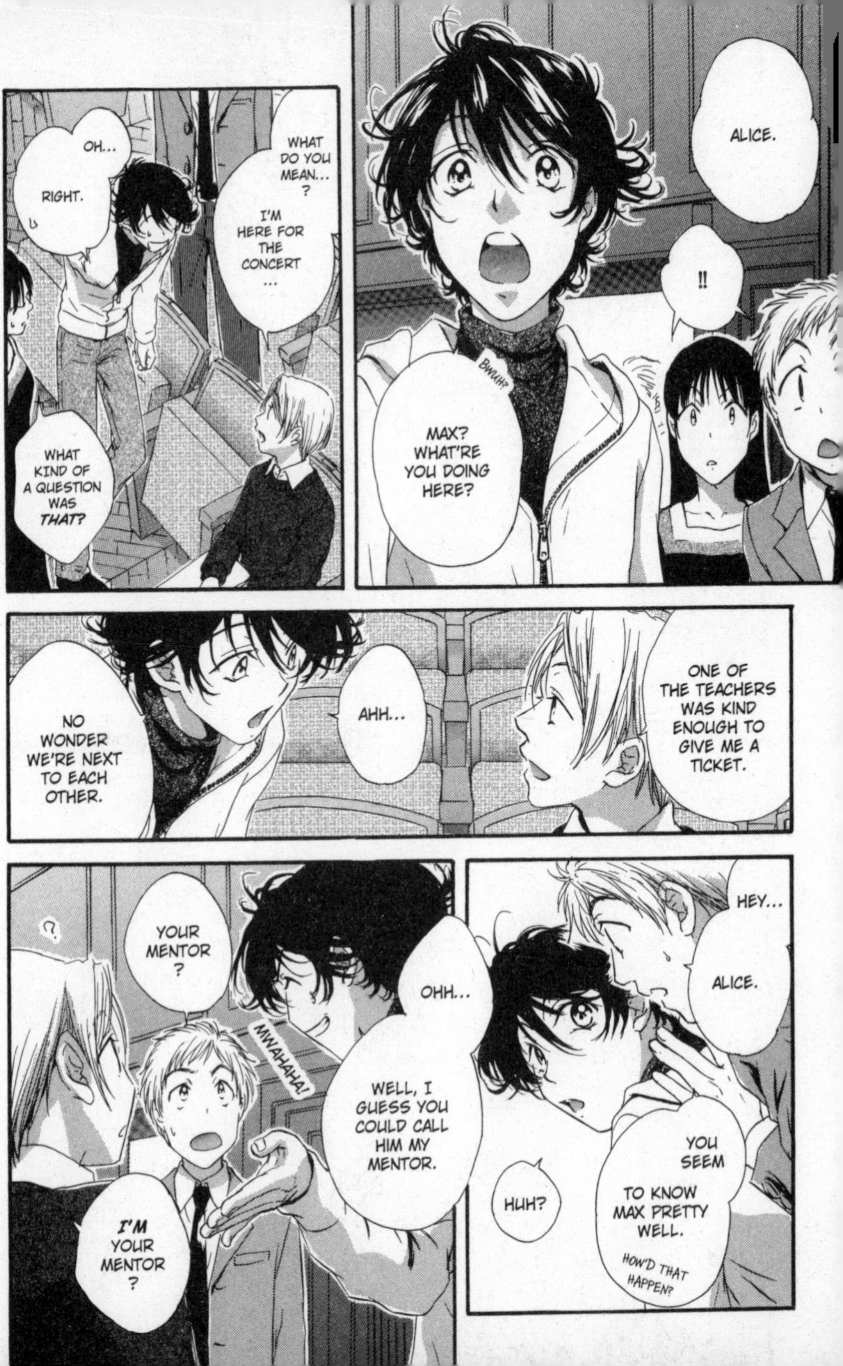
ALICE.
!!
BWUH?
MAX? WHAT'RE YOU DOING HERE?
WHAT DO YOU MEAN...?
I'M HERE FOR THE CONCERT...
OH...
RIGHT.
WHAT KIND OF A QUESTION WAS *THAT?*
ONE OF THE TEACHERS WAS KIND ENOUGH TO GIVE ME A TICKET.
AHH...
NO WONDER WE'RE NEXT TO EACH OTHER.
HEY...
ALICE.
YOU SEEM
TO KNOW MAX PRETTY WELL.
HOW'D THAT HAPPEN?
HUH?
OHH...
WELL, I GUESS YOU COULD CALL HIM MY MENTOR.
YOUR MENTOR?
MWAHAHA!
?
I'M YOUR MENTOR?

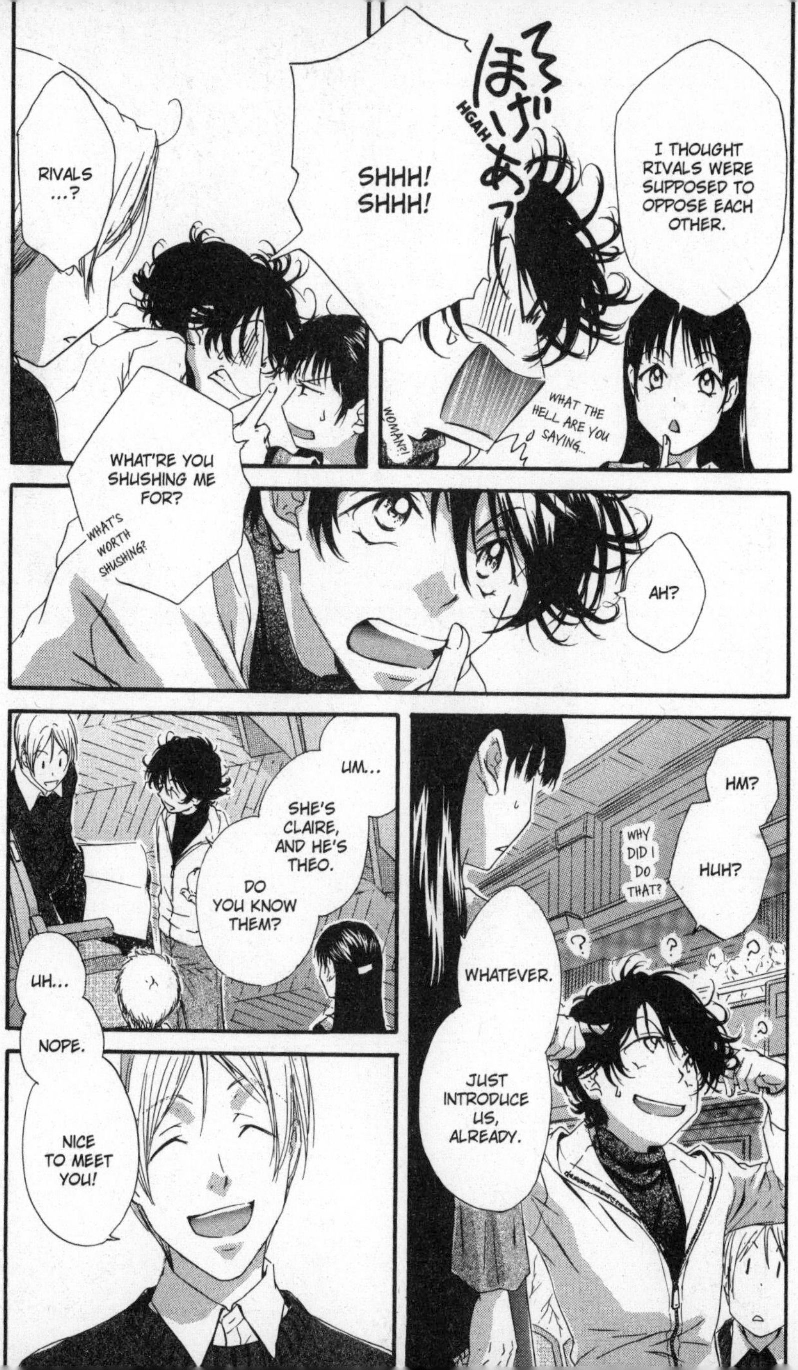
I THOUGHT RIVALS WERE SUPPOSED TO OPPOSE EACH OTHER.
ほげあっ
HGAH
WHAT THE HELL ARE YOU SAYING...
WOMAN?!
SHHH! SHHH!
RIVALS ...?
WHAT'RE YOU SHUSHING ME FOR?
WHAT'S WORTH SHUSHING?
AH?
HM?
HUH?
WHY DID I DO THAT?
WHATEVER.
JUST INTRODUCE US, ALREADY.
UM...
SHE'S CLAIRE, AND HE'S THEO.
DO YOU KNOW THEM?
UH...
NOPE.
NICE TO MEET YOU!

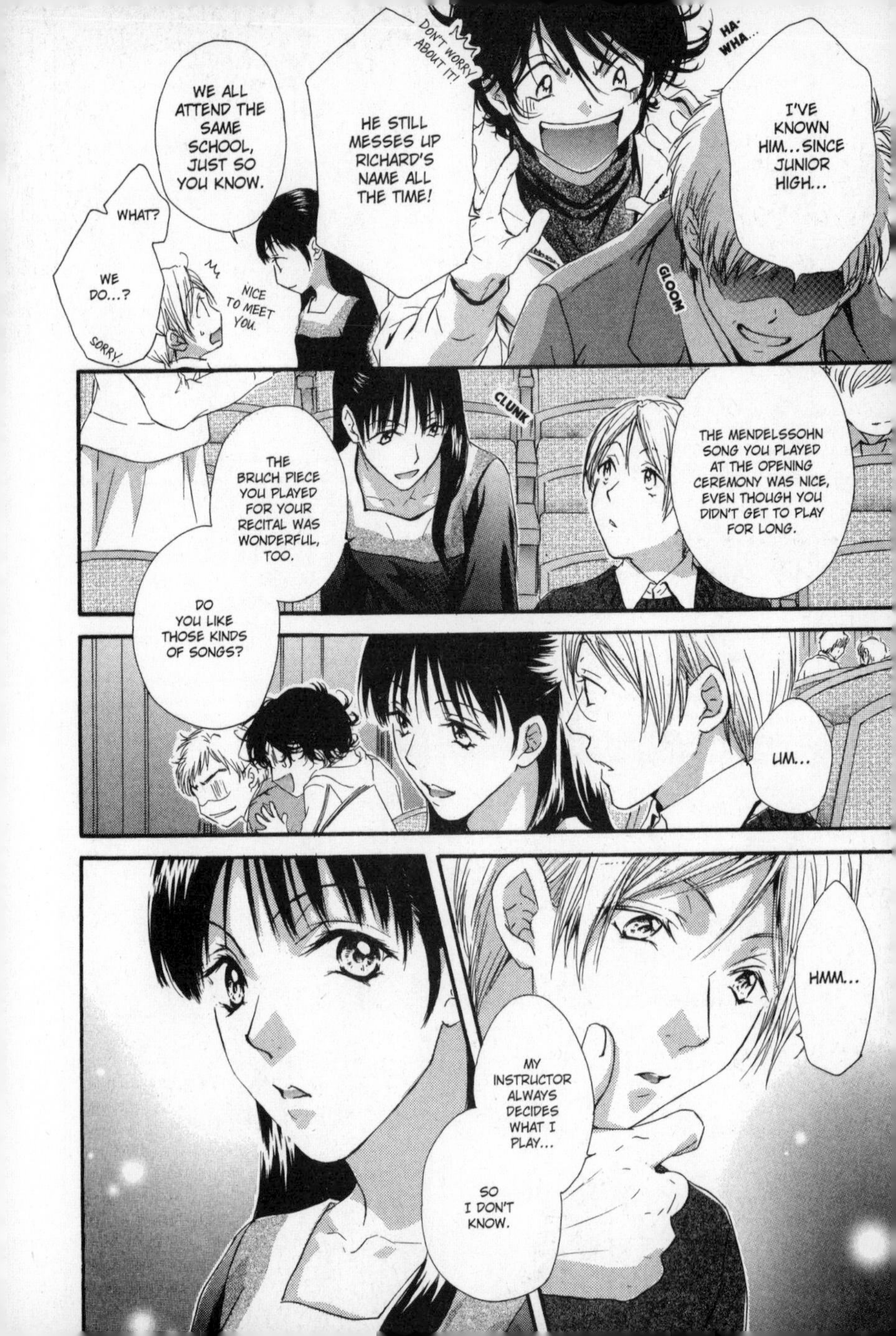
HA-WHA...
I'VE KNOWN HIM...SINCE JUNIOR HIGH...
GLOOM
DON'T WORRY ABOUT IT!
HE STILL MESSES UP RICHARD'S NAME ALL THE TIME!
WE ALL ATTEND THE SAME SCHOOL, JUST SO YOU KNOW.
WHAT?
NICE TO MEET YOU.
WE DO...?
SORRY.
THE MENDELSSOHN SONG YOU PLAYED AT THE OPENING CEREMONY WAS NICE, EVEN THOUGH YOU DIDN'T GET TO PLAY FOR LONG.
CLUNK
THE BRUCH PIECE YOU PLAYED FOR YOUR RECITAL WAS WONDERFUL, TOO.
DO YOU LIKE THOSE KINDS OF SONGS?
UM...
HMM...
MY INSTRUCTOR ALWAYS DECIDES WHAT I PLAY...
SO I DON'T KNOW.

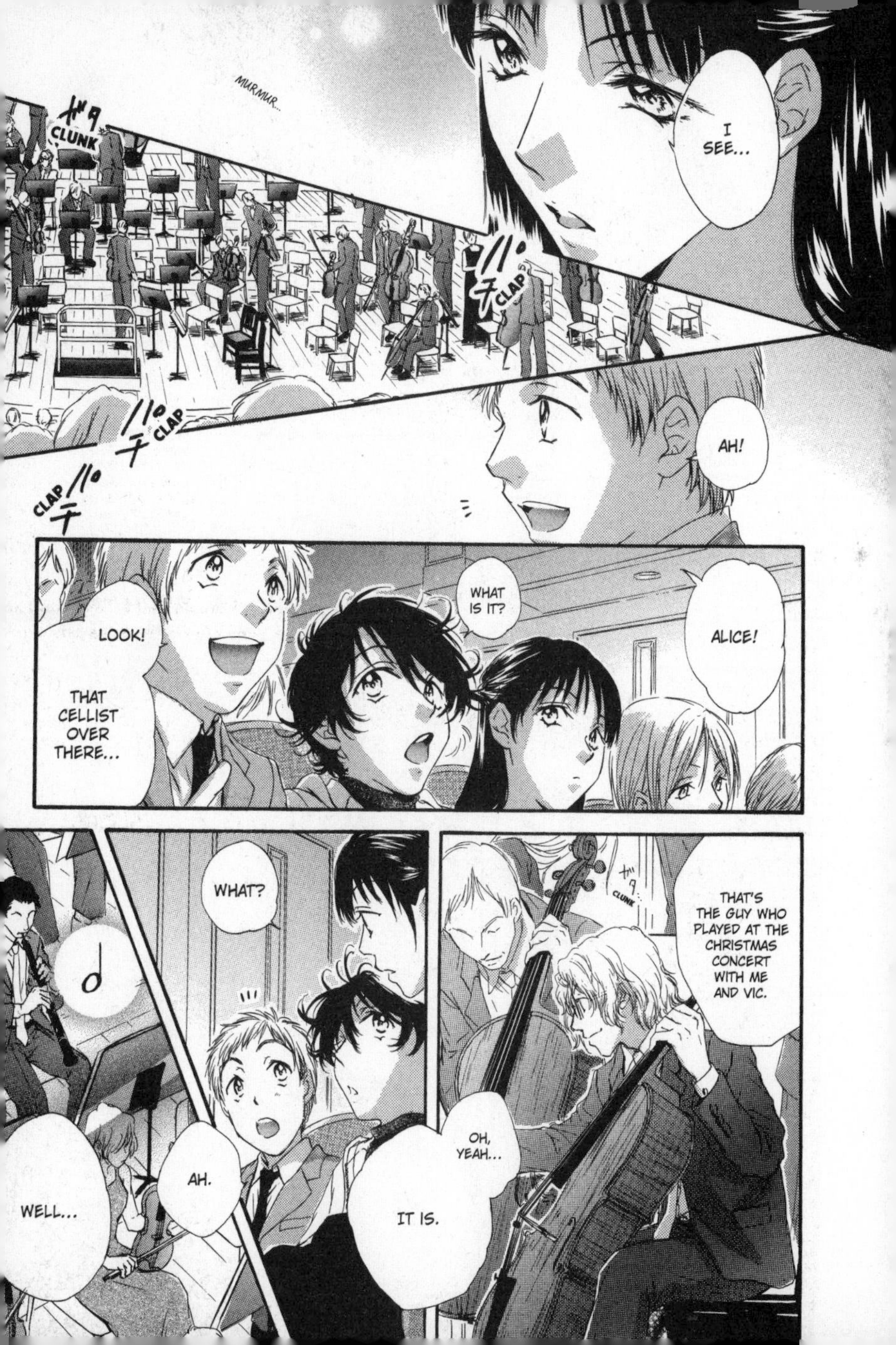
I SEE...
MURMUR...
CLUNK
CLAP
CLAP
AH!
CLAP
ALICE!
WHAT IS IT?
LOOK!
THAT CELLIST OVER THERE...
THAT'S THE GUY WHO PLAYED AT THE CHRISTMAS CONCERT WITH ME AND VIC.
CLUNK
OH, YEAH...
IT IS.
WHAT?
AH.
WELL...

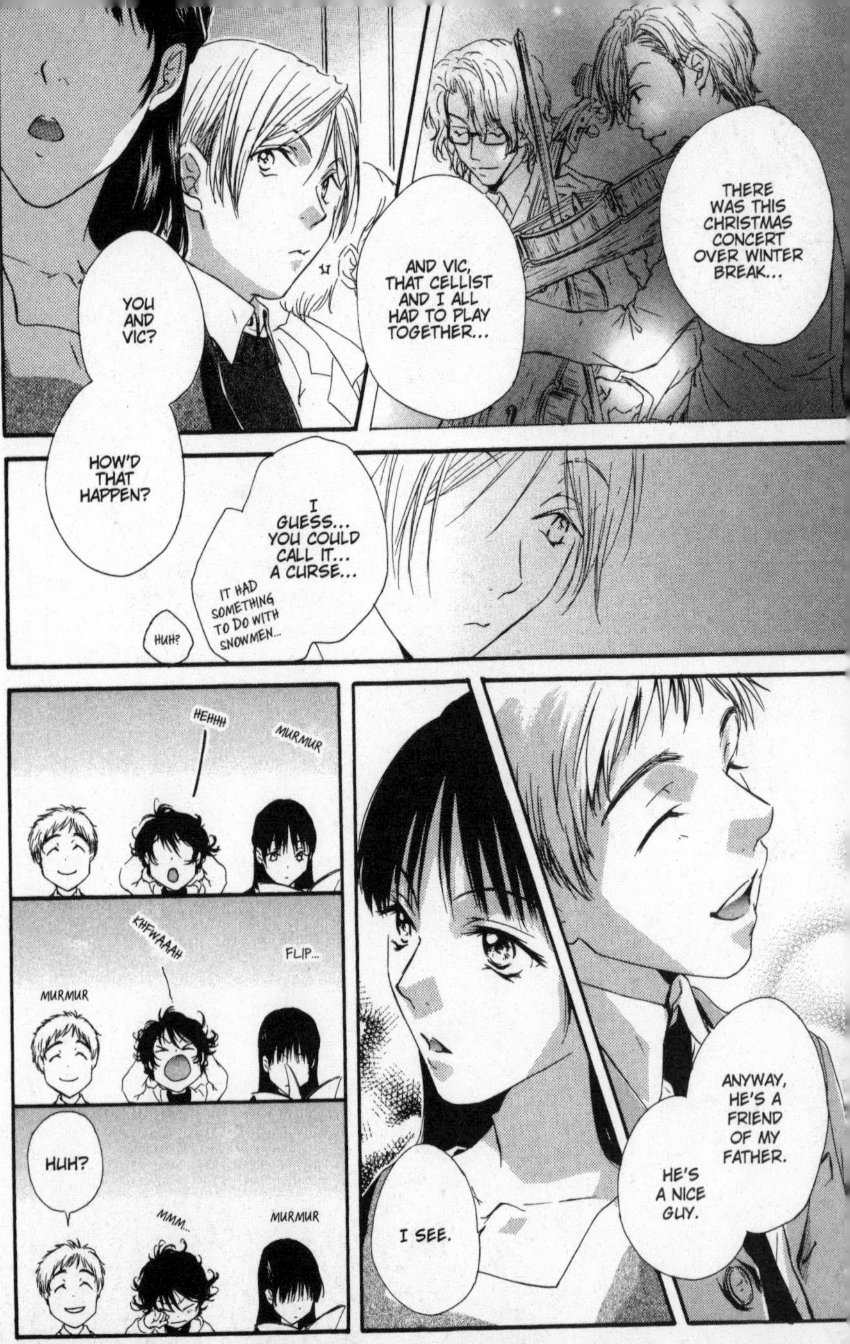
THERE WAS THIS CHRISTMAS CONCERT OVER WINTER BREAK...
AND VIC, THAT CELLIST AND I ALL HAD TO PLAY TOGETHER...
YOU AND VIC?
HOW'D THAT HAPPEN?
I GUESS... YOU COULD CALL IT... A CURSE...
IT HAD SOMETHING TO DO WITH SNOWMEN...
HUH?
ANYWAY, HE'S A FRIEND OF MY FATHER.
HE'S A NICE GUY.
I SEE.
MURMUR
HEHHH
FLIP...
KHFWAAAH
MURMUR
MURMUR
MMM...
HUH?

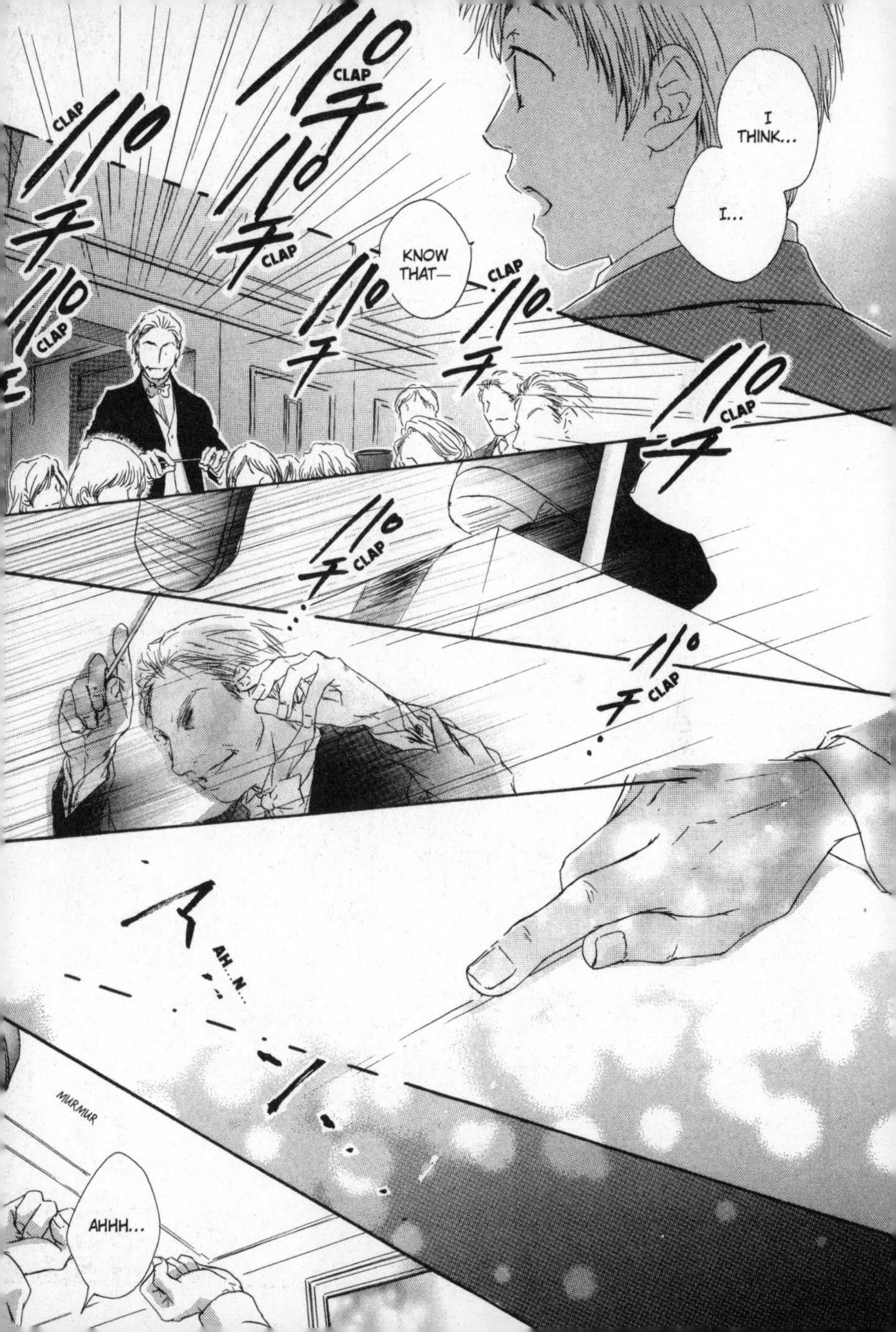
I THINK...
I...
KNOW THAT—
CLAP
CLAP
CLAP
CLAP
CLAP
CLAP
CLAP
CLAP
AH...N...
MURMUR
AHHH...

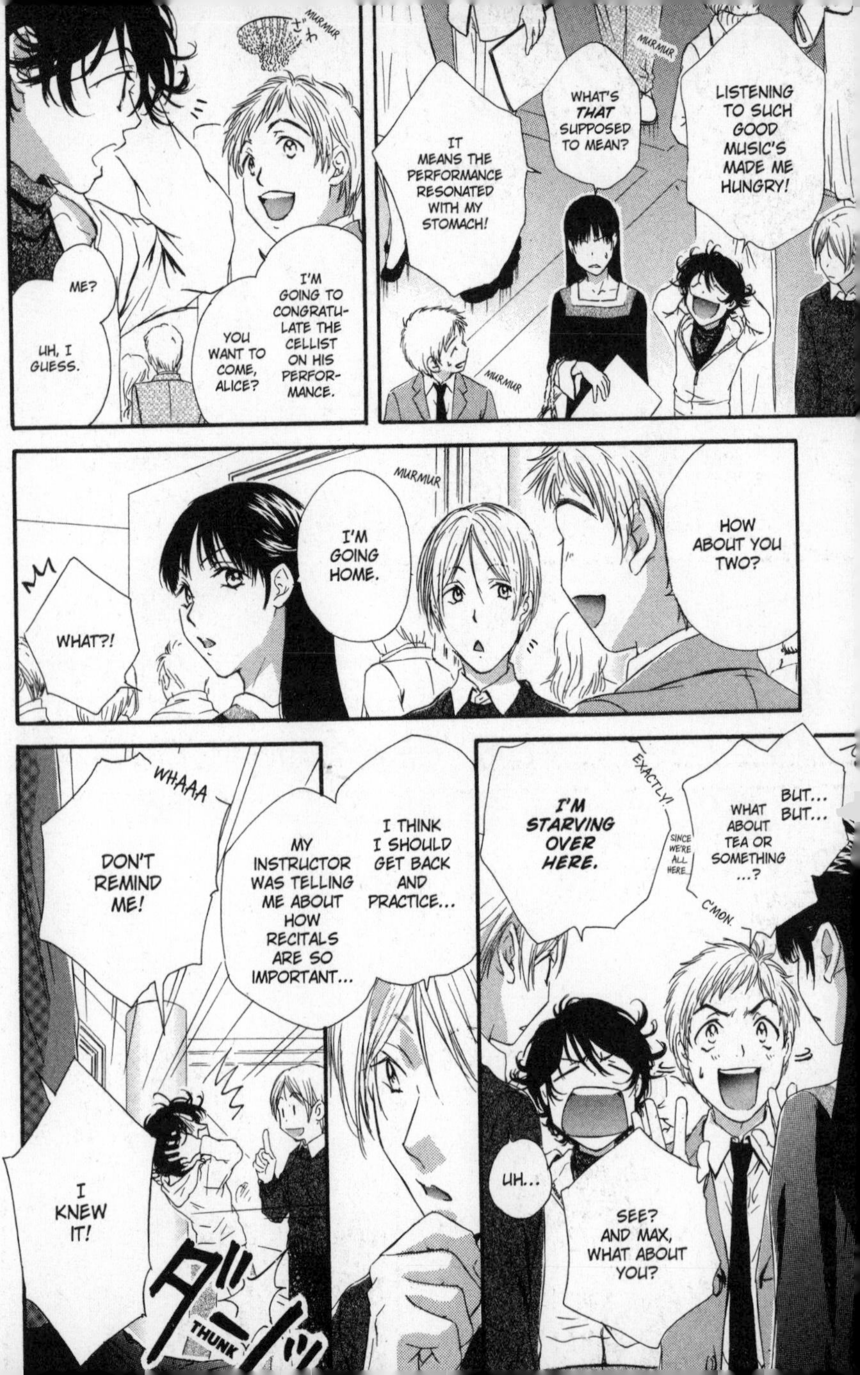
MURMUR
LISTENING TO SUCH GOOD MUSIC'S MADE ME HUNGRY!
WHAT'S *THAT* SUPPOSED TO MEAN?
IT MEANS THE PERFORMANCE RESONATED WITH MY STOMACH!
MURMUR
MURMUR ざわ
I'M GOING TO CONGRATULATE THE CELLIST ON HIS PERFORMANCE.
YOU WANT TO COME, ALICE?
ME?
UH, I GUESS.
HOW ABOUT YOU TWO?
MURMUR
I'M GOING HOME.
WHAT?!
BUT... BUT...
WHAT ABOUT TEA OR SOMETHING ...?
SINCE WE'RE ALL HERE...
EXACTLY!
I'M STARVING OVER HERE.
C'MON.
UH...
SEE? AND MAX, WHAT ABOUT YOU?
I THINK I SHOULD GET BACK AND PRACTICE...
MY INSTRUCTOR WAS TELLING ME ABOUT HOW RECITALS ARE SO IMPORTANT...
WHAAAA
DON'T REMIND ME!
I KNEW IT!
THUNK

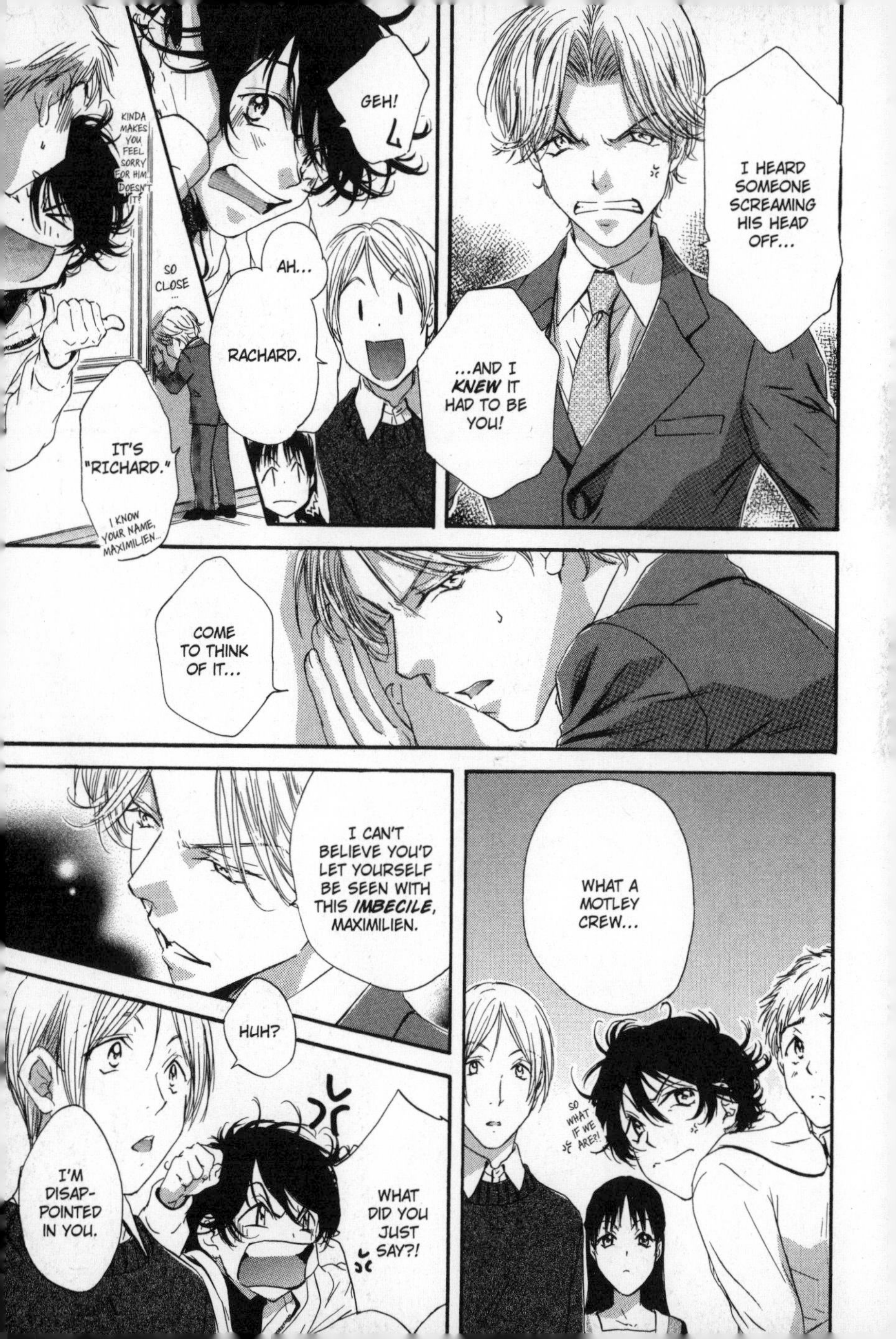
I HEARD SOMEONE SCREAMING HIS HEAD OFF...
...AND I *KNEW* IT HAD TO BE YOU!
GEH!
KINDA MAKES YOU FEEL SORRY FOR HIM, DOESN'T IT?
AH...
RACHARD.
SO CLOSE...
IT'S "RICHARD."
I KNOW YOUR NAME, MAXIMILIEN...
COME TO THINK OF IT...
WHAT A MOTLEY CREW...
SO WHAT IF WE ARE?!
I CAN'T BELIEVE YOU'D LET YOURSELF BE SEEN WITH THIS *IMBECILE*, MAXIMILIEN.
HUH?
I'M DISAP-POINTED IN YOU.
WHAT DID YOU JUST SAY?!

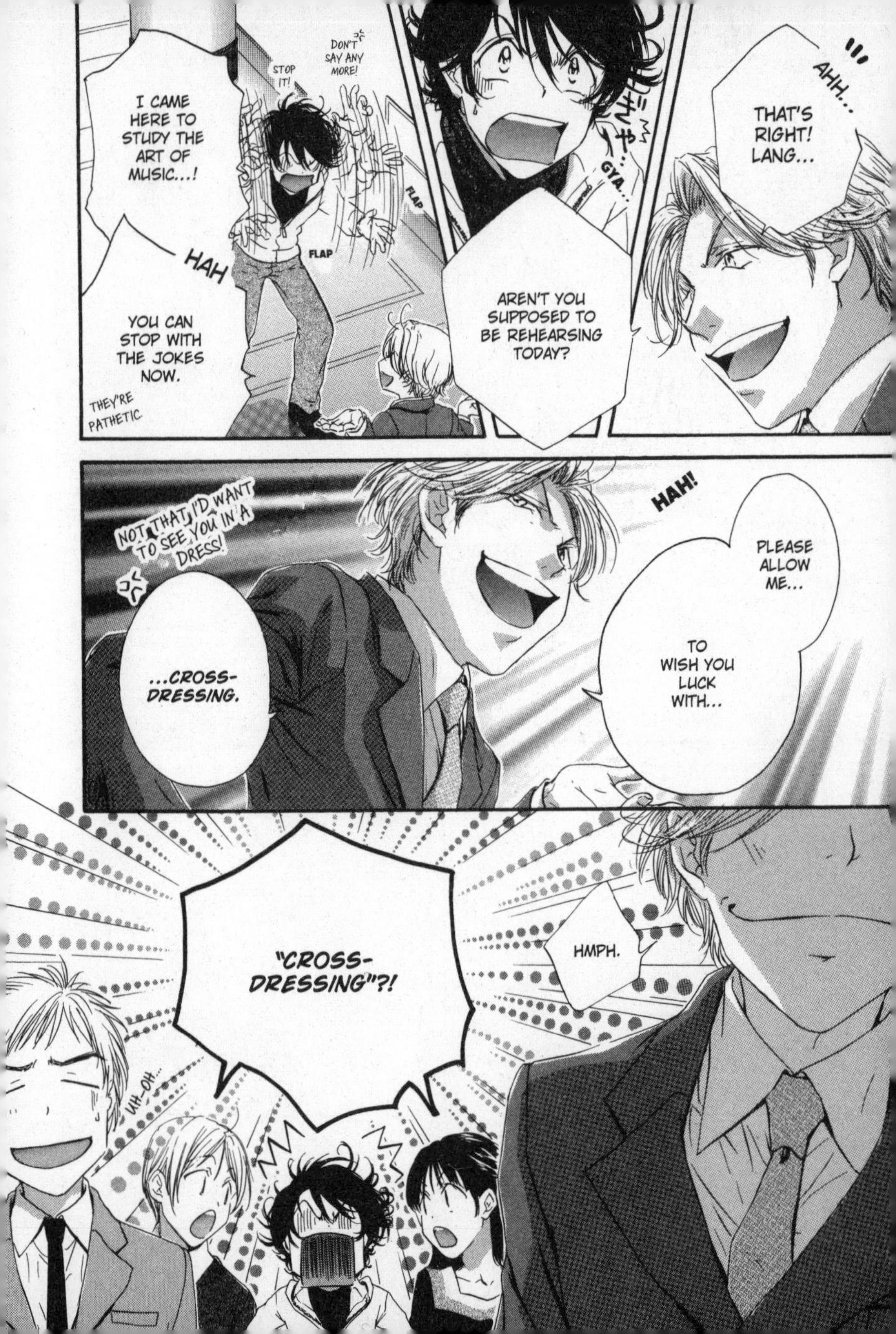
AHH...
THAT'S RIGHT! LANG...
GYA...
AREN'T YOU SUPPOSED TO BE REHEARSING TODAY?
DON'T SAY ANY MORE!
STOP IT!
I CAME HERE TO STUDY THE ART OF MUSIC...!
FLAP
FLAP
HAH
YOU CAN STOP WITH THE JOKES NOW.
THEY'RE PATHETIC.
HAH!
PLEASE ALLOW ME...
TO WISH YOU LUCK WITH...
...CROSS-DRESSING.
NOT THAT I'D WANT TO SEE YOU IN A DRESS!
HMPH.
"CROSS-DRESSING"?!
UH-OH...

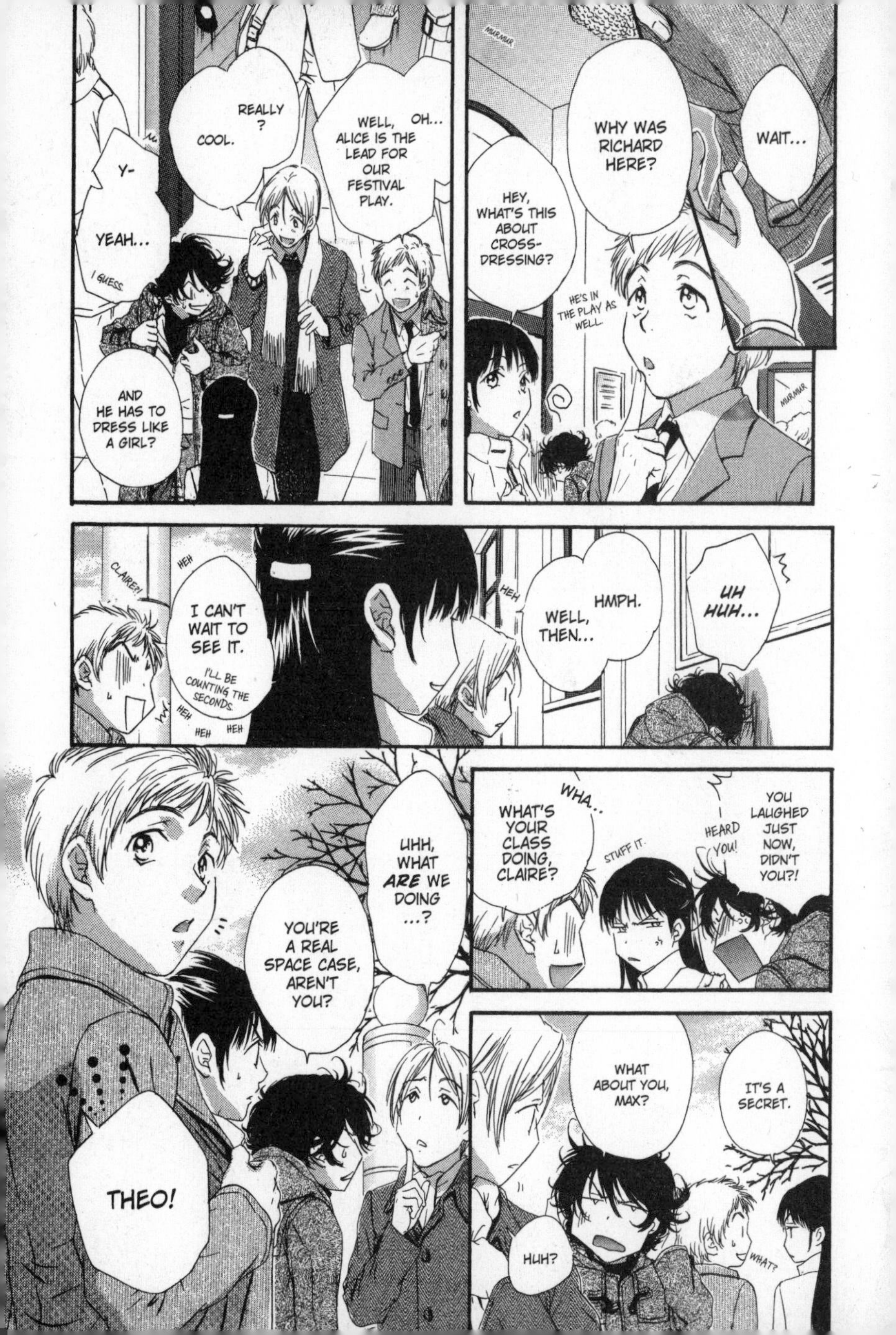
MURMUR
WAIT...
WHY WAS RICHARD HERE?
HEY, WHAT'S THIS ABOUT CROSS-DRESSING?
HE'S IN THE PLAY AS WELL.
MURMUR
OH...
WELL, ALICE IS THE LEAD FOR OUR FESTIVAL PLAY.
REALLY?
COOL.
Y-
YEAH...
I GUESS.
AND HE HAS TO DRESS LIKE A GIRL?
UH HUH...
HMPH. WELL, THEN...
HEH
I CAN'T WAIT TO SEE IT.
I'LL BE COUNTING THE SECONDS.
HEH
HEH HEH
CLAIRE?!
HEH
YOU LAUGHED JUST NOW, DIDN'T YOU?!
I HEARD YOU!
STUFF IT.
WHA...
WHAT'S YOUR CLASS DOING, CLAIRE?
IT'S A SECRET.
WHAT ABOUT YOU, MAX?
WHAT?
HUH?
UHH, WHAT ARE WE DOING...?
YOU'RE A REAL SPACE CASE, AREN'T YOU?
THEO!

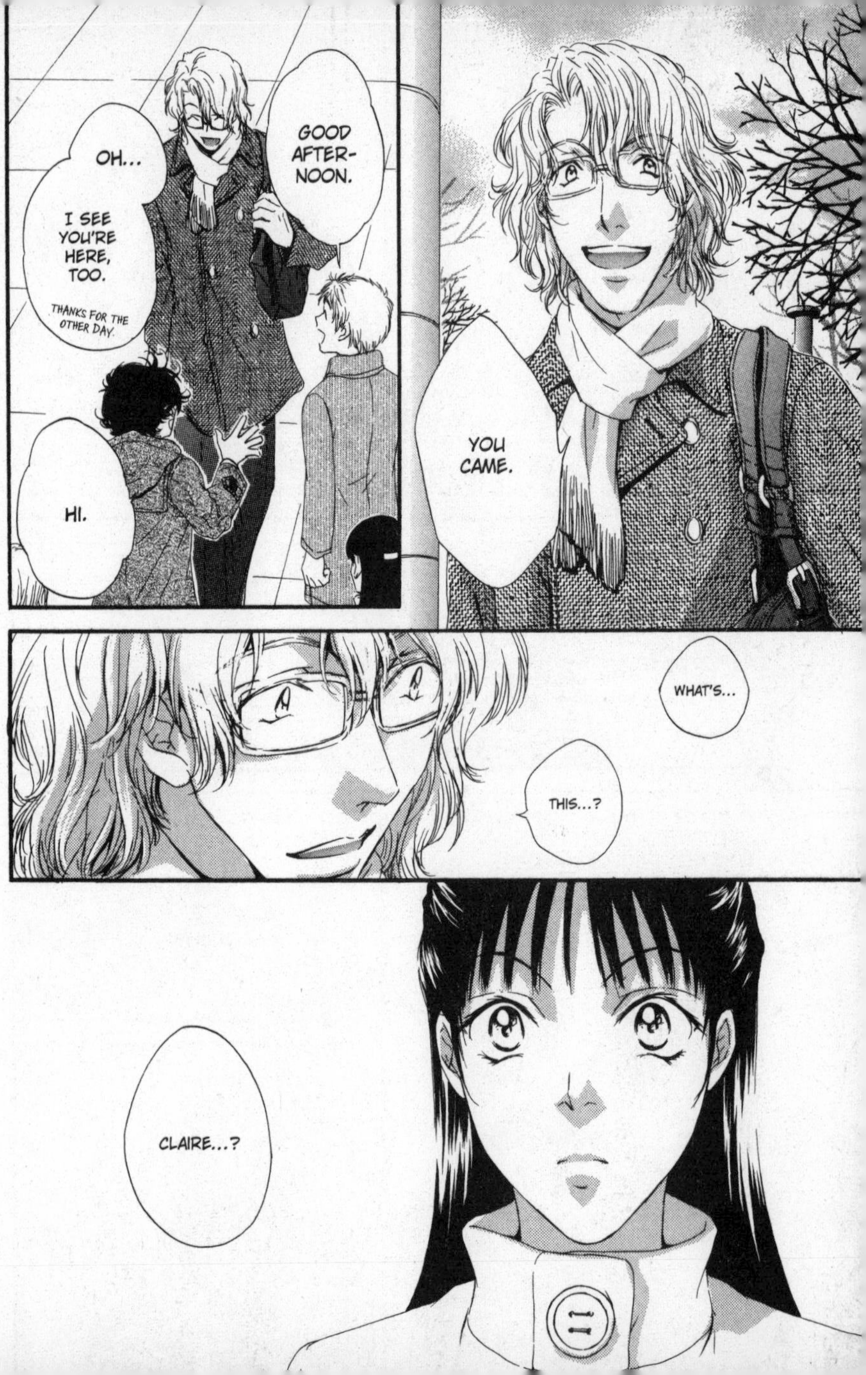
YOU CAME.
GOOD AFTER-NOON.
OH...
I SEE YOU'RE HERE, TOO.
THANKS FOR THE OTHER DAY.
HI.
WHAT'S...
THIS...?
CLAIRE...?

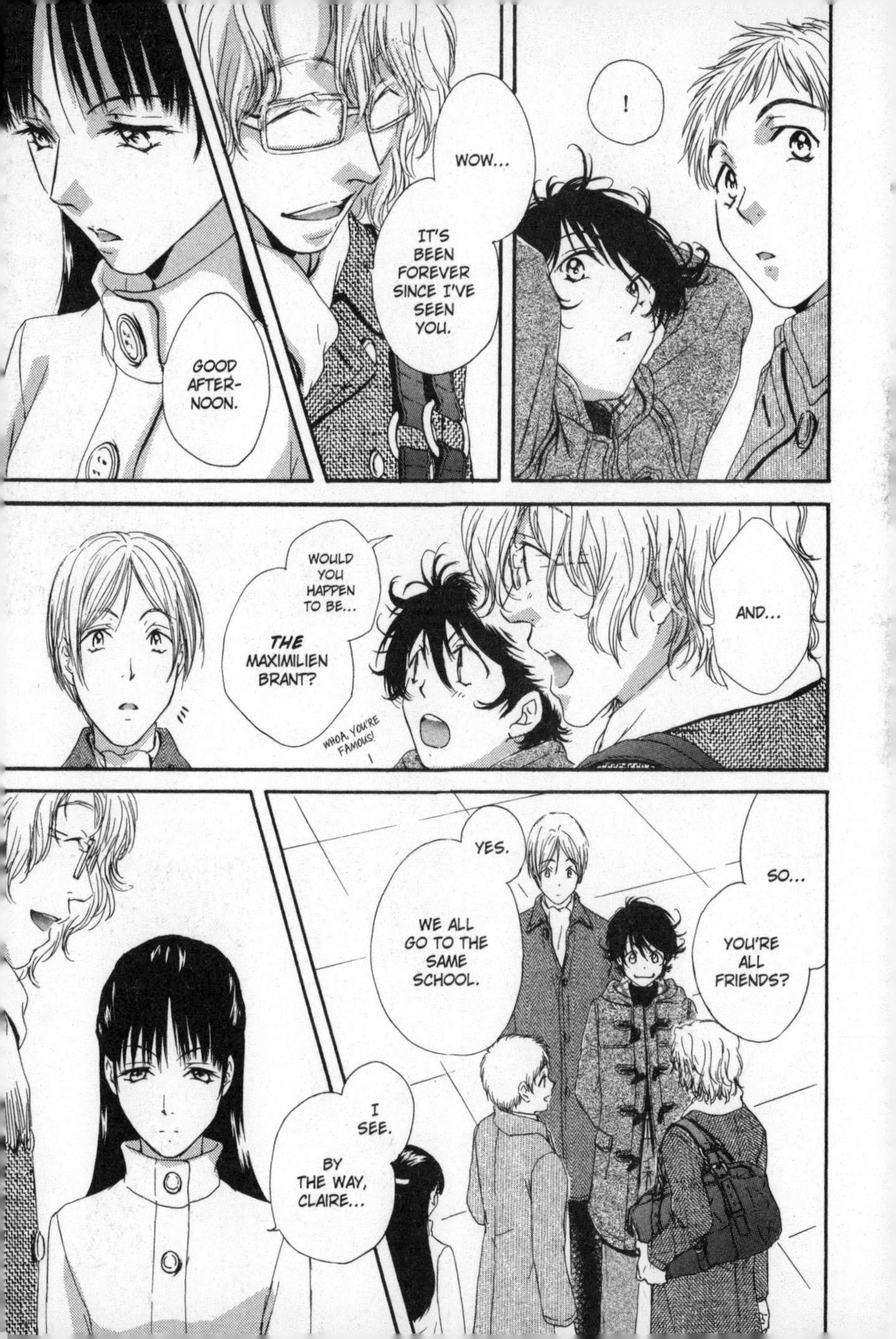
!
WOW...
IT'S BEEN FOREVER SINCE I'VE SEEN YOU.
GOOD AFTER-NOON.
AND...
WOULD YOU HAPPEN TO BE... *THE* MAXIMILIEN BRANT?
WHOA, YOU'RE FAMOUS!
SO... YOU'RE ALL FRIENDS?
YES. WE ALL GO TO THE SAME SCHOOL.
I SEE. BY THE WAY, CLAIRE...

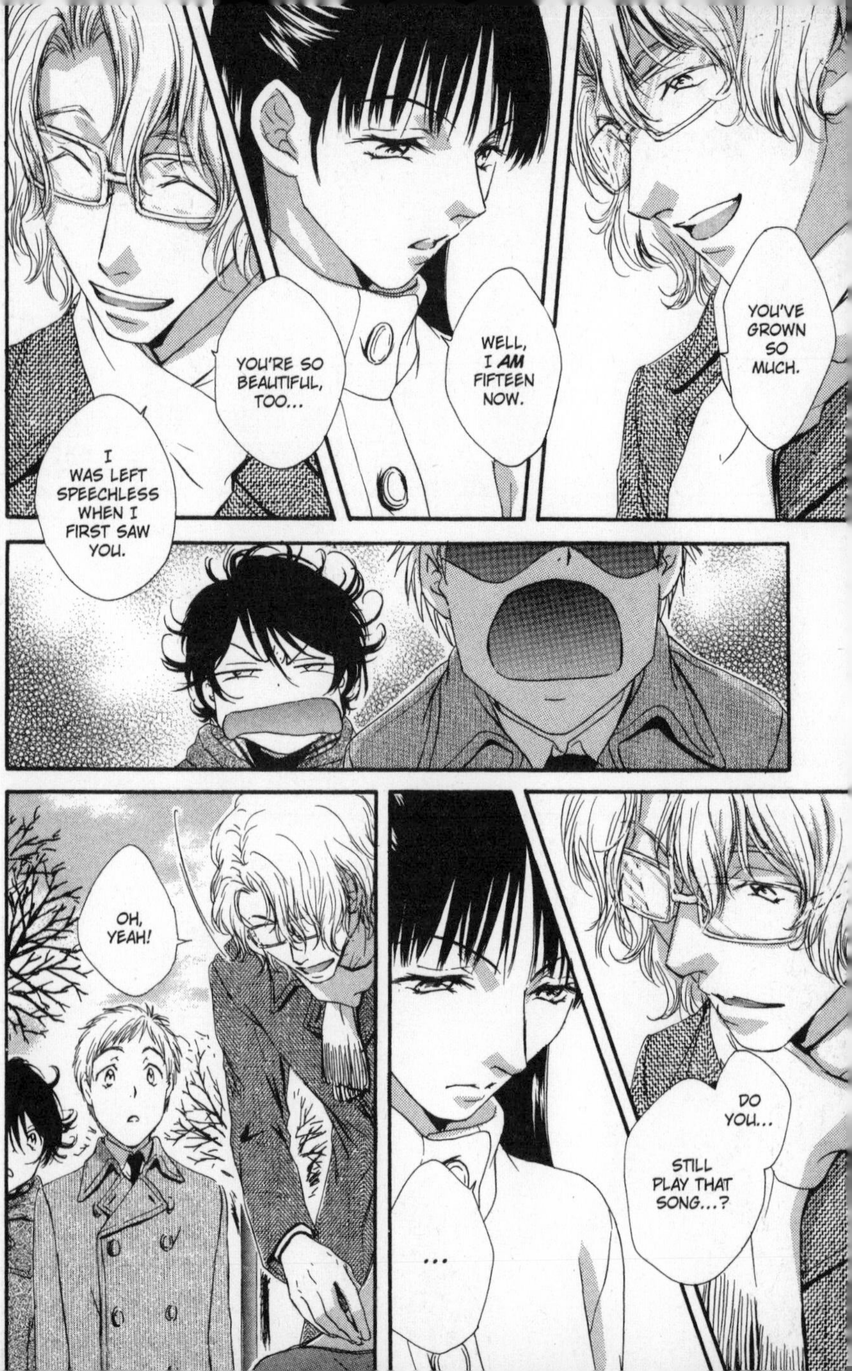
YOU'VE GROWN SO MUCH.
WELL, I *AM* FIFTEEN NOW.
YOU'RE SO BEAUTIFUL, TOO...
I WAS LEFT SPEECHLESS WHEN I FIRST SAW YOU.
DO YOU...
STILL PLAY THAT SONG...?
...
OH, YEAH!

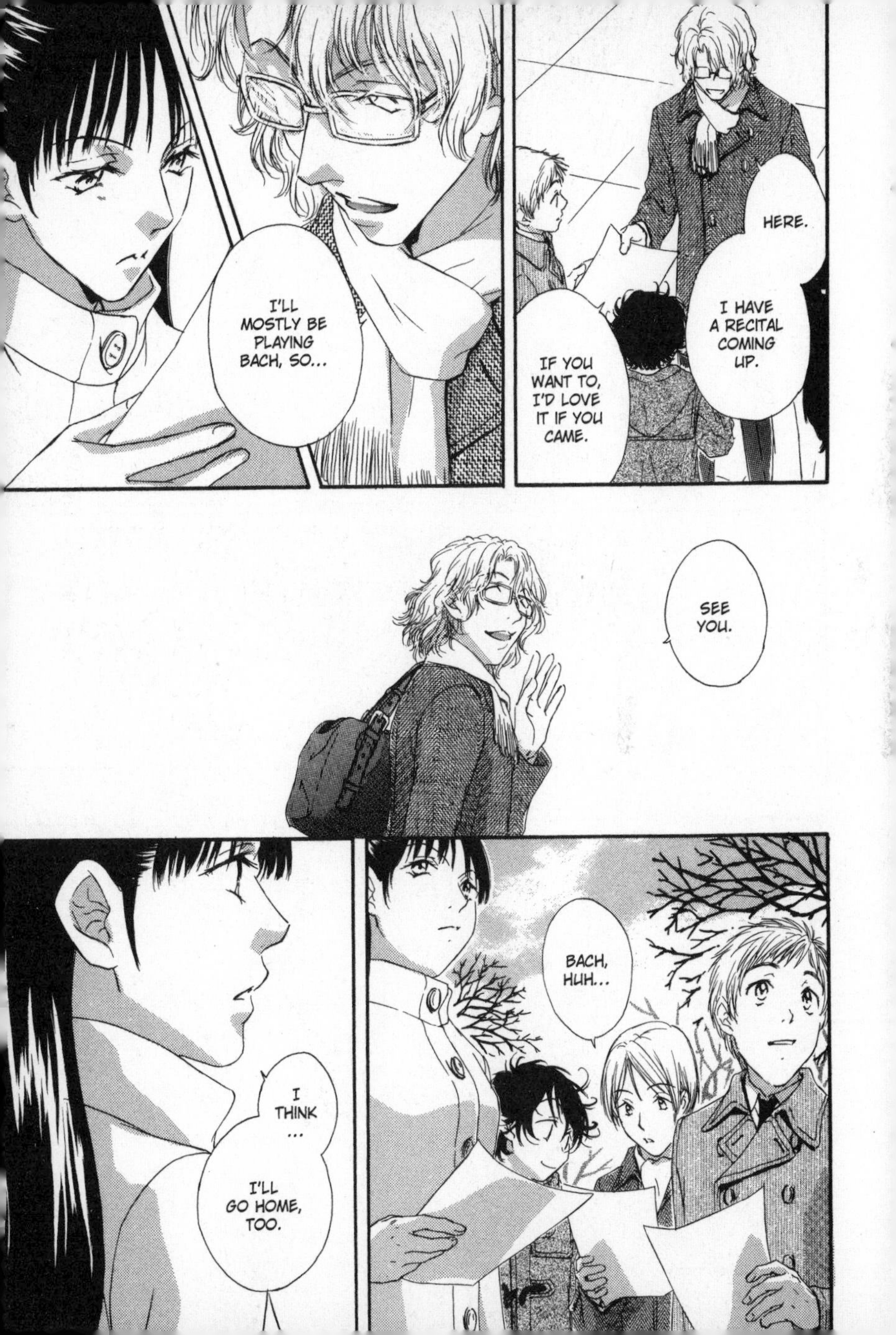
HERE.
I HAVE A RECITAL COMING UP.
IF YOU WANT TO, I'D LOVE IT IF YOU CAME.
I'LL MOSTLY BE PLAYING BACH, SO...
SEE YOU.
BACH, HUH...
I THINK...
I'LL GO HOME, TOO.

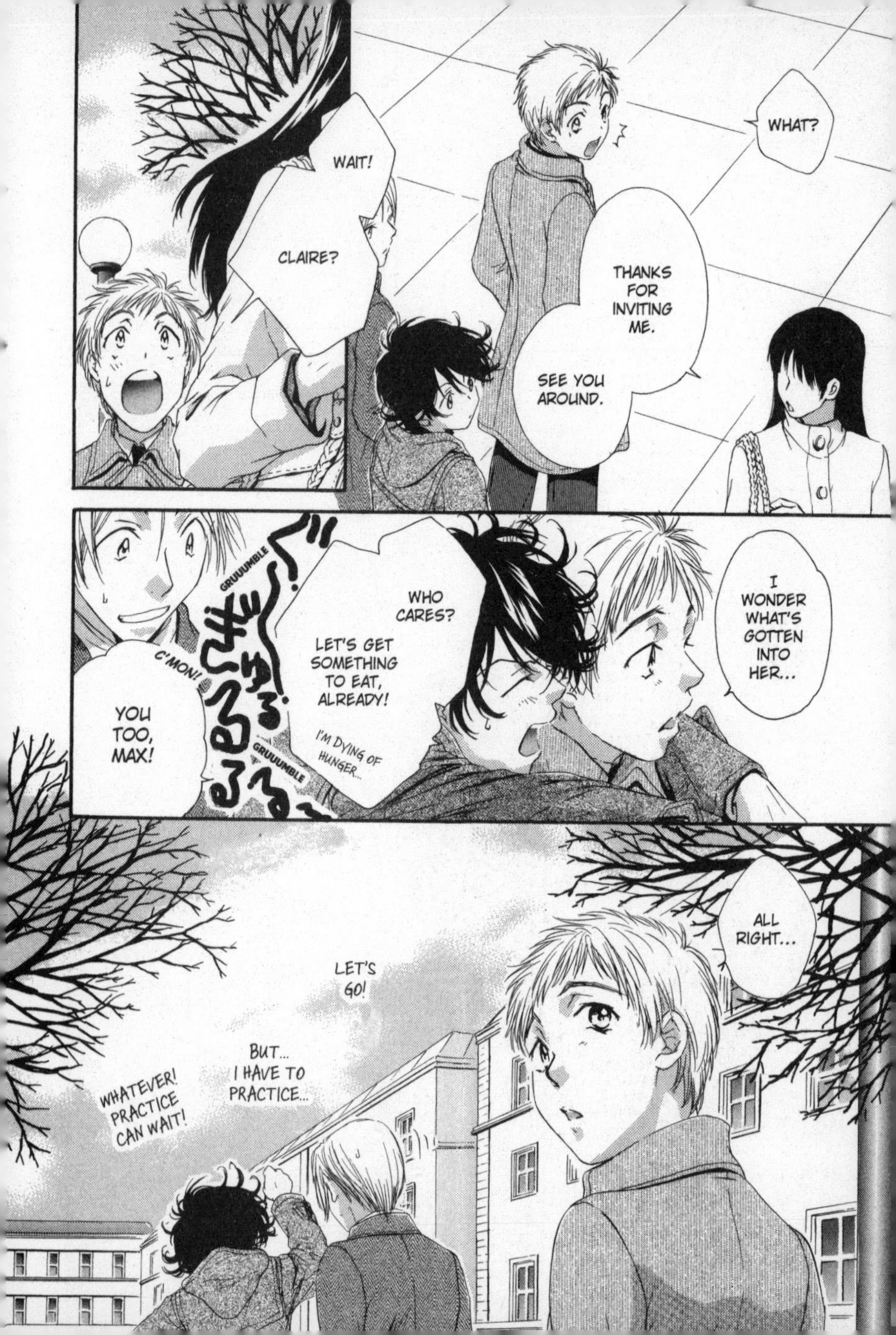
WHAT?
THANKS FOR INVITING ME.
SEE YOU AROUND.
WAIT!
CLAIRE?
I WONDER WHAT'S GOTTEN INTO HER...
WHO CARES?
LET'S GET SOMETHING TO EAT, ALREADY!
I'M DYING OF HUNGER...
GRUUUMBLE
GRUUUMBLE
C'MON!
YOU TOO, MAX!
ALL RIGHT...
LET'S GO!
BUT... I HAVE TO PRACTICE...
WHATEVER! PRACTICE CAN WAIT!

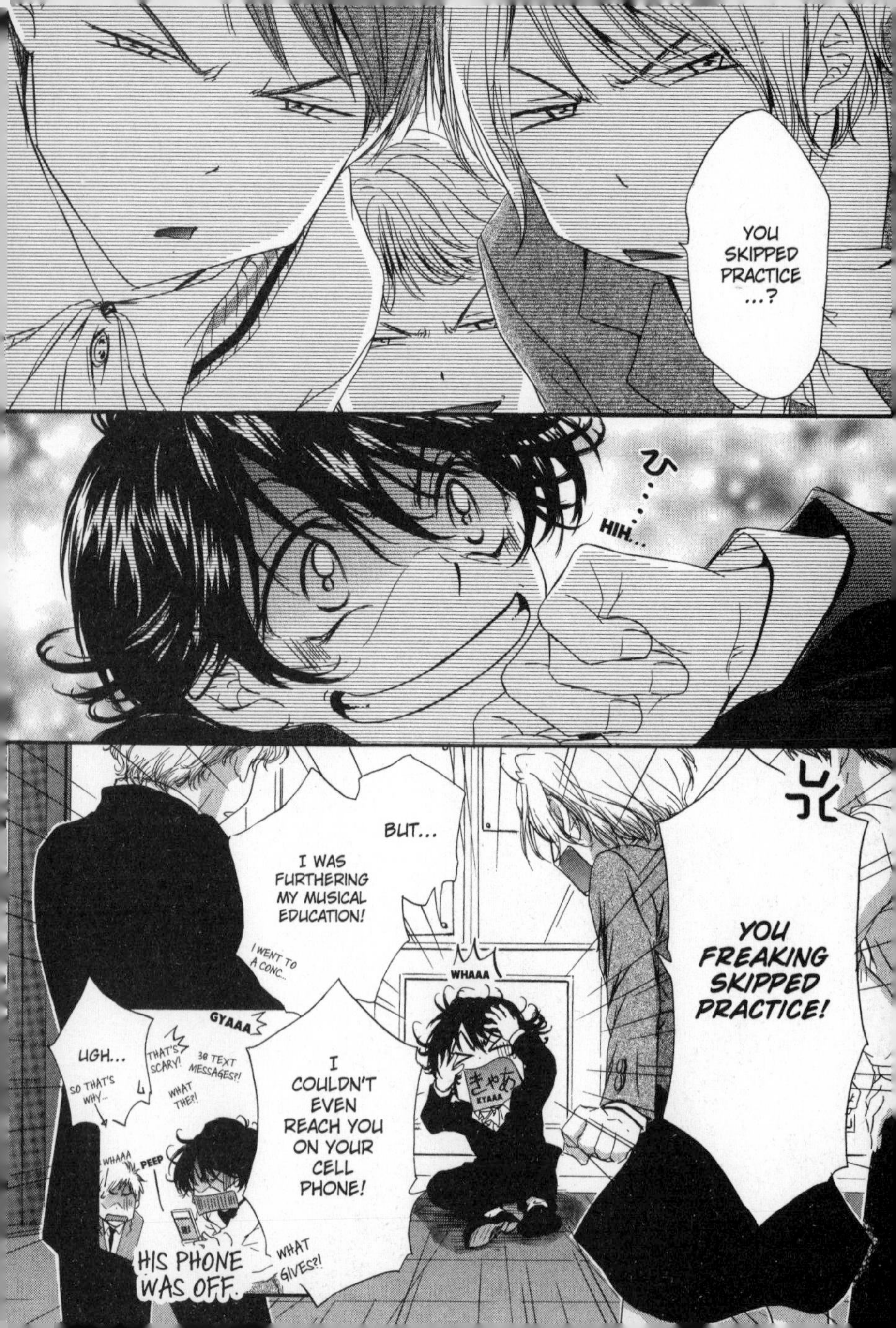
YOU SKIPPED PRACTICE ...?
ひ...
HIH...
YOU FREAKING SKIPPED PRACTICE!
WHAAA
きゃあ
KYAAA
BUT...
I WAS FURTHERING MY MUSICAL EDUCATION!
I WENT TO A CONC...
I COULDN'T EVEN REACH YOU ON YOUR CELL PHONE!
GYAAA
30 TEXT MESSAGES?!
THAT'S SCARY!
WHAT THE?!
UGH...
SO THAT'S WHY...
PEEP
WHAAA
WHAT GIVES?!
HIS PHONE WAS OFF.

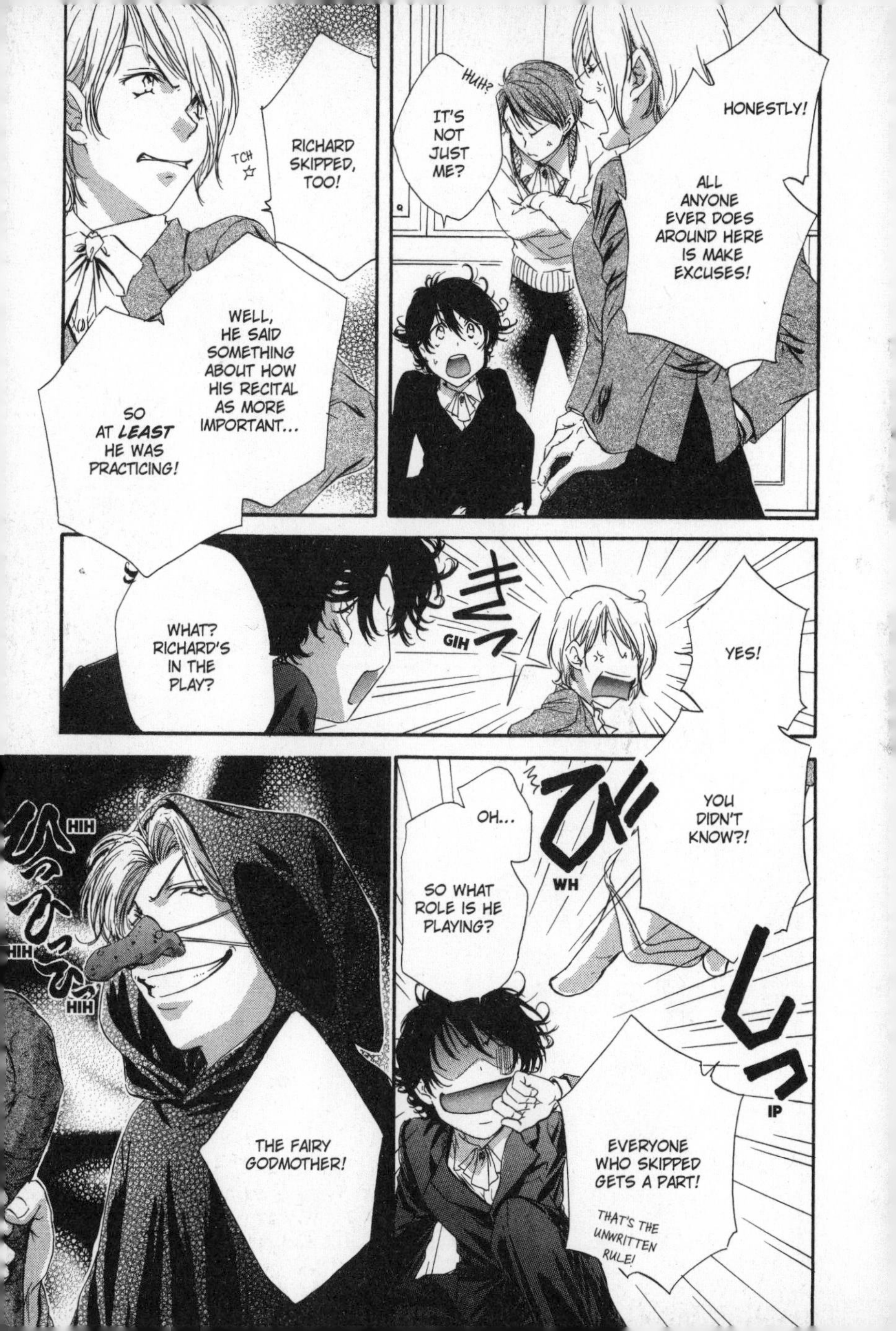
HONESTLY!
ALL ANYONE EVER DOES AROUND HERE IS MAKE EXCUSES!
HUH?
IT'S NOT JUST ME?
RICHARD SKIPPED, TOO!
TCH ☆
WELL, HE SAID SOMETHING ABOUT HOW HIS RECITAL AS MORE IMPORTANT...
SO AT *LEAST* HE WAS PRACTICING!
YES!
GIH
WHAT? RICHARD'S IN THE PLAY?
YOU DIDN'T KNOW?!
WH
IP
OH...
SO WHAT ROLE IS HE PLAYING?
EVERYONE WHO SKIPPED GETS A PART!
THAT'S THE UNWRITTEN RULE!
HIH
HIH
HIH
THE FAIRY GODMOTHER!

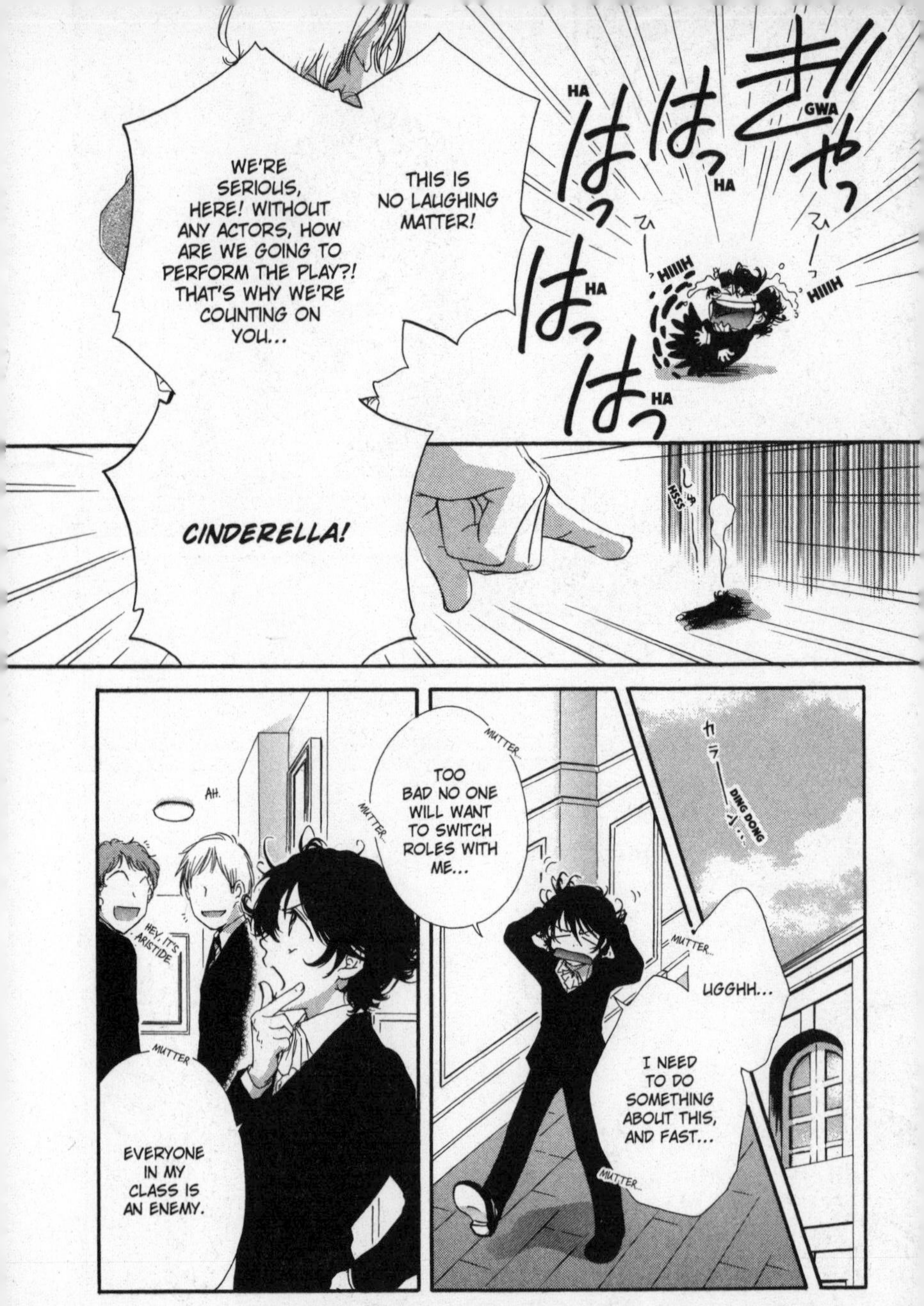
ぎゃっ
GWA
はっはっ
HA
HA
はっはっ
HA
HA
ひー
HIIIH
ひーっ
HIIIH
THIS IS NO LAUGHING MATTER!
WE'RE SERIOUS, HERE! WITHOUT ANY ACTORS, HOW ARE WE GOING TO PERFORM THE PLAY?! THAT'S WHY WE'RE COUNTING ON YOU...
しゅ
HSSS
CINDERELLA!
カラーン
DING DONG
MUTTER...
UGGHH...
I NEED TO DO SOMETHING ABOUT THIS, AND FAST...
MUTTER...
MUTTER...
TOO BAD NO ONE WILL WANT TO SWITCH ROLES WITH ME...
MUTTER...
AH.
HEY, IT'S ARISTIDE.
MUTTER
EVERYONE IN MY CLASS IS AN ENEMY.

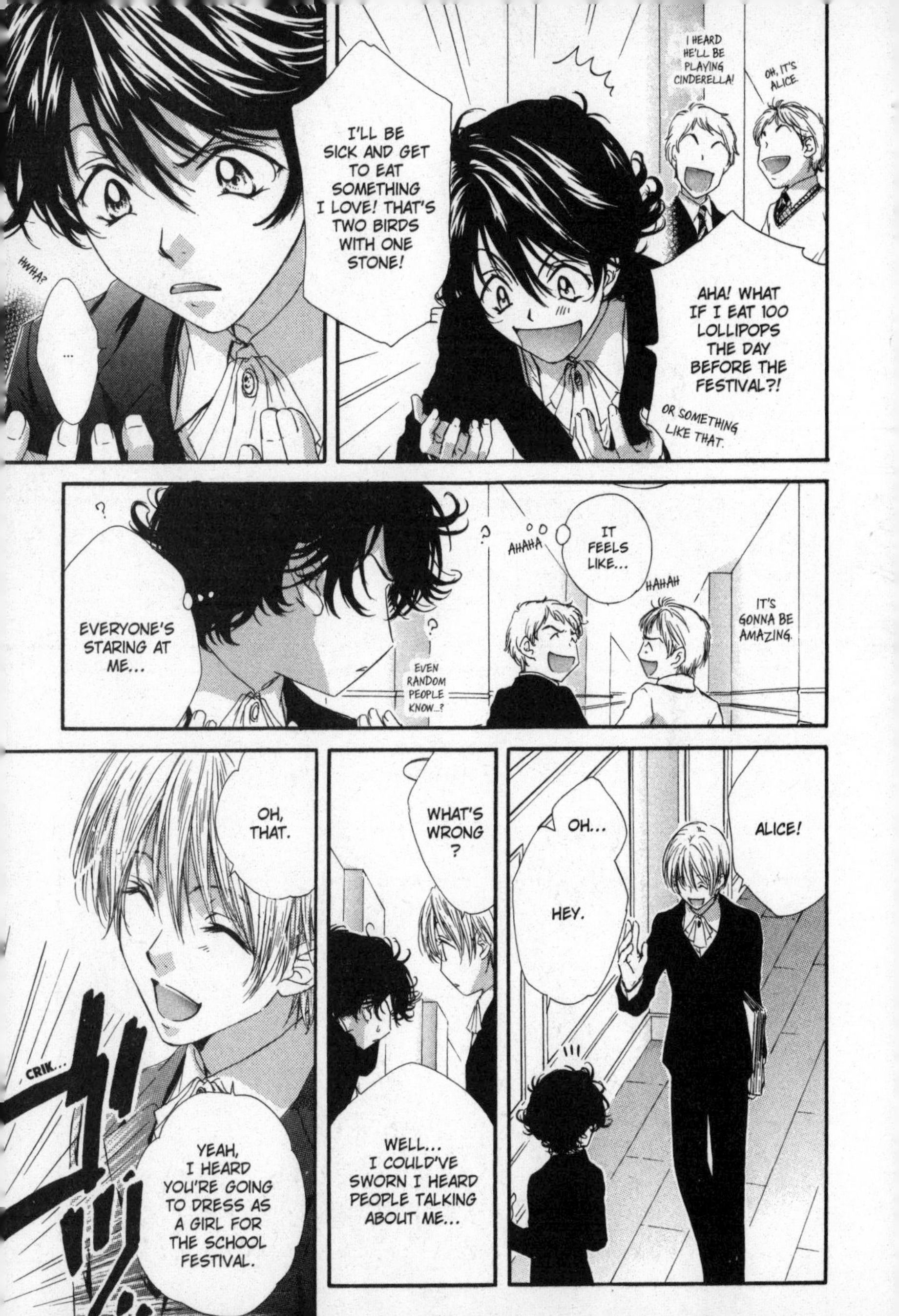
OH, IT'S ALICE.
I HEARD HE'LL BE PLAYING CINDERELLA!
AHA! WHAT IF I EAT 100 LOLLIPOPS THE DAY BEFORE THE FESTIVAL?!
OR SOMETHING LIKE THAT.
I'LL BE SICK AND GET TO EAT SOMETHING I LOVE! THAT'S TWO BIRDS WITH ONE STONE!
HWHA?
...
IT'S GONNA BE AMAZING.
HAHAH
IT FEELS LIKE...
AHAHA
?
?
EVEN RANDOM PEOPLE KNOW...?
EVERYONE'S STARING AT ME...
?
ALICE!
OH...
HEY.
WHAT'S WRONG ?
WELL... I COULD'VE SWORN I HEARD PEOPLE TALKING ABOUT ME...
OH, THAT.
YEAH, I HEARD YOU'RE GOING TO DRESS AS A GIRL FOR THE SCHOOL FESTIVAL.
CRIK...

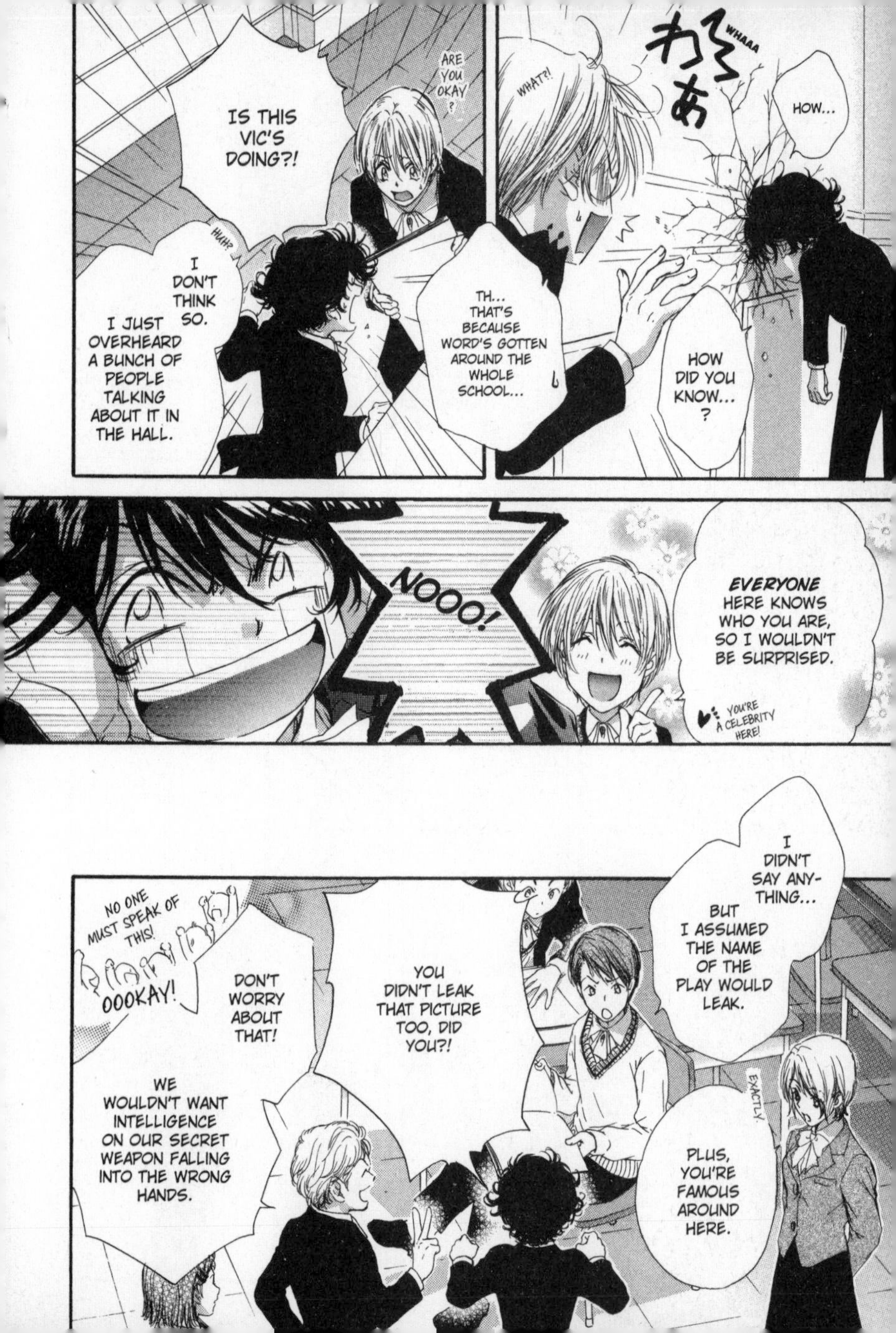

HOW...
わぁあ
WHAAA
HOW DID YOU KNOW...?
WHAT?!
TH... THAT'S BECAUSE WORD'S GOTTEN AROUND THE WHOLE SCHOOL...
ARE YOU OKAY?
IS THIS VIC'S DOING?!
HUH?
I DON'T THINK SO.
I JUST OVERHEARD A BUNCH OF PEOPLE TALKING ABOUT IT IN THE HALL.
EVERYONE HERE KNOWS WHO YOU ARE, SO I WOULDN'T BE SURPRISED.
YOU'RE A CELEBRITY HERE!
NOOOO!
I DIDN'T SAY ANY-THING... BUT I ASSUMED THE NAME OF THE PLAY WOULD LEAK.
EXACTLY
PLUS, YOU'RE FAMOUS AROUND HERE.
YOU DIDN'T LEAK THAT PICTURE TOO, DID YOU?!
DON'T WORRY ABOUT THAT!
WE WOULDN'T WANT INTELLIGENCE ON OUR SECRET WEAPON FALLING INTO THE WRONG HANDS.
NO ONE MUST SPEAK OF THIS!
OOOKAY!

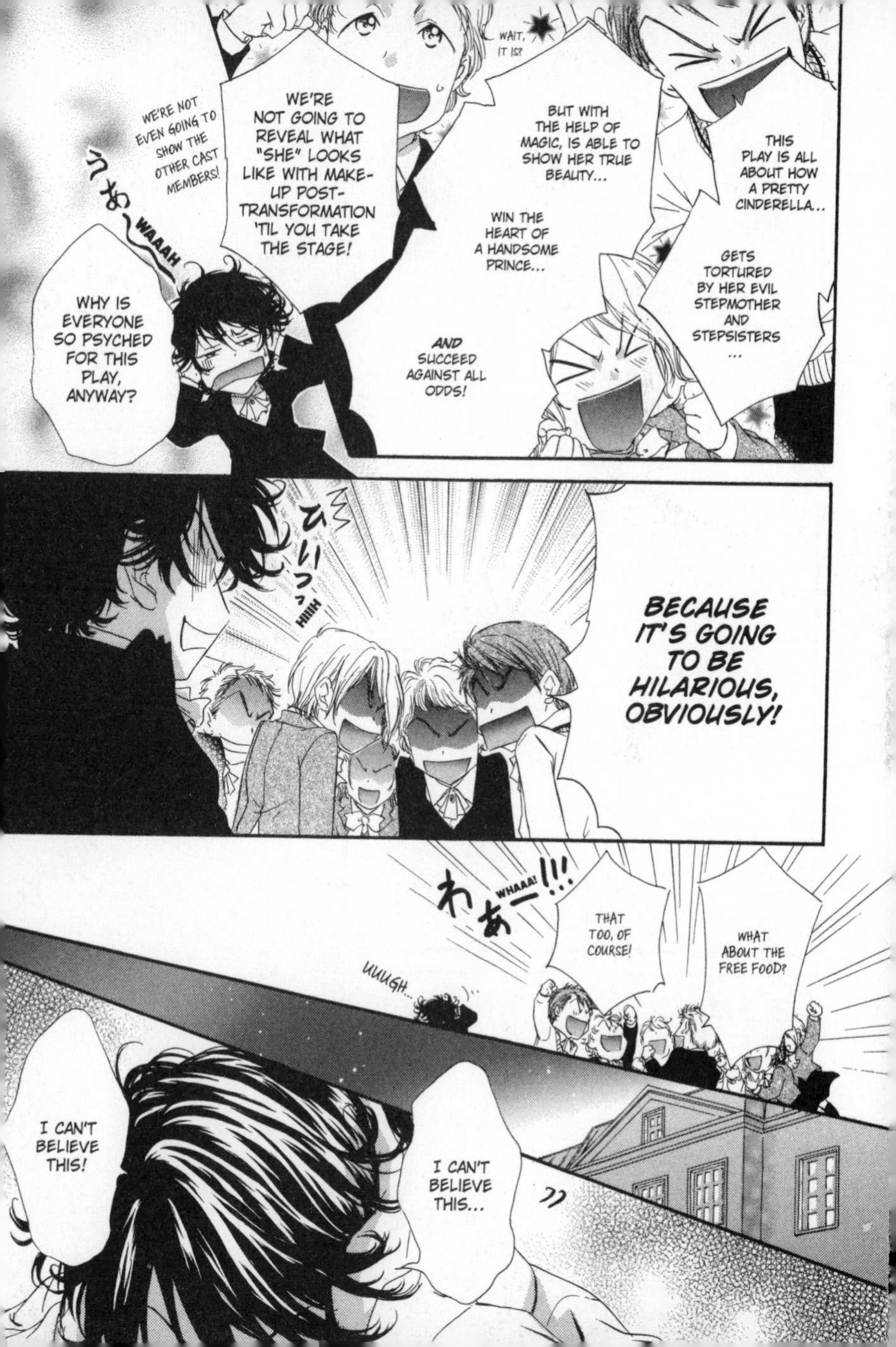
THIS PLAY IS ALL ABOUT HOW A PRETTY CINDERELLA...
GETS TORTURED BY HER EVIL STEPMOTHER AND STEPSISTERS...
WAIT, IT IS?
BUT WITH THE HELP OF MAGIC, IS ABLE TO SHOW HER TRUE BEAUTY...
WIN THE HEART OF A HANDSOME PRINCE...
AND SUCCEED AGAINST ALL ODDS!
WE'RE NOT GOING TO REVEAL WHAT "SHE" LOOKS LIKE WITH MAKE-UP POST-TRANSFORMATION 'TIL YOU TAKE THE STAGE!
WE'RE NOT EVEN GOING TO SHOW THE OTHER CAST MEMBERS!
うあ〜 WAAAH
WHY IS EVERYONE SO PSYCHED FOR THIS PLAY, ANYWAY?
BECAUSE IT'S GOING TO BE HILARIOUS, OBVIOUSLY!
ひいっっ HIIIH
WHAT ABOUT THE FREE FOOD?
THAT TOO, OF COURSE!
わあー WHAAA!!!!
UUUGH...
I CAN'T BELIEVE THIS...
I CAN'T BELIEVE THIS!
フフ

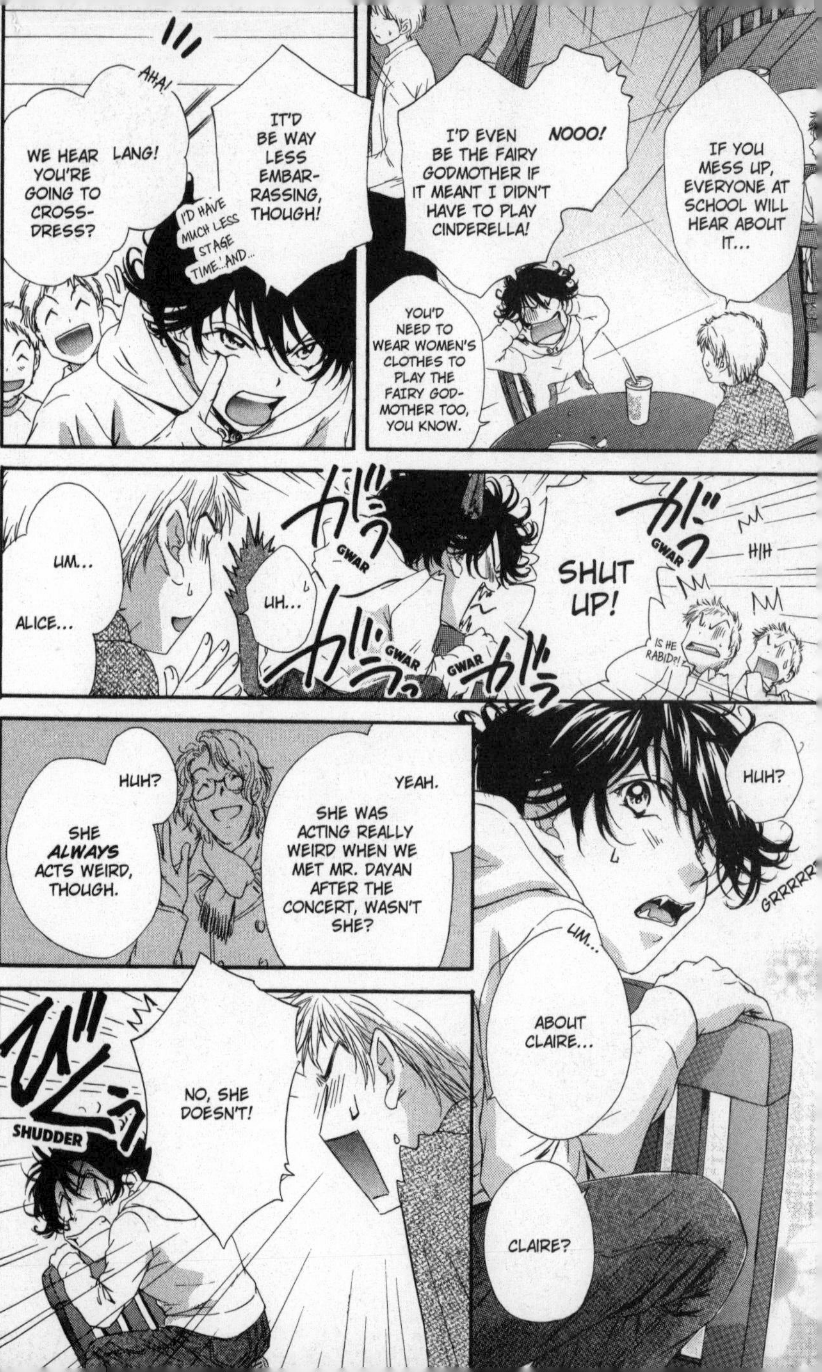

IF YOU MESS UP, EVERYONE AT SCHOOL WILL HEAR ABOUT IT...
NOOO!
I'D EVEN BE THE FAIRY GODMOTHER IF IT MEANT I DIDN'T HAVE TO PLAY CINDERELLA!
YOU'D NEED TO WEAR WOMEN'S CLOTHES TO PLAY THE FAIRY GOD-MOTHER TOO, YOU KNOW.
IT'D BE WAY LESS EMBAR-RASSING, THOUGH!
I'D HAVE MUCH LESS STAGE TIME...AND...
AHA!
LANG! WE HEAR YOU'RE GOING TO CROSS-DRESS?
GWAR
SHUT UP!
IS HE RABID?!
GWAR
GWAR
GWAR
UH...
UM...
ALICE...
HUH?
GRRRRR
UM...
ABOUT CLAIRE...
CLAIRE?
YEAH.
SHE WAS ACTING REALLY WEIRD WHEN WE MET MR. DAYAN AFTER THE CONCERT, WASN'T SHE?
HUH?
SHE *ALWAYS* ACTS WEIRD, THOUGH.
NO, SHE DOESN'T!
SHUDDER

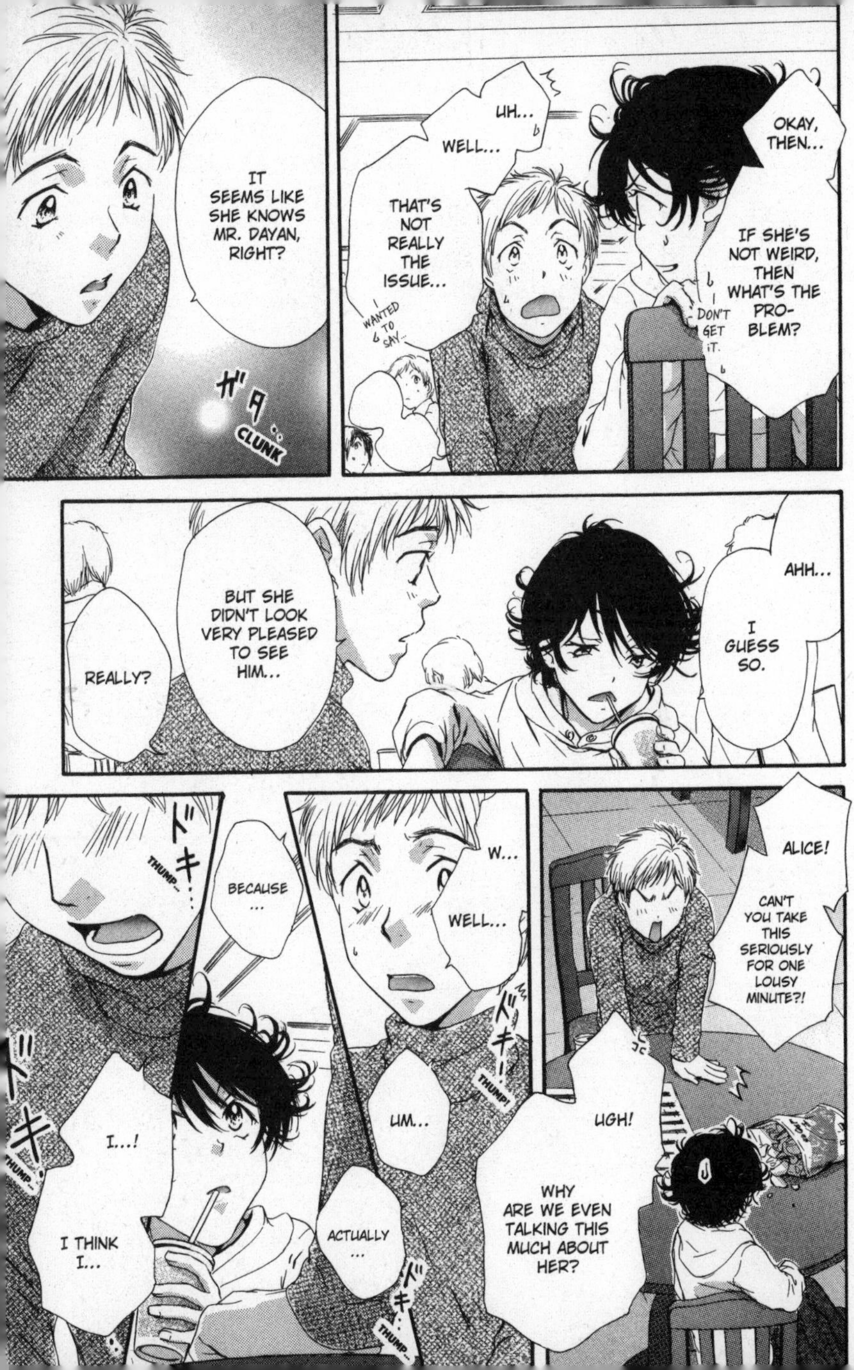
OKAY, THEN...
IF SHE'S NOT WEIRD, THEN WHAT'S THE PRO- BLEM?
I DON'T GET IT.
UH...
WELL...
THAT'S NOT REALLY THE ISSUE...
I WANTED TO SAY...
IT SEEMS LIKE SHE KNOWS MR. DAYAN, RIGHT?
ガタ
CLUNK
AHH...
I GUESS SO.
BUT SHE DIDN'T LOOK VERY PLEASED TO SEE HIM...
REALLY?
ALICE!
CAN'T YOU TAKE THIS SERIOUSLY FOR ONE LOUSY MINUTE?!
UGH!
WHY ARE WE EVEN TALKING THIS MUCH ABOUT HER?
W...
WELL...
ドキー
THUMP!
UM...
ACTUALLY...
ドキ
THUMP...
ドキ
THUMP...
BECAUSE...
I...!
I THINK I...
ドキ
THUMP...

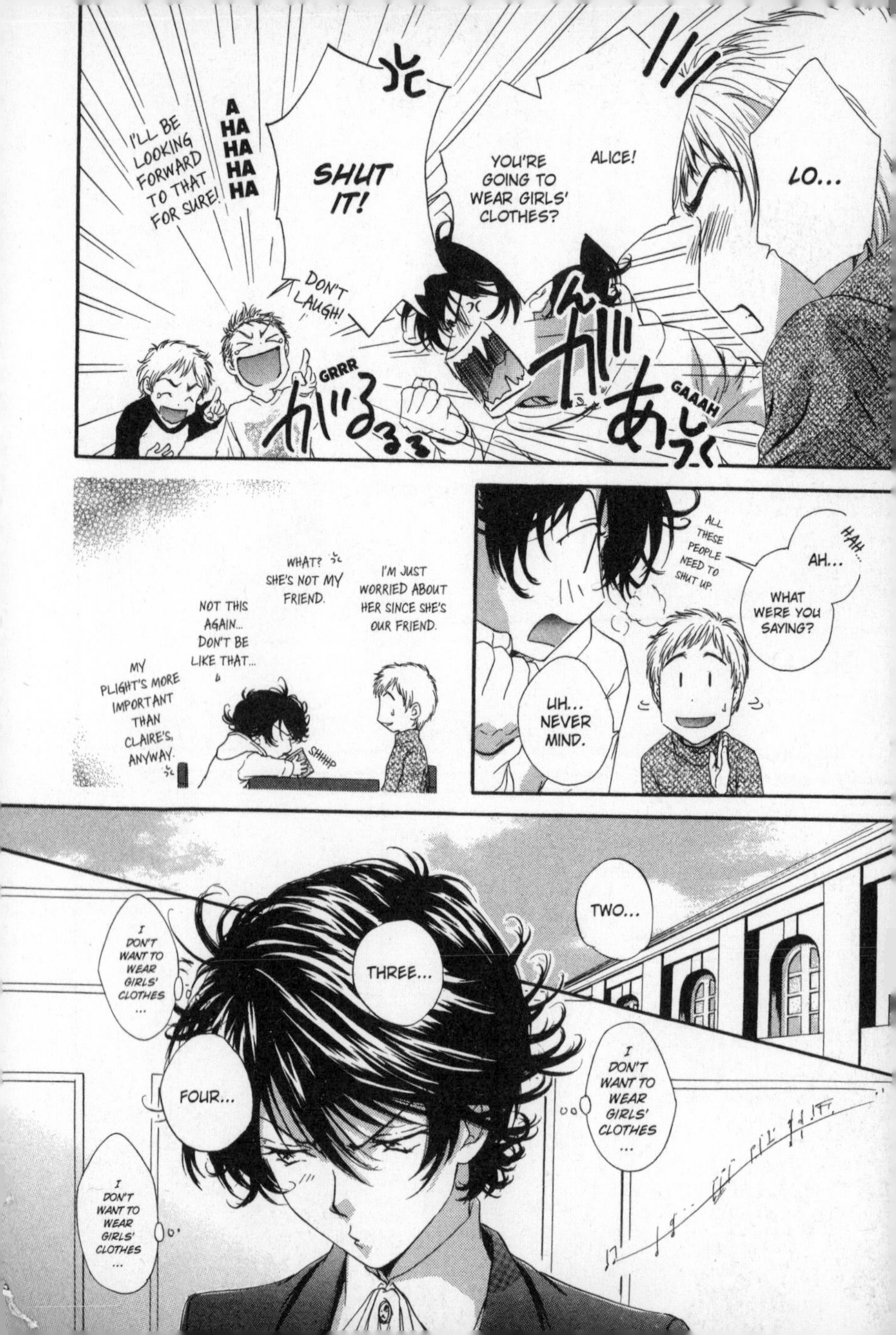
LO...
ALICE!
YOU'RE GOING TO WEAR GIRLS' CLOTHES?
SHUT IT!
DON'T LAUGH!
A HA HA HA HA HA
I'LL BE LOOKING FORWARD TO THAT FOR SURE!
GAAAH
GRRR
ALL THESE PEOPLE NEED TO SHUT UP.
HAH...
AH... WHAT WERE YOU SAYING?
UH... NEVER MIND.
I'M JUST WORRIED ABOUT HER SINCE SHE'S OUR FRIEND.
WHAT? SHE'S NOT MY FRIEND.
NOT THIS AGAIN... DON'T BE LIKE THAT...
MY PLIGHT'S MORE IMPORTANT THAN CLAIRE'S, ANYWAY.
SHHHP
TWO...
I DON'T WANT TO WEAR GIRLS' CLOTHES...
THREE...
I DON'T WANT TO WEAR GIRLS' CLOTHES...
FOUR...
I DON'T WANT TO WEAR GIRLS' CLOTHES...

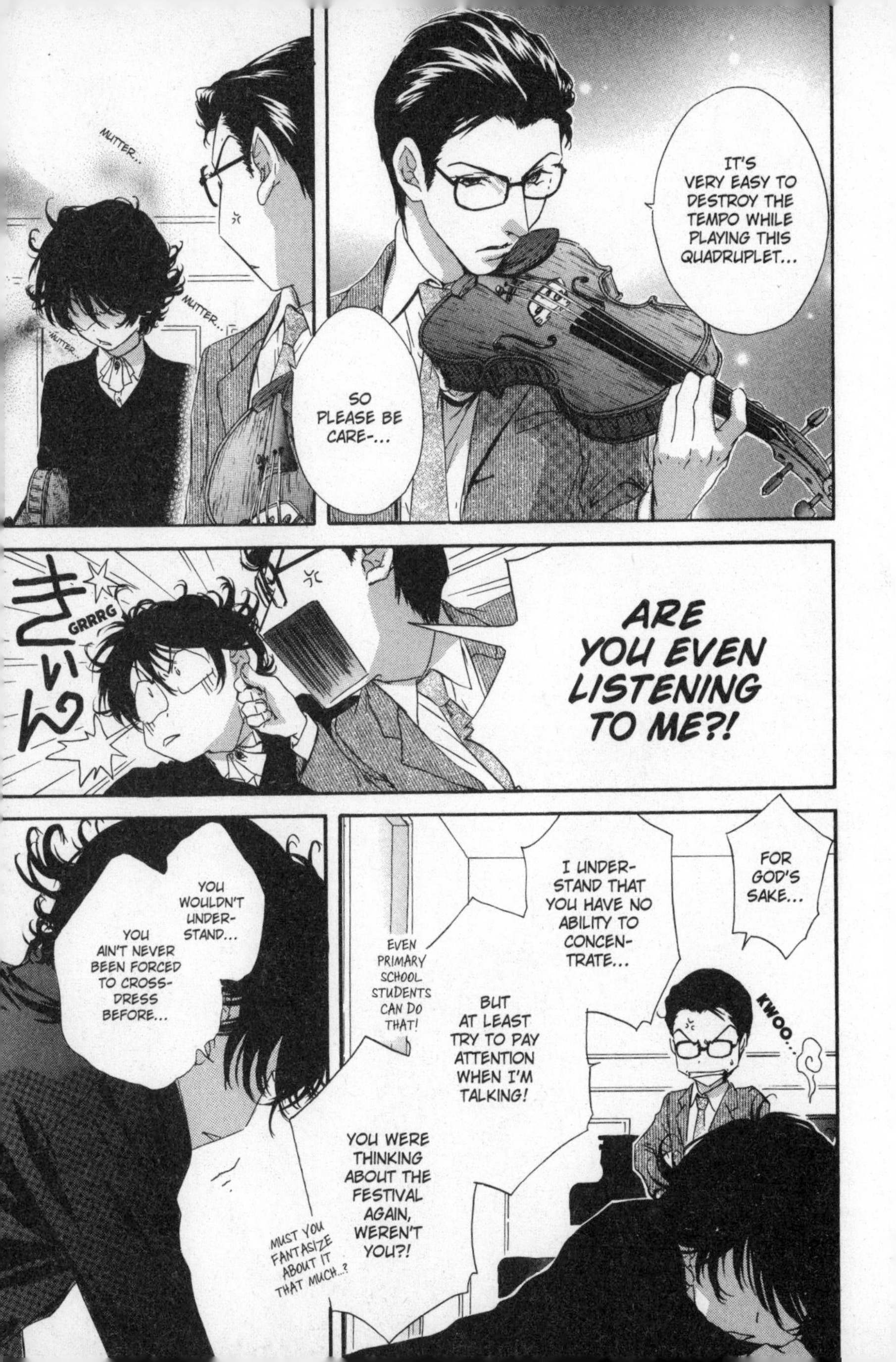
IT'S VERY EASY TO DESTROY THE TEMPO WHILE PLAYING THIS QUADRUPLET...
SO PLEASE BE CARE-...
MUTTER...
MUTTER...
MUTTER...
ARE YOU EVEN LISTENING TO ME?!
GRRRG
FOR GOD'S SAKE...
I UNDER-STAND THAT YOU HAVE NO ABILITY TO CONCEN-TRATE...
EVEN PRIMARY SCHOOL STUDENTS CAN DO THAT!
BUT AT LEAST TRY TO PAY ATTENTION WHEN I'M TALKING!
KWOO...
YOU WERE THINKING ABOUT THE FESTIVAL AGAIN, WEREN'T YOU?!
MUST YOU FANTASIZE ABOUT IT THAT MUCH...?
YOU WOULDN'T UNDER-STAND...
YOU AIN'T NEVER BEEN FORCED TO CROSS-DRESS BEFORE...

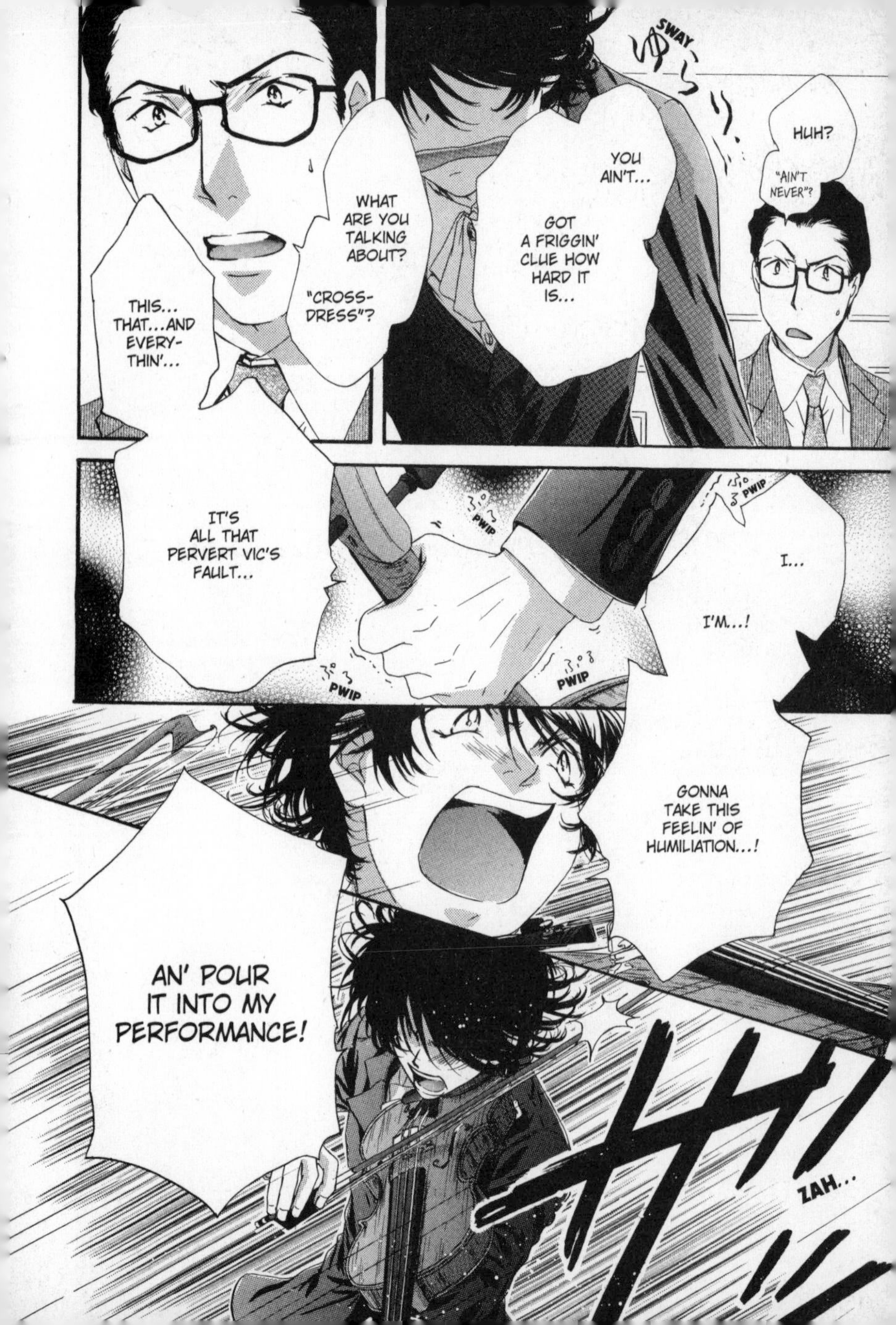
SWAY
HUH?
"AIN'T NEVER"?
YOU AIN'T...
GOT A FRIGGIN' CLUE HOW HARD IT IS...
WHAT ARE YOU TALKING ABOUT? "CROSS-DRESS"?
THIS... THAT...AND EVERY-THIN'...
PWIP
I...
I'M...!
PWIP
PWIP
IT'S ALL THAT PERVERT VIC'S FAULT...
PWIP
GONNA TAKE THIS FEELIN' OF HUMILIATION...!
AN' POUR IT INTO MY PERFORMANCE!
ZAH...

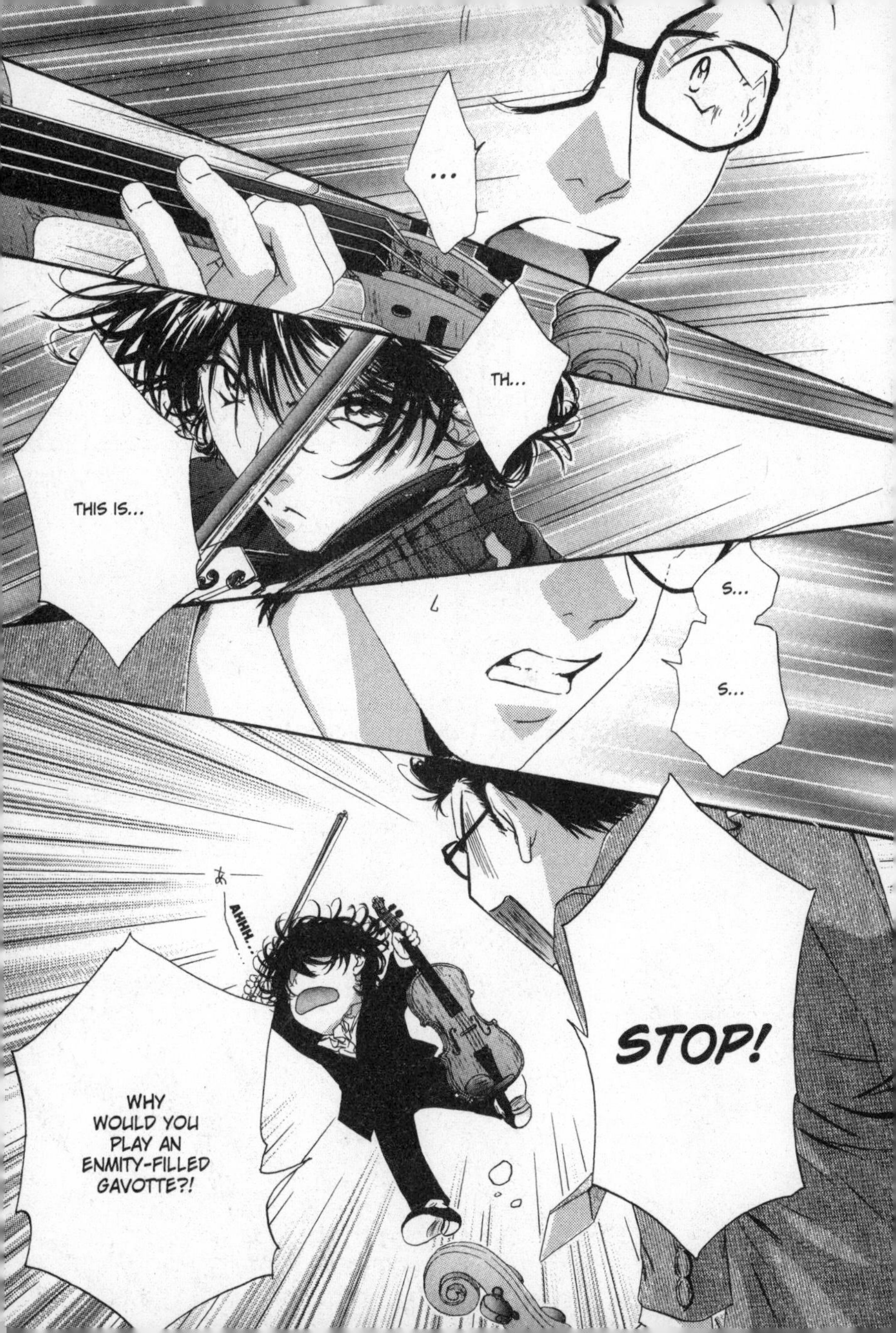
...
TH...
THIS IS...
S...
S...
STOP!
あ—
AHHH...
WHY WOULD YOU PLAY AN ENMITY-FILLED GAVOTTE?!

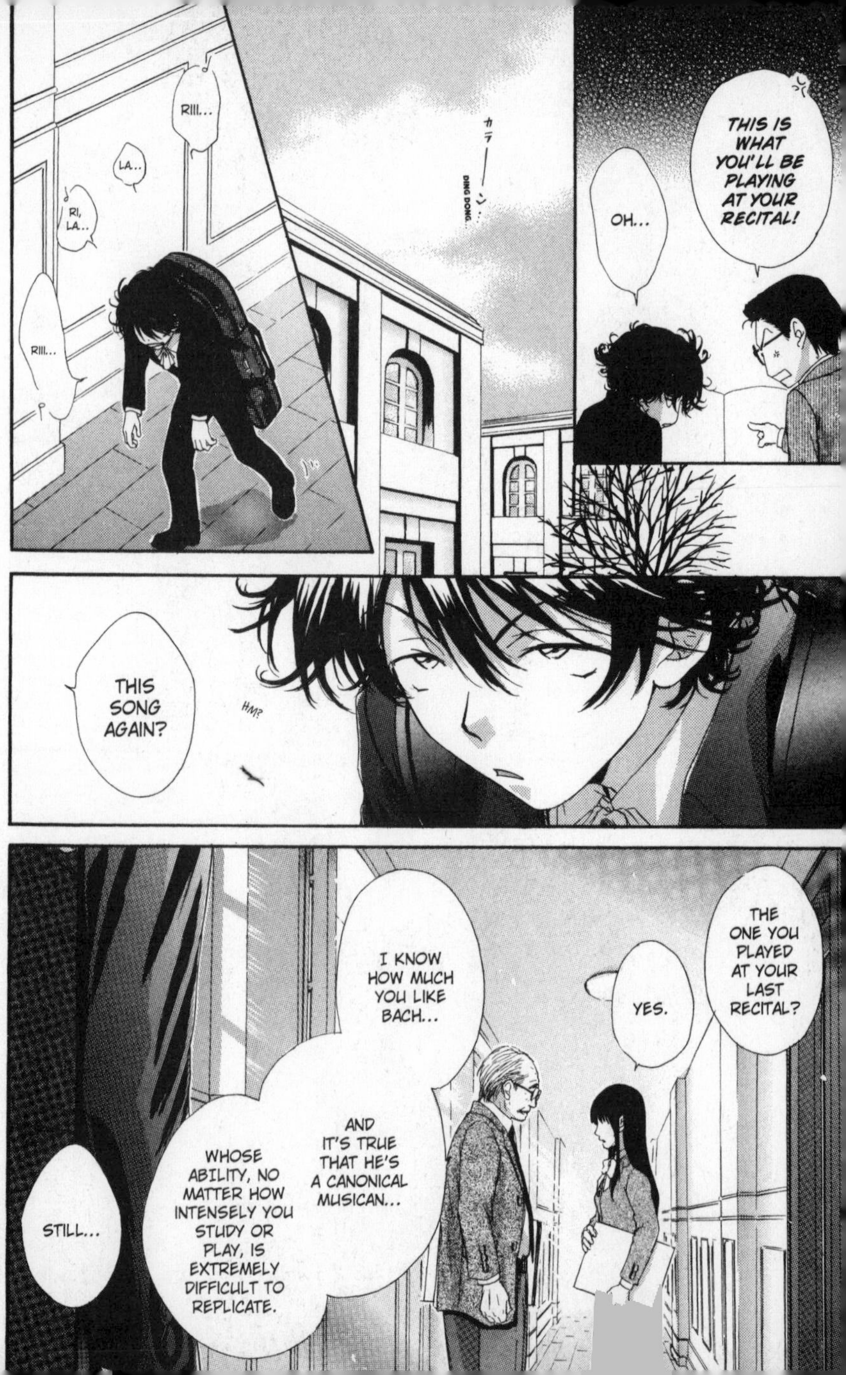
THIS IS WHAT YOU'LL BE PLAYING AT YOUR RECITAL!
OH...
カラ—ン…
DING DONG...
RIII...
LA...
RI, LA...
RIII...
HM?
THIS SONG AGAIN?
THE ONE YOU PLAYED AT YOUR LAST RECITAL?
YES.
I KNOW HOW MUCH YOU LIKE BACH...
AND IT'S TRUE THAT HE'S A CANONICAL MUSICAN...
WHOSE ABILITY, NO MATTER HOW INTENSELY YOU STUDY OR PLAY, IS EXTREMELY DIFFICULT TO REPLICATE.
STILL...

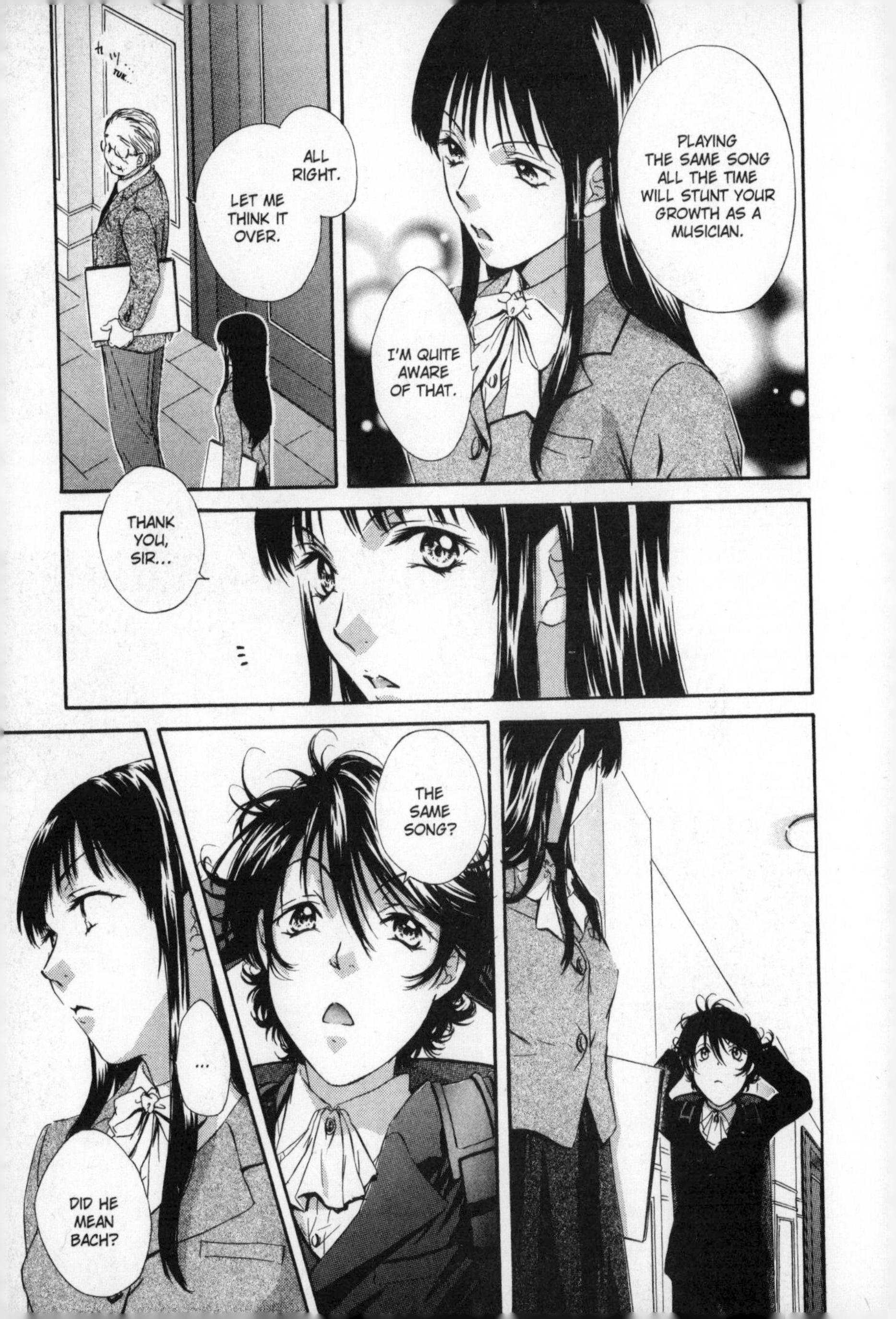
PLAYING THE SAME SONG ALL THE TIME WILL STUNT YOUR GROWTH AS A MUSICIAN.
I'M QUITE AWARE OF THAT.
TUK...
ALL RIGHT.
LET ME THINK IT OVER.
THANK YOU, SIR...
THE SAME SONG?
...
DID HE MEAN BACH?

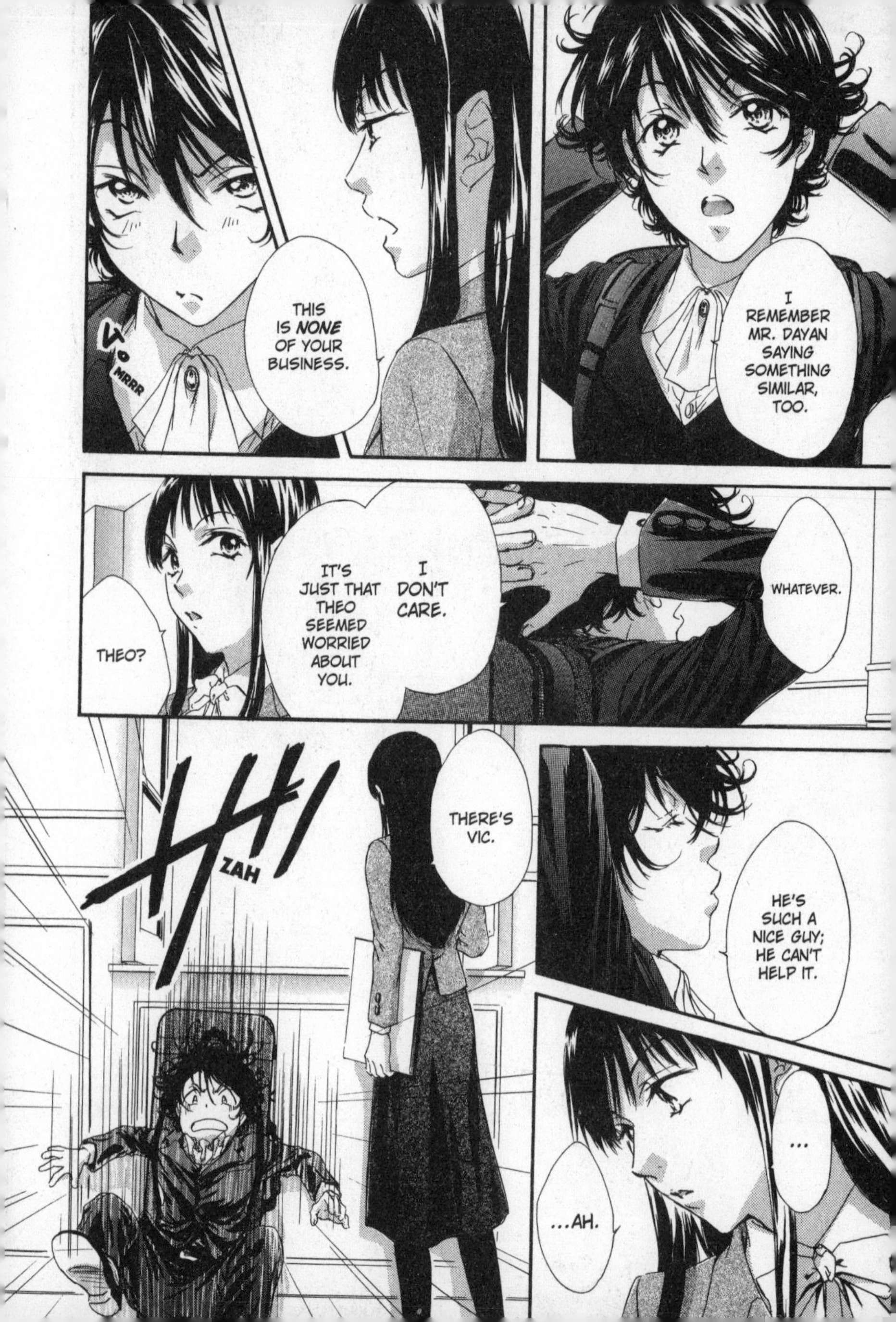
I REMEMBER MR. DAYAN SAYING SOMETHING SIMILAR, TOO.
THIS IS *NONE* OF YOUR BUSINESS.
MRRR
WHATEVER.
I DON'T CARE.
IT'S JUST THAT THEO SEEMED WORRIED ABOUT YOU.
THEO?
HE'S SUCH A NICE GUY; HE CAN'T HELP IT.
...
...AH.
THERE'S VIC.
ZAH

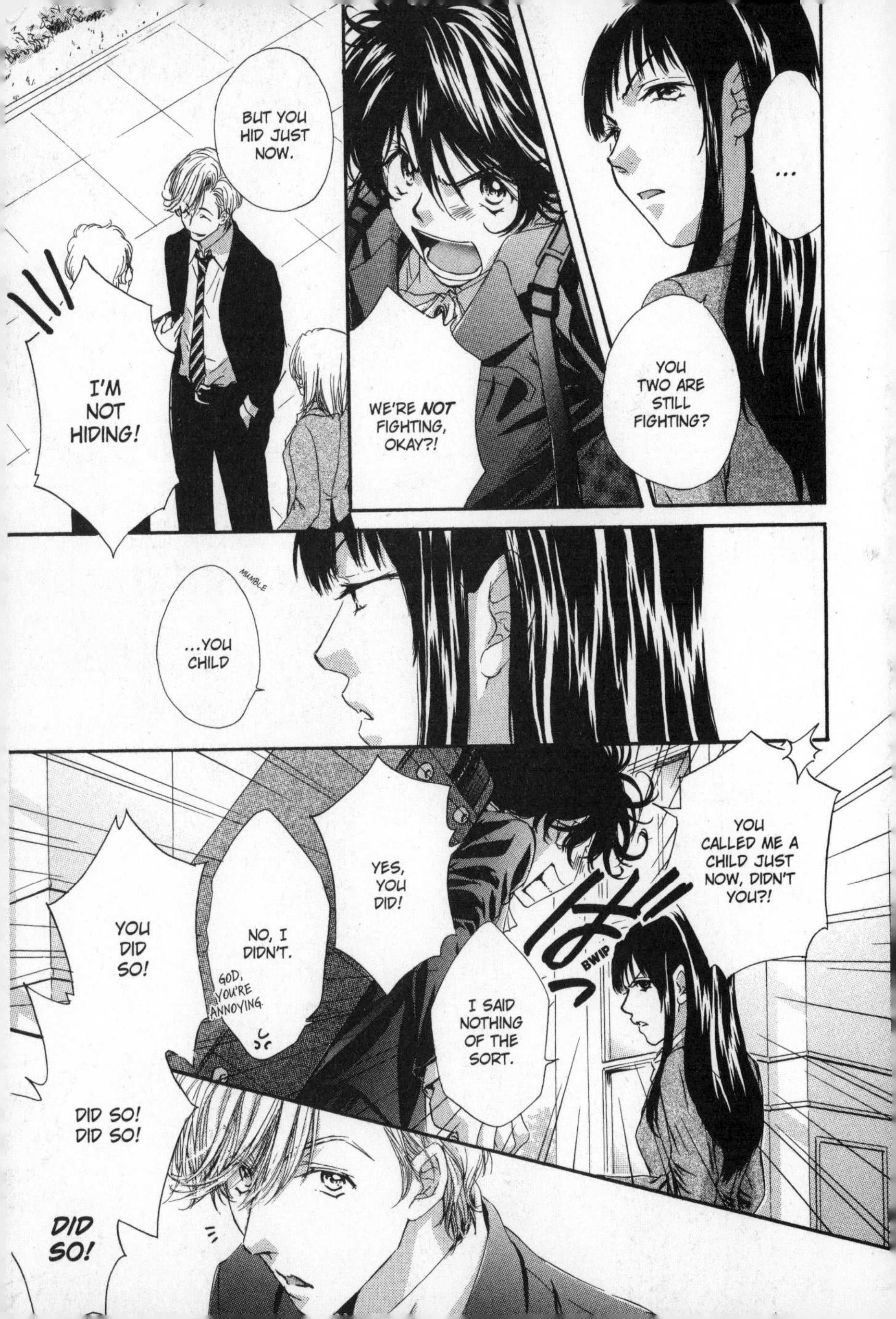
...
YOU TWO ARE STILL FIGHTING?
WE'RE NOT FIGHTING, OKAY?!
BUT YOU HID JUST NOW.
I'M NOT HIDING!
MMMBLE
...YOU CHILD
YOU CALLED ME A CHILD JUST NOW, DIDN'T YOU?!
BWIP
I SAID NOTHING OF THE SORT.
YES, YOU DID!
NO, I DIDN'T.
GOD, YOU'RE ANNOYING.
YOU DID SO!
DID SO! DID SO!
DID SO!

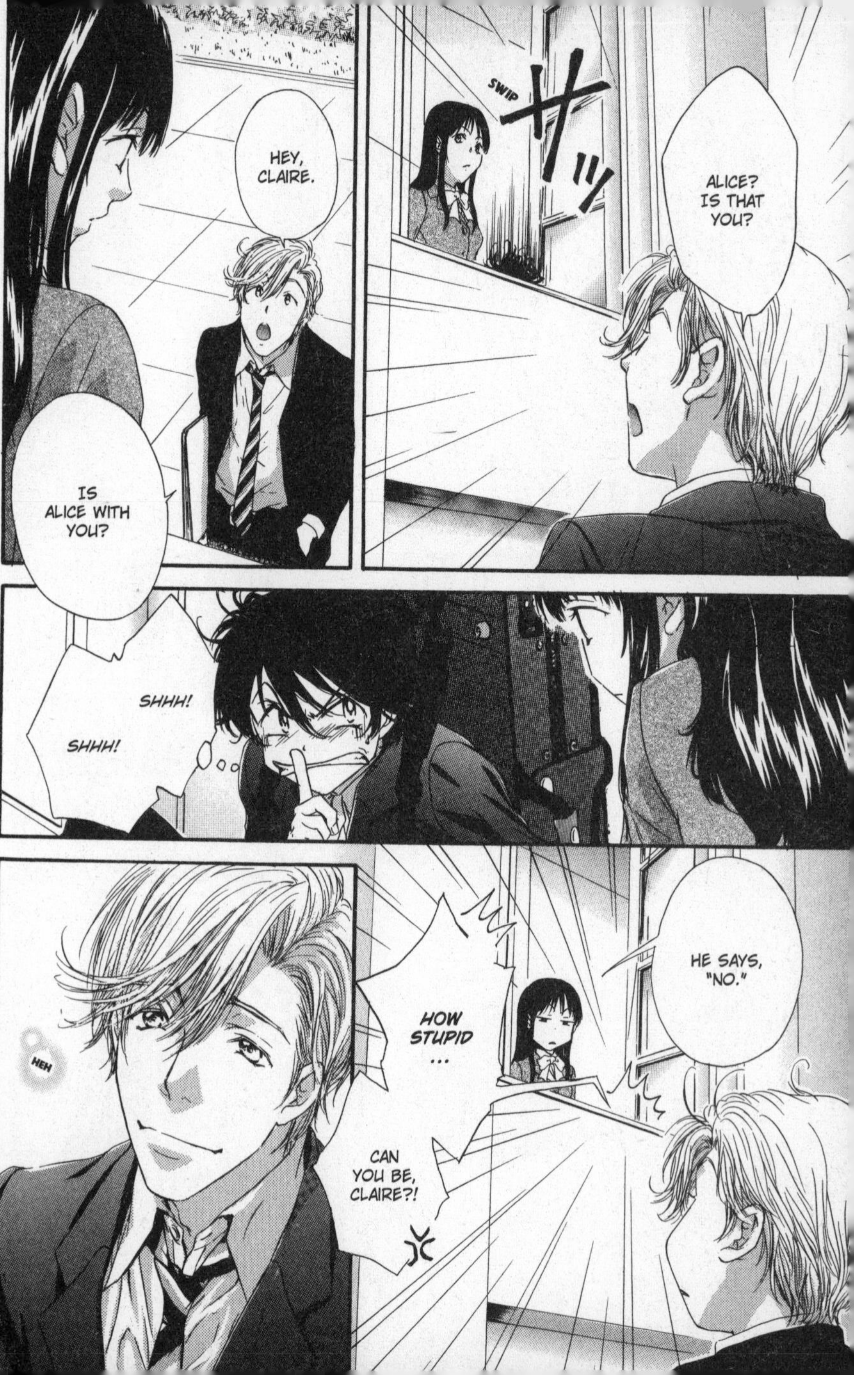
SWIP
ALICE? IS THAT YOU?
HEY, CLAIRE.
IS ALICE WITH YOU?
SHHH!
SHHH!
HE SAYS, "NO."
HOW STUPID ...
CAN YOU BE, CLAIRE?!
HEH

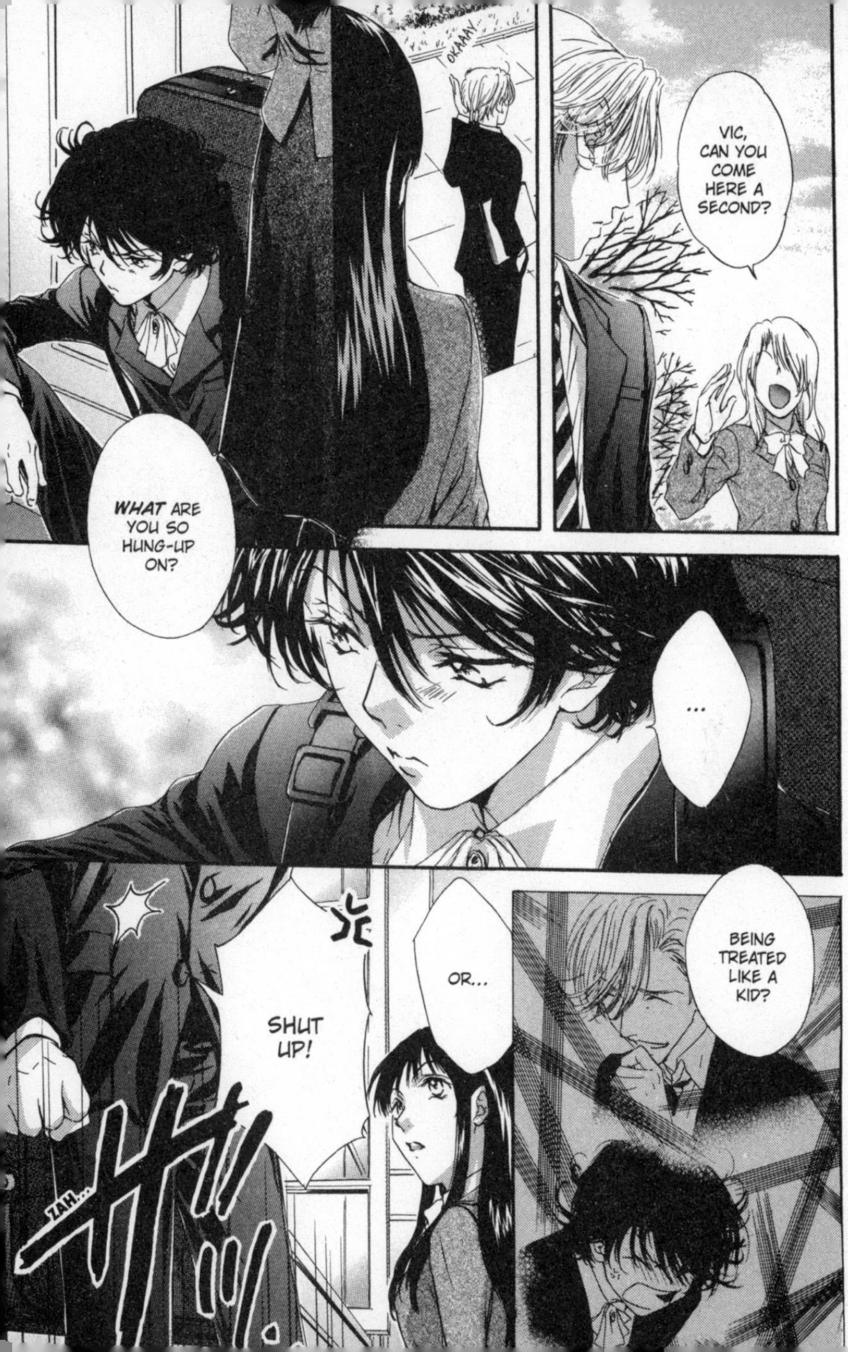
VIC, CAN YOU COME HERE A SECOND?
OKAAAY
WHAT ARE YOU SO HUNG-UP ON?
...
BEING TREATED LIKE A KID?
OR...
SHUT UP!
ZAH...

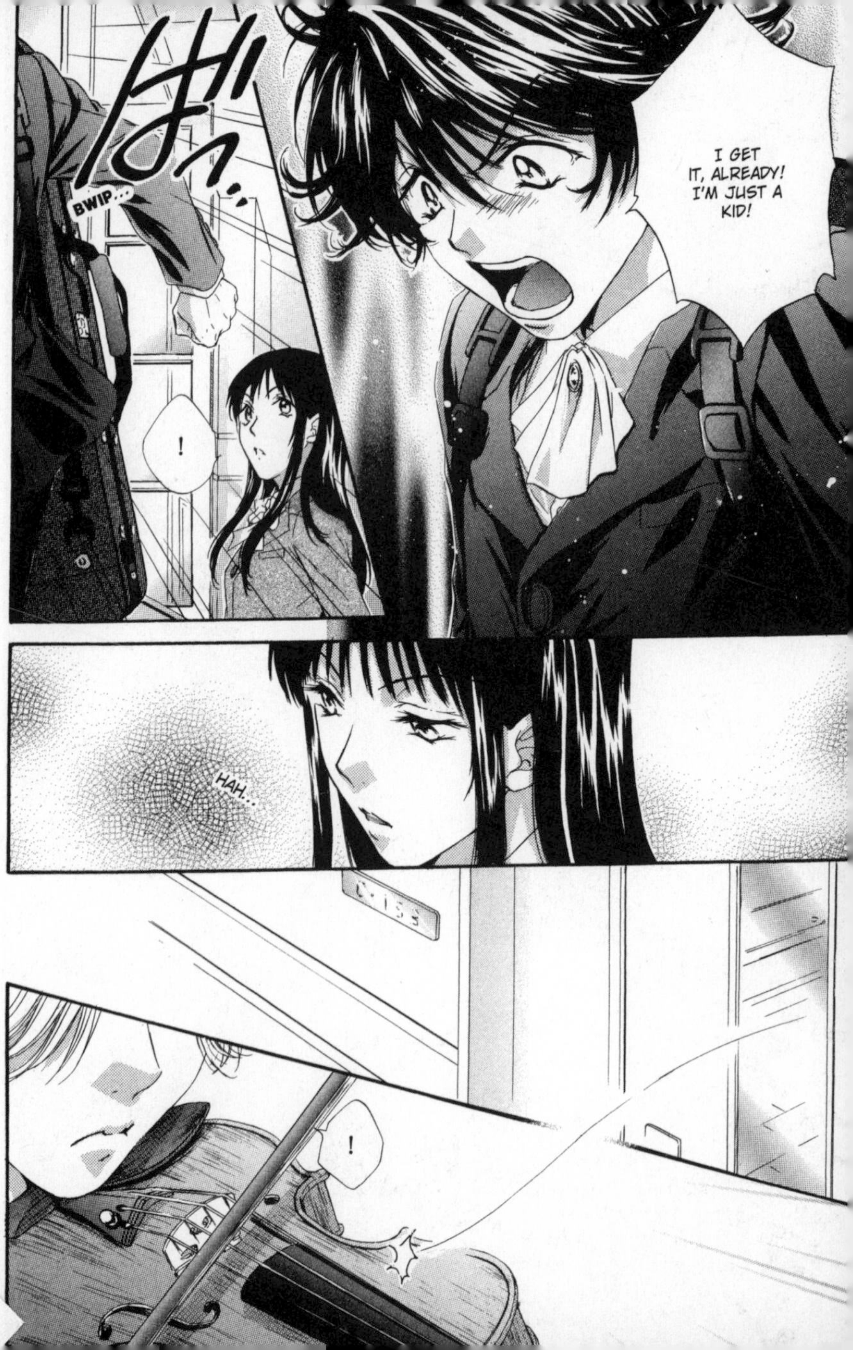
I GET IT, ALREADY! I'M JUST A KID!
ぱっ
BWIP...
!
HAH...
!

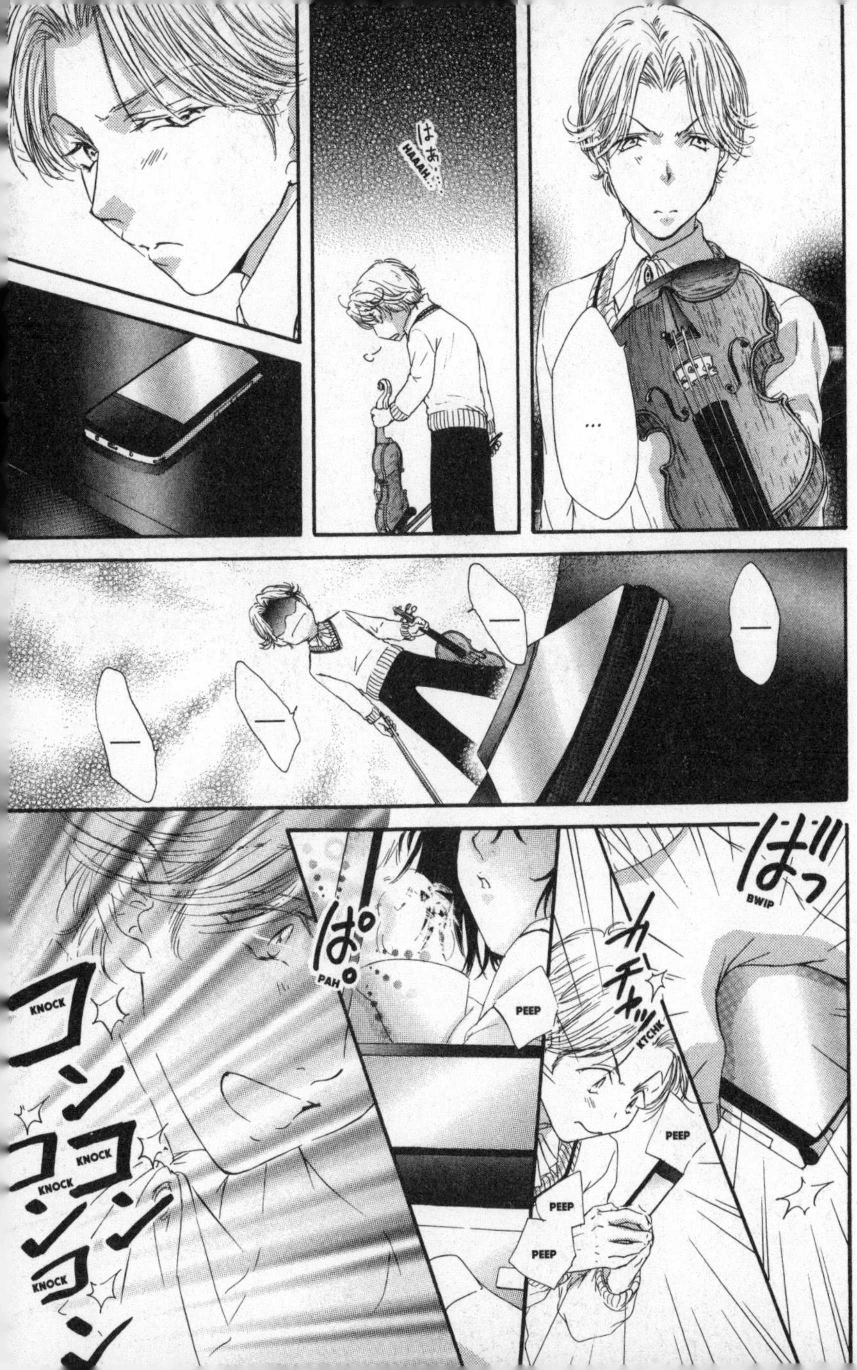
…
はぁ
HAAAH…
—
—
—
—
ばっ
BWIP
カチャッ
KTCHK
PEEP
PEEP
PEEP
ぱ。
PAH
PEEP
コンコン
コンコン
KNOCK
KNOCK
KNOCK
KNOCK

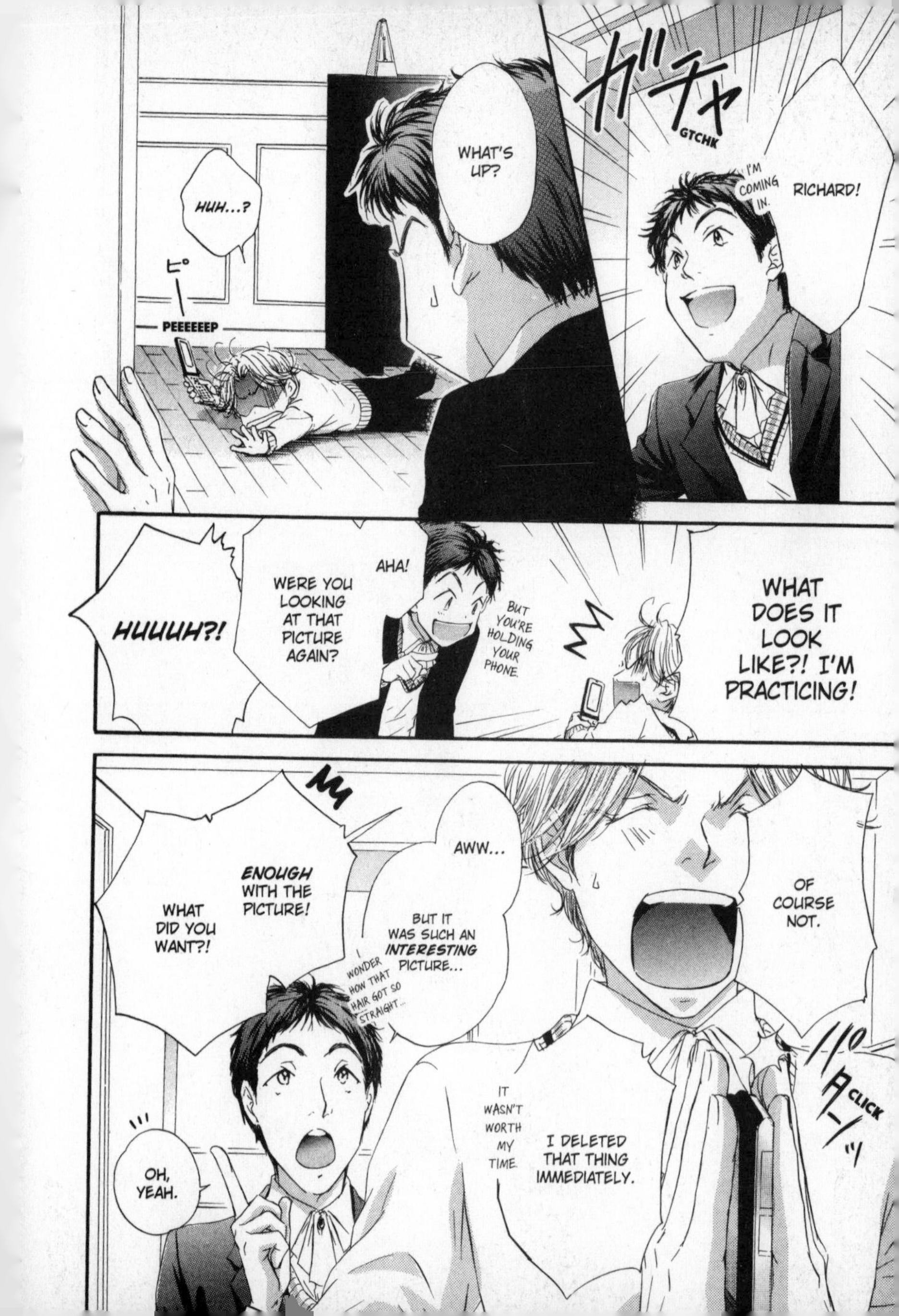

ガチャ
GTCHK
RICHARD!
I'M COMING IN.
WHAT'S UP?
HUH...?
ピー
PEEEEEEP
WHAT DOES IT LOOK LIKE?! I'M PRACTICING!
BUT YOU'RE HOLDING YOUR PHONE.
AHA!
WERE YOU LOOKING AT THAT PICTURE AGAIN?
HUUUH?!
OF COURSE NOT.
CLICK
I DELETED THAT THING IMMEDIATELY.
IT WASN'T WORTH MY TIME.
AWW...
BUT IT WAS SUCH AN INTERESTING PICTURE...
I WONDER HOW THAT HAIR GOT SO STRAIGHT...
ENOUGH WITH THE PICTURE!
WHAT DID YOU WANT?!
OH, YEAH.

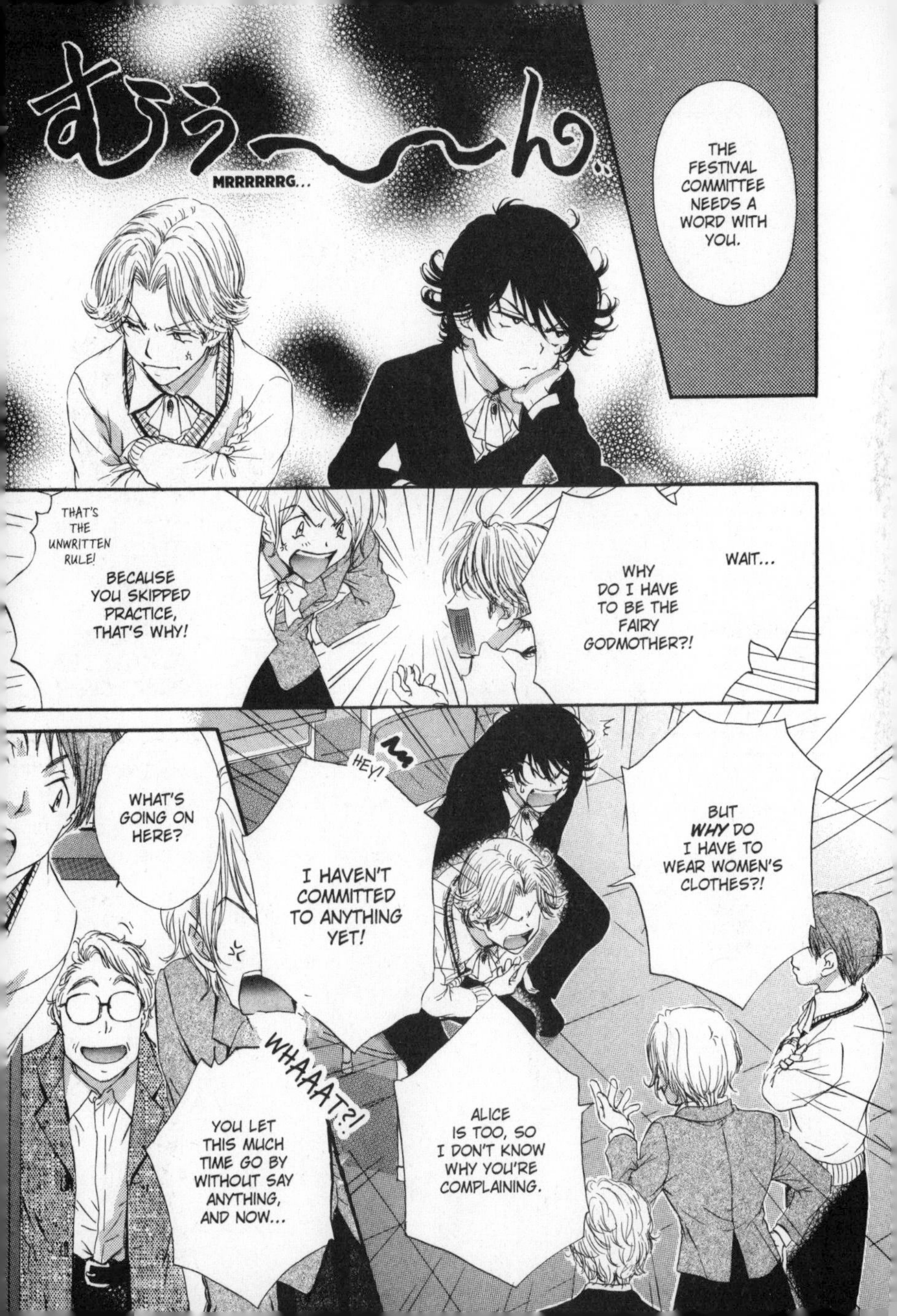
THE FESTIVAL COMMITTEE NEEDS A WORD WITH YOU.
むぅ〜ん
MRRRRRRG...
WAIT...
WHY DO I HAVE TO BE THE FAIRY GODMOTHER?!
BECAUSE YOU SKIPPED PRACTICE, THAT'S WHY!
THAT'S THE UNWRITTEN RULE!
BUT WHY DO I HAVE TO WEAR WOMEN'S CLOTHES?!
HEY!
I HAVEN'T COMMITTED TO ANYTHING YET!
WHAT'S GOING ON HERE?
ALICE IS TOO, SO I DON'T KNOW WHY YOU'RE COMPLAINING.
WHAAAAT?!
YOU LET THIS MUCH TIME GO BY WITHOUT SAY ANYTHING, AND NOW...

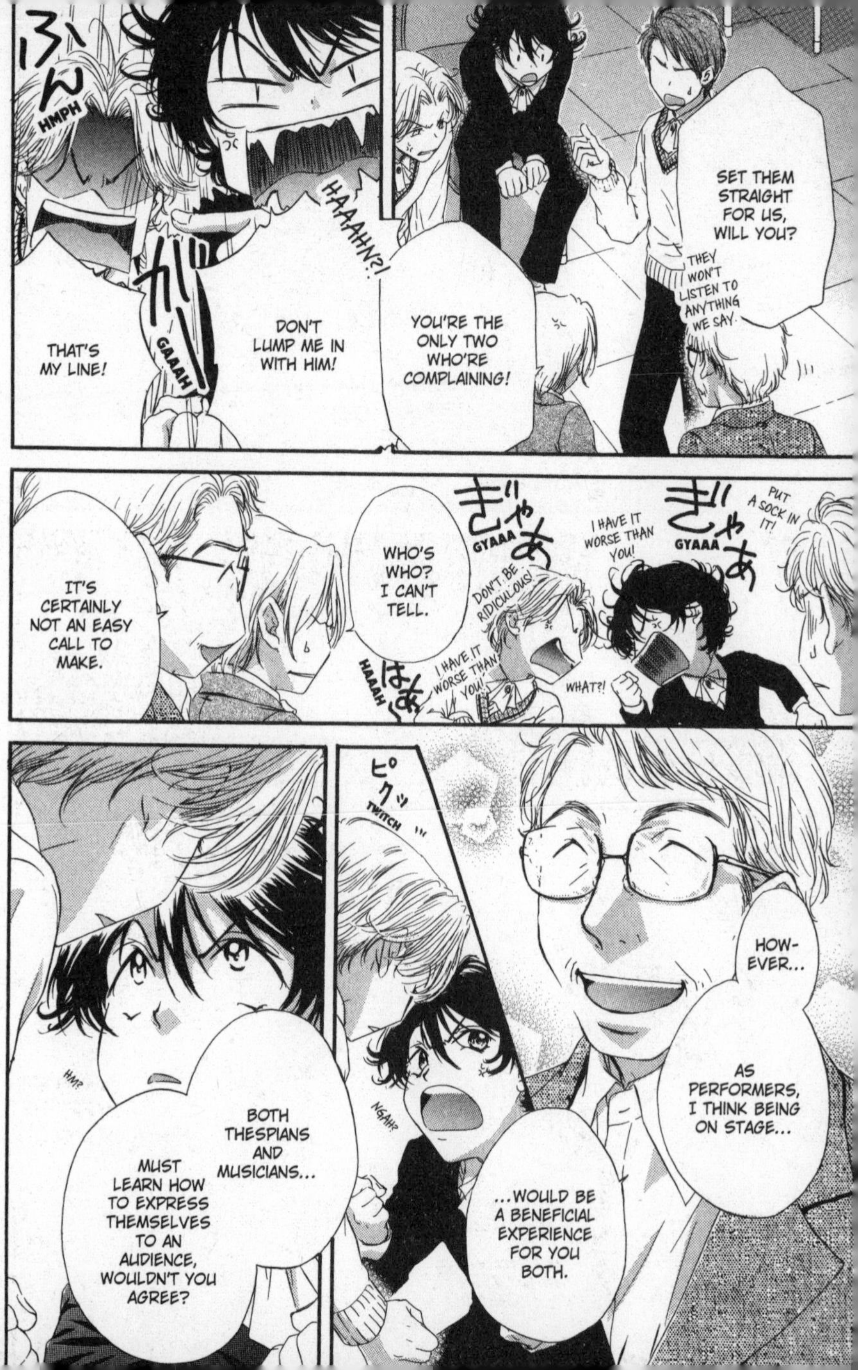
SET THEM STRAIGHT FOR US, WILL YOU?
THEY WON'T LISTEN TO ANYTHING WE SAY.
YOU'RE THE ONLY TWO WHO'RE COMPLAINING!
HAAAHN?!
DON'T LUMP ME IN WITH HIM!
ふん
HMPH
THAT'S MY LINE!
ガー
GAAAH
PUT A SOCK IN IT!
ぎゃあ
GYAAA
I HAVE IT WORSE THAN YOU!
WHAT?!
ぎゃあ
GYAAA
DON'T BE RIDICULOUS!
I HAVE IT WORSE THAN YOU!
WHO'S WHO? I CAN'T TELL.
はぁ
HAAAH
IT'S CERTAINLY NOT AN EASY CALL TO MAKE.
HOW-EVER...
AS PERFORMERS, I THINK BEING ON STAGE...
...WOULD BE A BENEFICIAL EXPERIENCE FOR YOU BOTH.
ピクッ
TWITCH
NGAH?
BOTH THESPIANS AND MUSICIANS...
MUST LEARN HOW TO EXPRESS THEMSELVES TO AN AUDIENCE, WOULDN'T YOU AGREE?
HM?

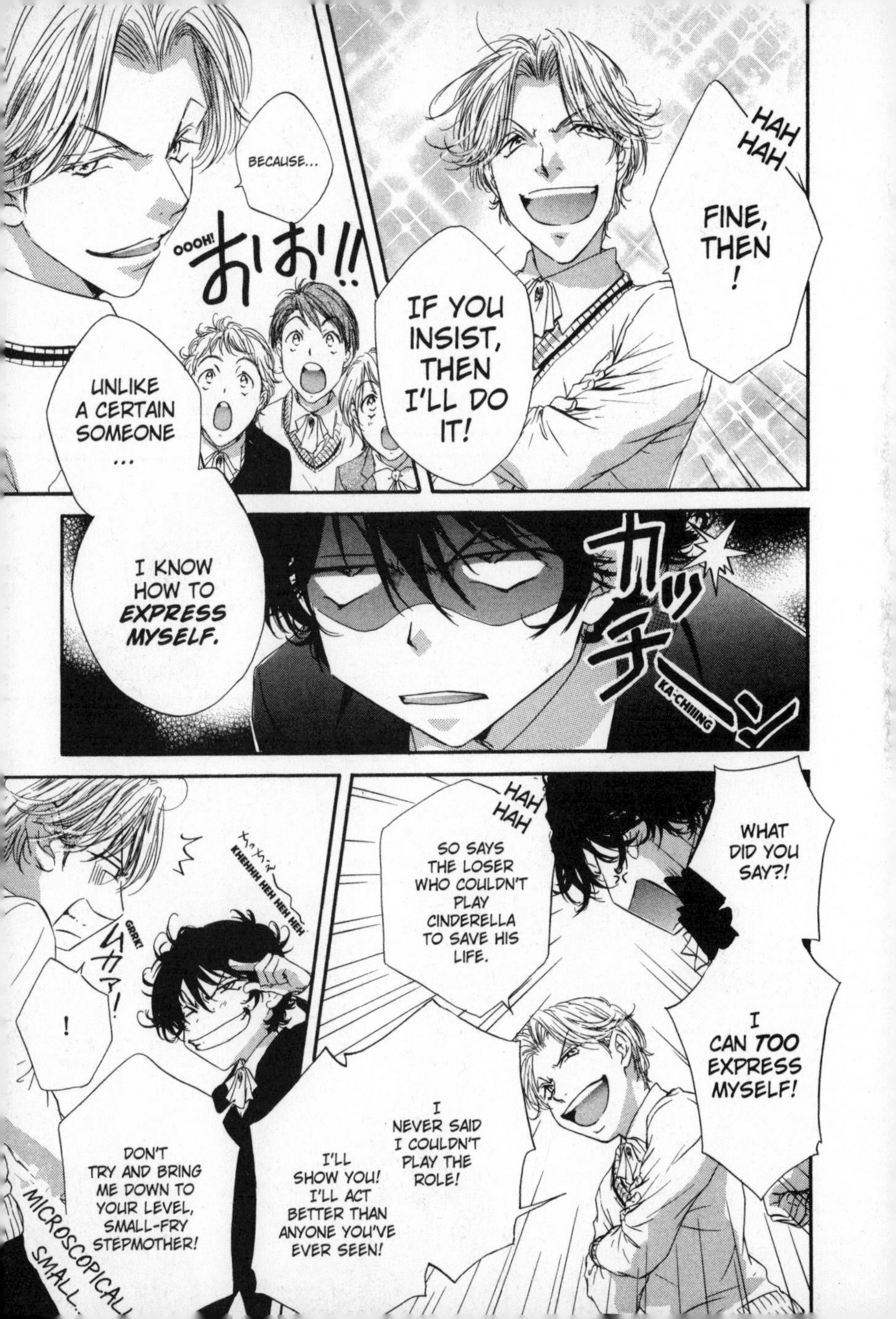
HAH HAH
FINE, THEN!
IF YOU INSIST, THEN I'LL DO IT!
BECAUSE...
OOOH!
おお!!
UNLIKE A CERTAIN SOMEONE...
I KNOW HOW TO EXPRESS MYSELF.
カッチーン
KA-CHIING
WHAT DID YOU SAY?!
HAH HAH
SO SAYS THE LOSER WHO COULDN'T PLAY CINDERELLA TO SAVE HIS LIFE.
I CAN TOO EXPRESS MYSELF!
I NEVER SAID I COULDN'T PLAY THE ROLE!
I'LL SHOW YOU! I'LL ACT BETTER THAN ANYONE YOU'VE EVER SEEN!
KHENHH HEH HEH HEH
ムカァ!
GRRK!
!
DON'T TRY AND BRING ME DOWN TO YOUR LEVEL, SMALL-FRY STEPMOTHER!
MICROSCOPICALLY SMALL...

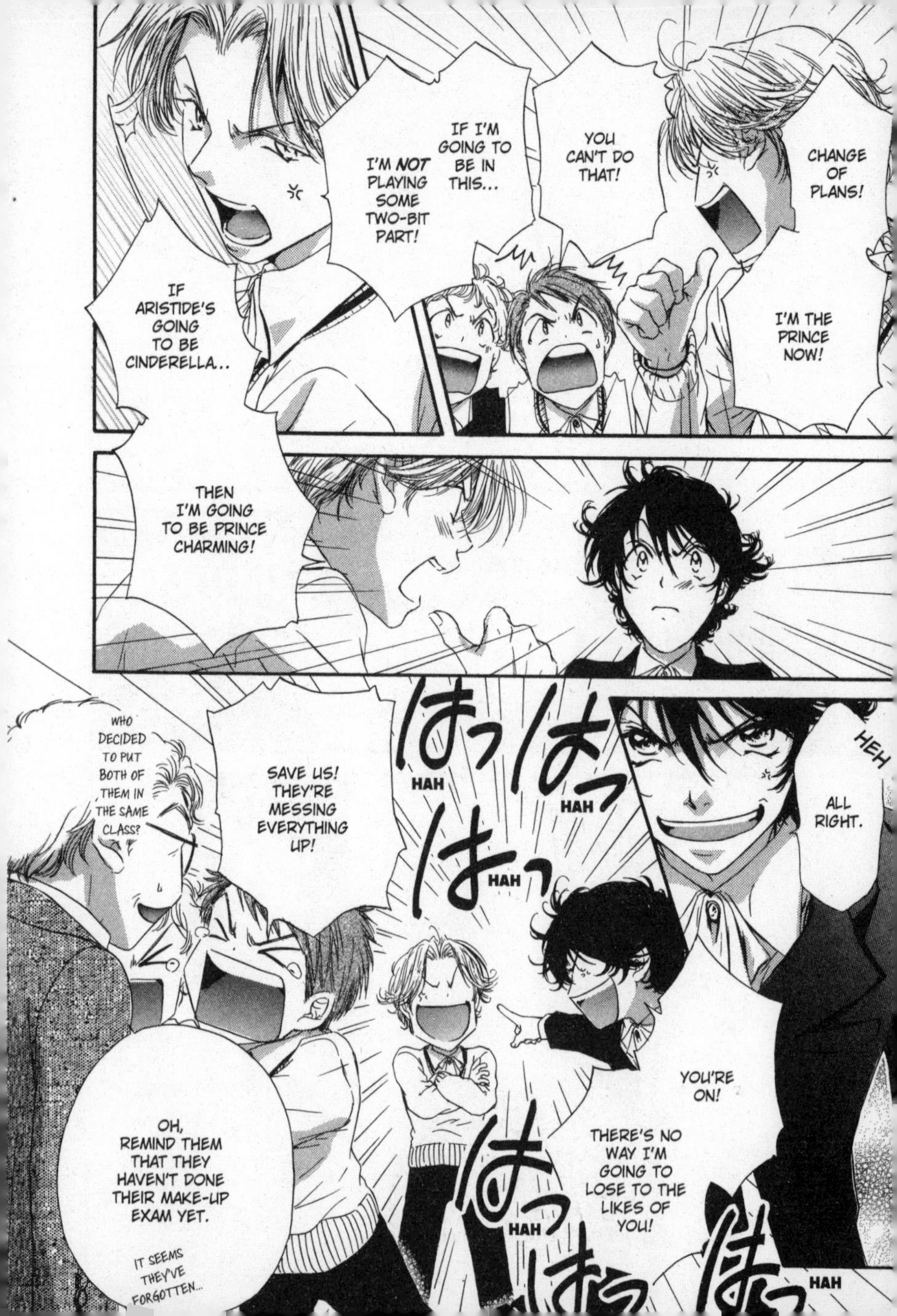
CHANGE OF PLANS!
I'M THE PRINCE NOW!
YOU CAN'T DO THAT!
IF I'M GOING TO BE IN THIS...
I'M *NOT* PLAYING SOME TWO-BIT PART!
IF ARISTIDE'S GOING TO BE CINDERELLA...
THEN I'M GOING TO BE PRINCE CHARMING!
HEH
ALL RIGHT.
YOU'RE ON!
THERE'S NO WAY I'M GOING TO LOSE TO THE LIKES OF YOU!
はっはっはっ
HAH HAH HAH
はっはっはっ
HAH HAH
SAVE US! THEY'RE MESSING EVERYTHING UP!
WHO DECIDED TO PUT BOTH OF THEM IN THE SAME CLASS?
OH, REMIND THEM THAT THEY HAVEN'T DONE THEIR MAKE-UP EXAM YET.
IT SEEMS THEY'VE FORGOTTEN...

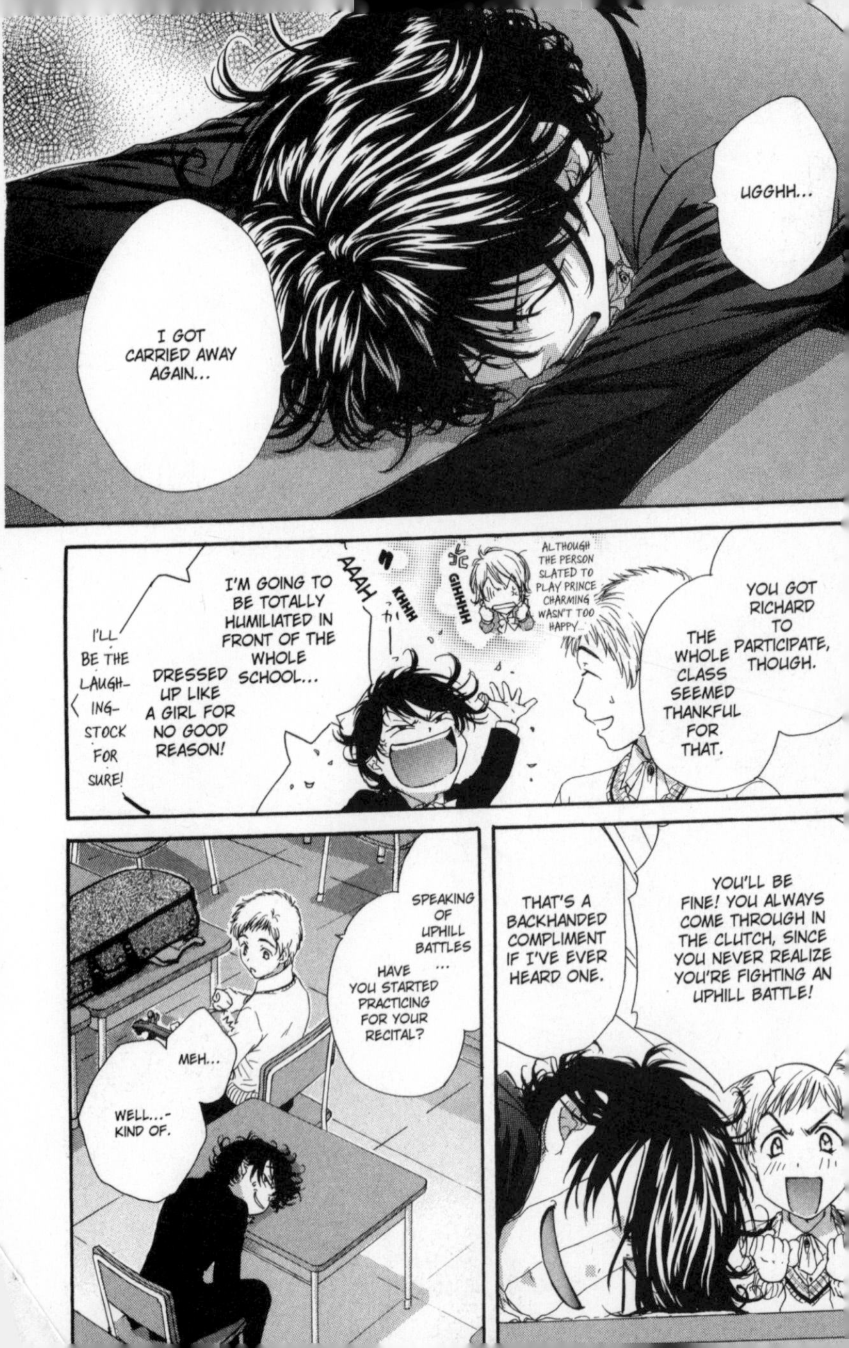
UGGHH...
I GOT CARRIED AWAY AGAIN...
YOU GOT RICHARD TO PARTICIPATE, THOUGH.
THE WHOLE CLASS SEEMED THANKFUL FOR THAT.
ALTHOUGH THE PERSON SLATED TO PLAY PRINCE CHARMING WASN'T TOO HAPPY...
GIHHHH
KHHH
AAAH
I'M GOING TO BE TOTALLY HUMILIATED IN FRONT OF THE WHOLE SCHOOL...
DRESSED UP LIKE A GIRL FOR NO GOOD REASON!
I'LL BE THE LAUGHING-STOCK FOR SURE!
YOU'LL BE FINE! YOU ALWAYS COME THROUGH IN THE CLUTCH, SINCE YOU NEVER REALIZE YOU'RE FIGHTING AN UPHILL BATTLE!
THAT'S A BACKHANDED COMPLIMENT IF I'VE EVER HEARD ONE.
SPEAKING OF UPHILL BATTLES...
HAVE YOU STARTED PRACTICING FOR YOUR RECITAL?
MEH...
WELL...- KIND OF.

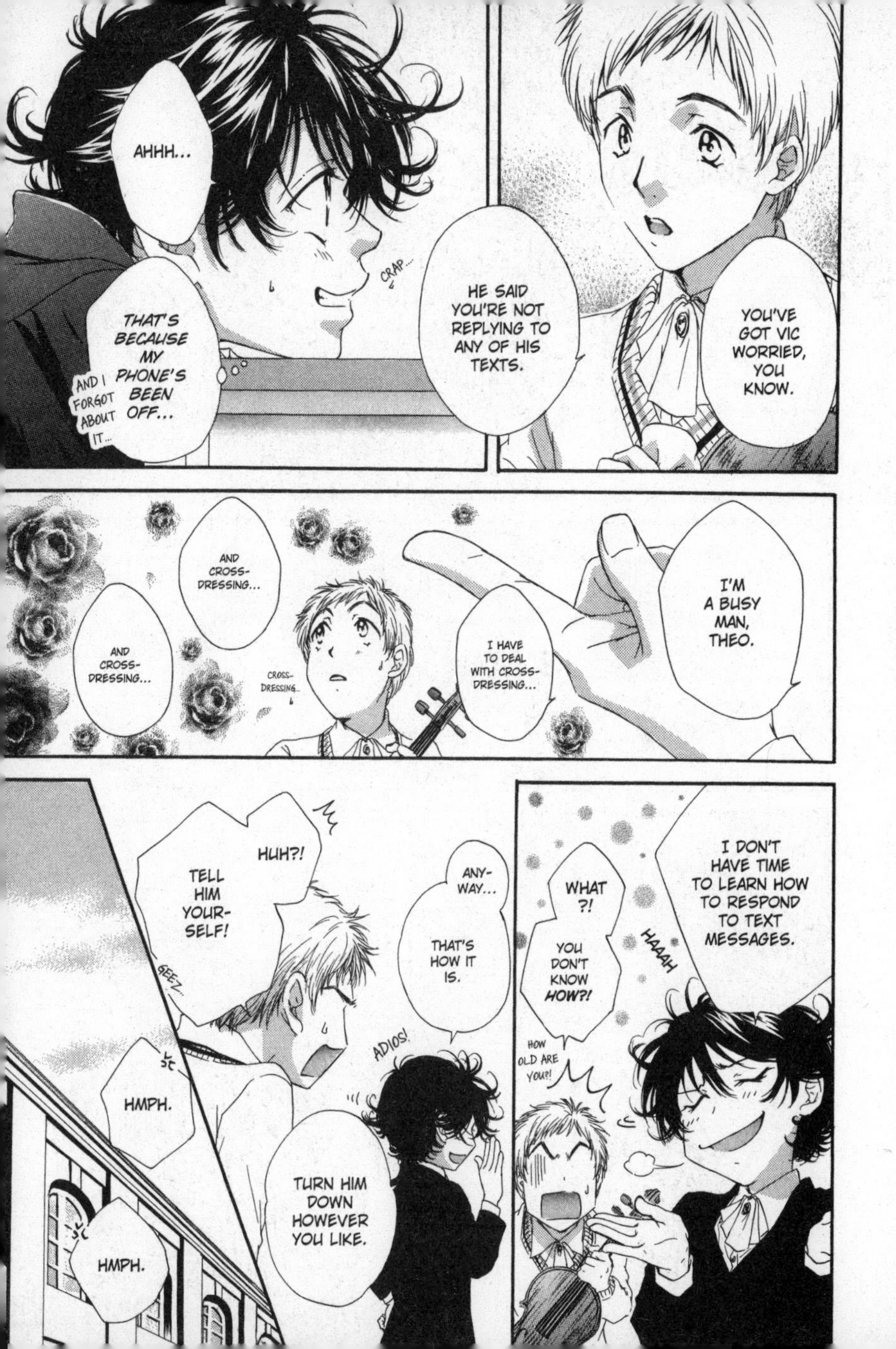
YOU'VE GOT VIC WORRIED, YOU KNOW.
HE SAID YOU'RE NOT REPLYING TO ANY OF HIS TEXTS.
CRAP...
AHHH...
THAT'S BECAUSE MY PHONE'S BEEN OFF...
AND I FORGOT ABOUT IT...
I'M A BUSY MAN, THEO.
I HAVE TO DEAL WITH CROSS-DRESSING...
CROSS-DRESSING...
AND CROSS-DRESSING...
AND CROSS-DRESSING...
I DON'T HAVE TIME TO LEARN HOW TO RESPOND TO TEXT MESSAGES.
HAAAH
WHAT?!
YOU DON'T KNOW *HOW?!*
HOW OLD ARE YOU?!
ANY-WAY...
THAT'S HOW IT IS.
HUH?!
TELL HIM YOUR-SELF!
GEEZ...
ADIOS!
TURN HIM DOWN HOWEVER YOU LIKE.
HMPH.
HMPH.

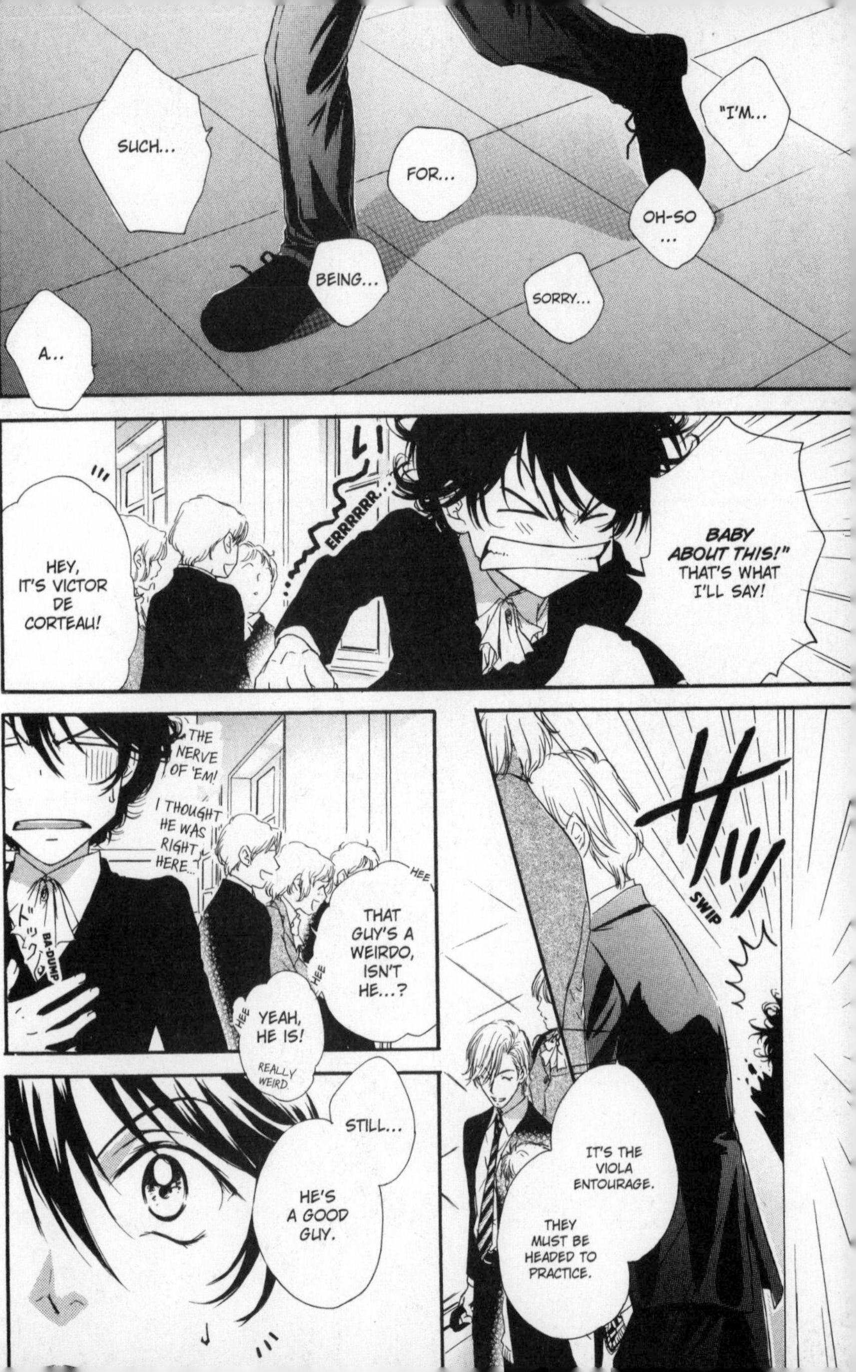
"I'M...
OH-SO
...
SORRY...
FOR...
BEING...
SUCH...
A...
BABY ABOUT THIS!" THAT'S WHAT I'LL SAY!
ERRRRRR...
HEY, IT'S VICTOR DE CORTEAU!
SWIP
IT'S THE VIOLA ENTOURAGE.
THEY MUST BE HEADED TO PRACTICE.
THE NERVE OF 'EM!
I THOUGHT HE WAS RIGHT HERE...
HEE
THAT GUY'S A WEIRDO, ISN'T HE...?
HEE
HEE
YEAH, HE IS!
REALLY WEIRD.
BA-DUMP
STILL...
HE'S A GOOD GUY.

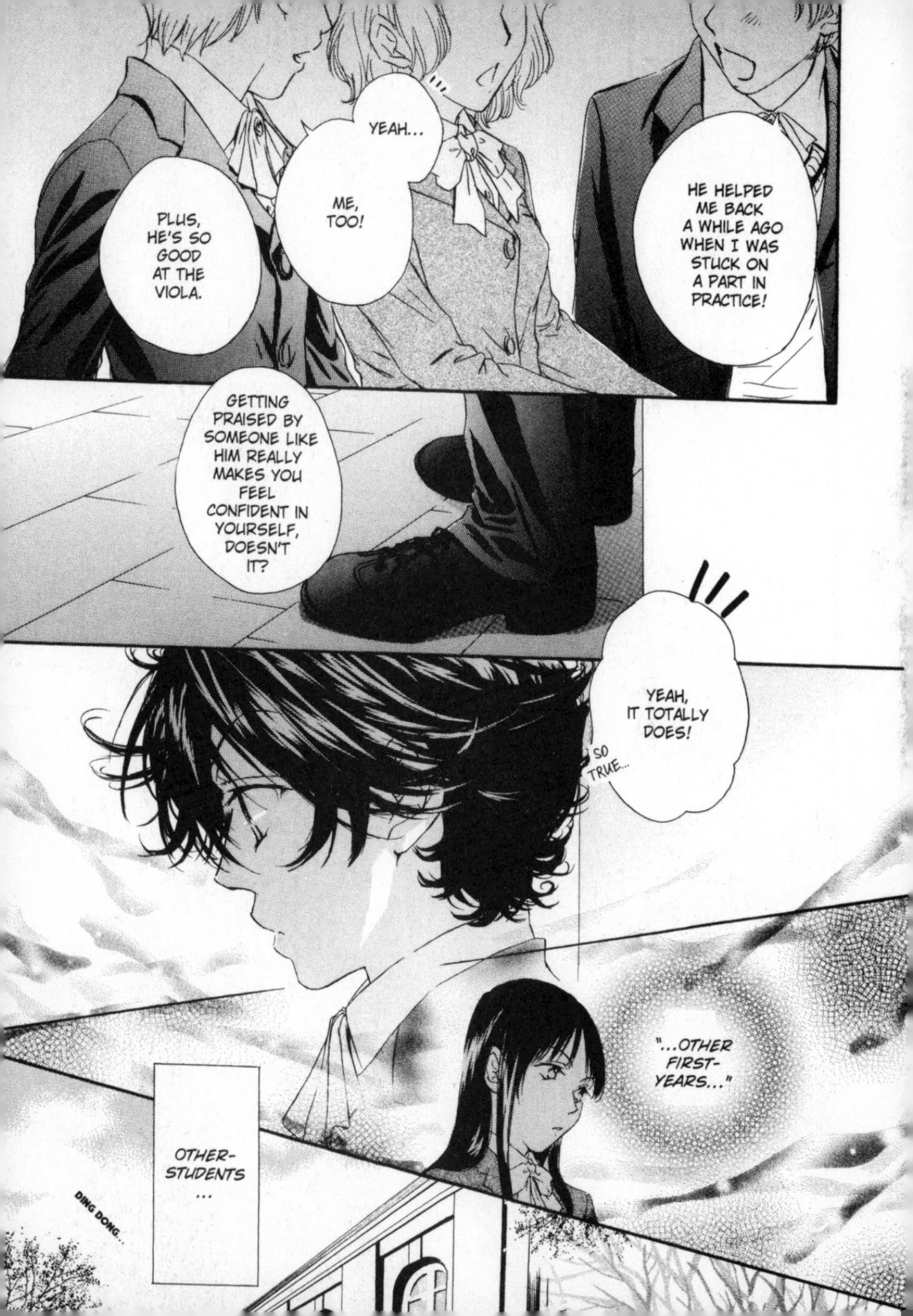
HE HELPED ME BACK A WHILE AGO WHEN I WAS STUCK ON A PART IN PRACTICE!
YEAH...
ME, TOO!
PLUS, HE'S SO GOOD AT THE VIOLA.
GETTING PRAISED BY SOMEONE LIKE HIM REALLY MAKES YOU FEEL CONFIDENT IN YOURSELF, DOESN'T IT?
YEAH, IT TOTALLY DOES!
SO TRUE...
"...OTHER FIRST-YEARS..."
OTHER-STUDENTS ...
DING DONG...

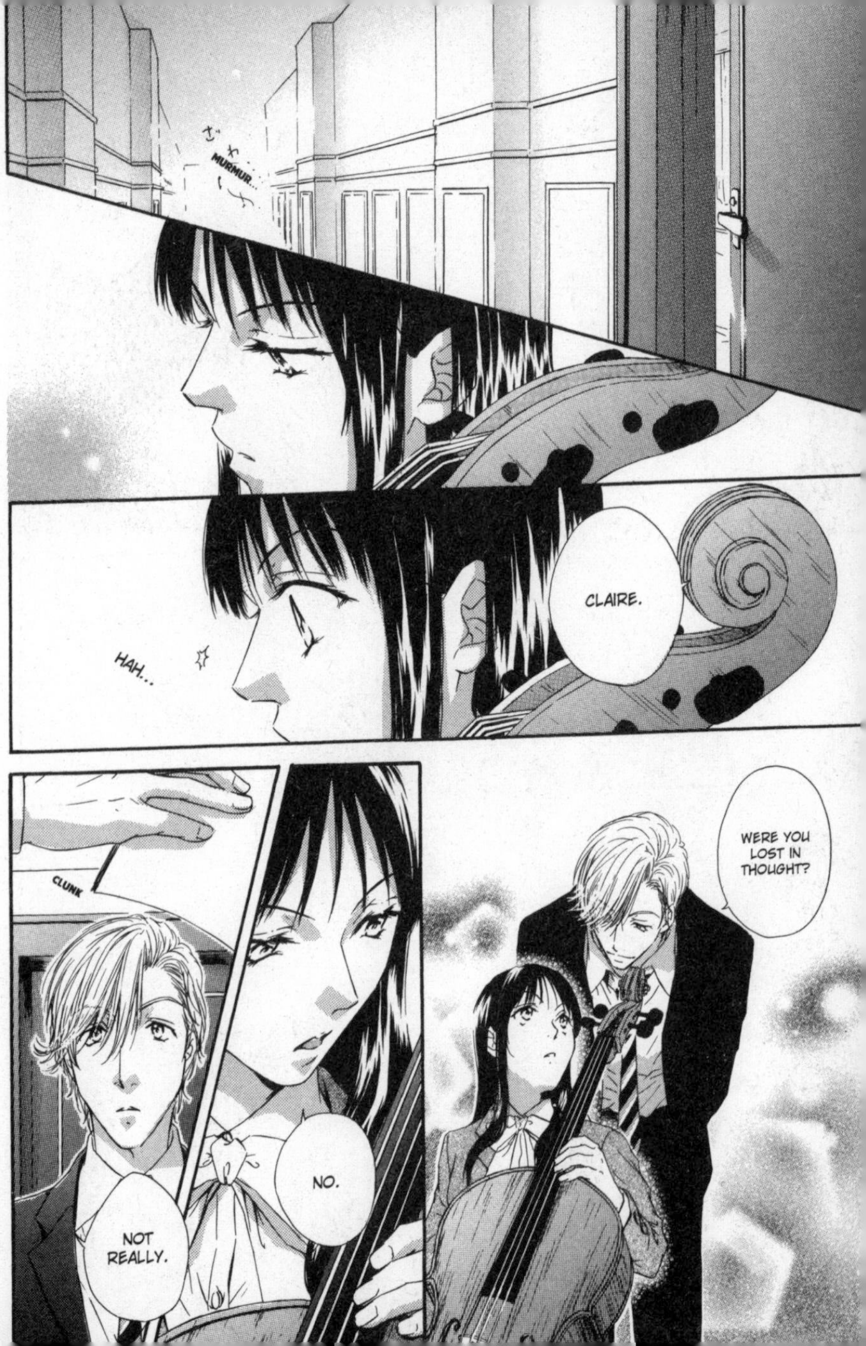
MURMUR...
CLAIRE.
HAH...
WERE YOU LOST IN THOUGHT?
CLUNK
NO.
NOT REALLY.

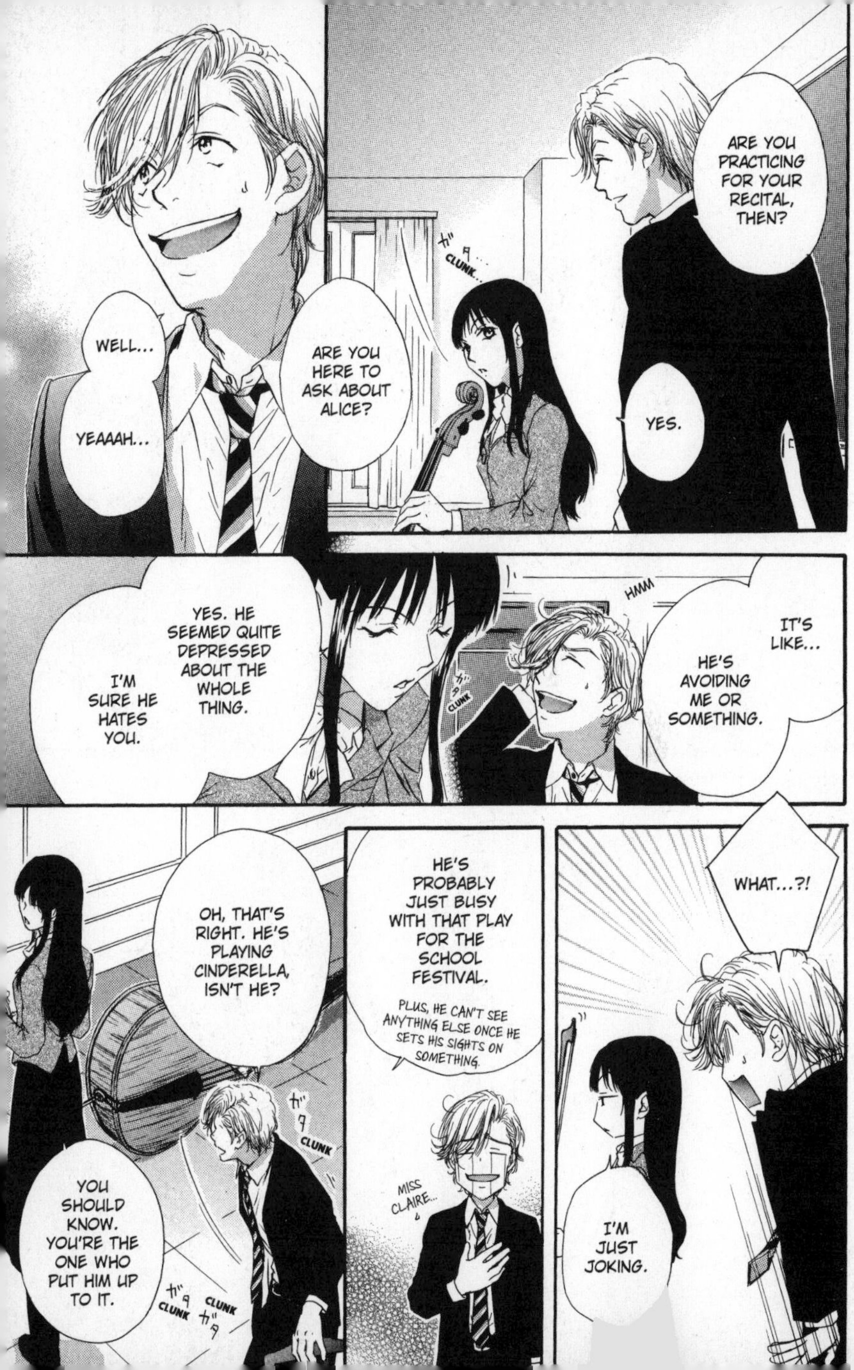
ARE YOU PRACTICING FOR YOUR RECITAL, THEN?
ガタ… CLUNK…
ARE YOU HERE TO ASK ABOUT ALICE?
YES.
WELL...
YEAAAH...
IT'S LIKE...
HE'S AVOIDING ME OR SOMETHING.
HMM
ガタ CLUNK
YES. HE SEEMED QUITE DEPRESSED ABOUT THE WHOLE THING.
I'M SURE HE HATES YOU.
WHAT...?!
I'M JUST JOKING.
HE'S PROBABLY JUST BUSY WITH THAT PLAY FOR THE SCHOOL FESTIVAL.
PLUS, HE CAN'T SEE ANYTHING ELSE ONCE HE SETS HIS SIGHTS ON SOMETHING.
MISS CLAIRE...
OH, THAT'S RIGHT. HE'S PLAYING CINDERELLA, ISN'T HE?
ガタ CLUNK
YOU SHOULD KNOW. YOU'RE THE ONE WHO PUT HIM UP TO IT.
ガタ CLUNK CLUNK ガタ

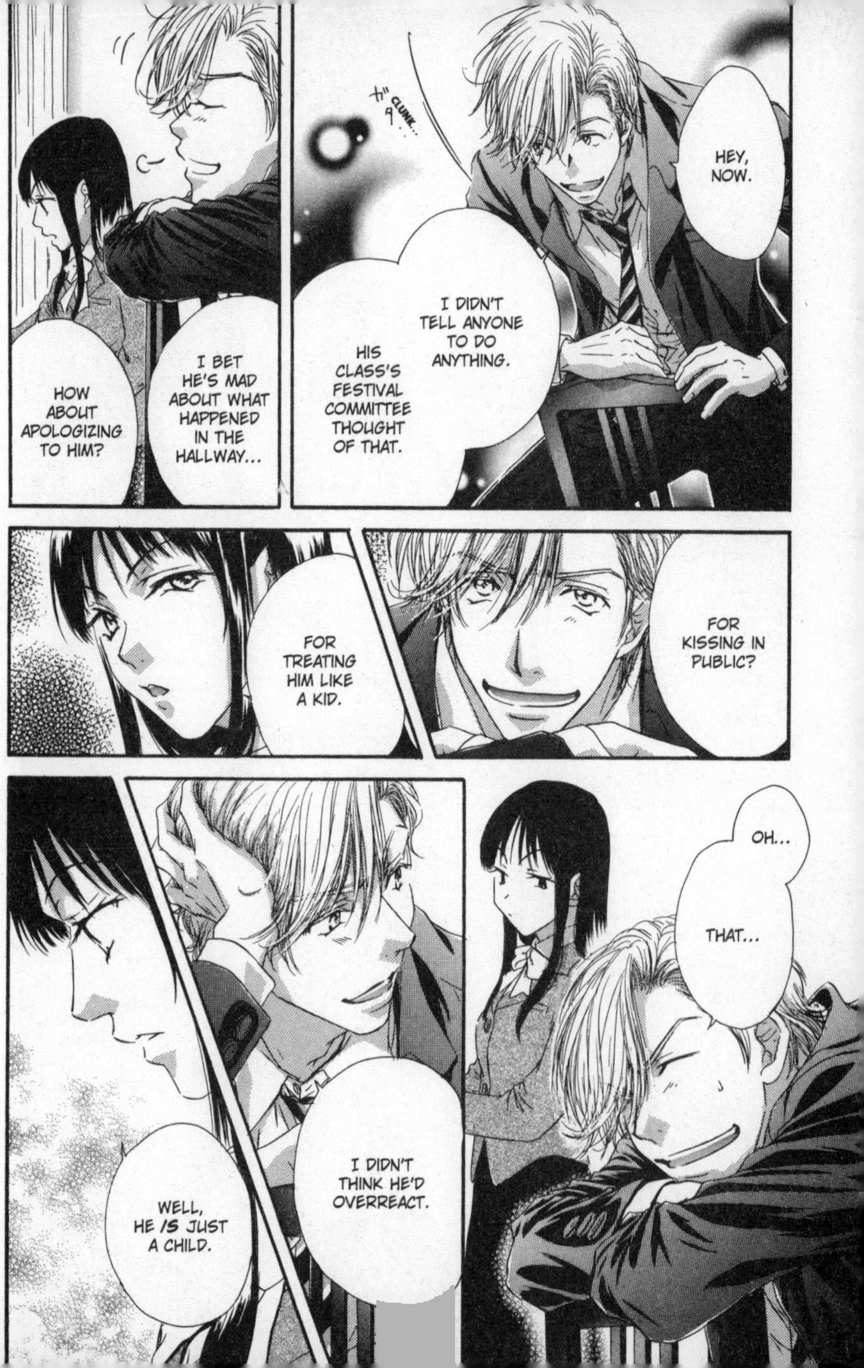
HEY, NOW.
ガッ
CLUNK...
I DIDN'T TELL ANYONE TO DO ANYTHING.
HIS CLASS'S FESTIVAL COMMITTEE THOUGHT OF THAT.
I BET HE'S MAD ABOUT WHAT HAPPENED IN THE HALLWAY...
HOW ABOUT APOLOGIZING TO HIM?
FOR KISSING IN PUBLIC?
FOR TREATING HIM LIKE A KID.
OH...
THAT...
I DIDN'T THINK HE'D OVERREACT.
WELL, HE *IS* JUST A CHILD.

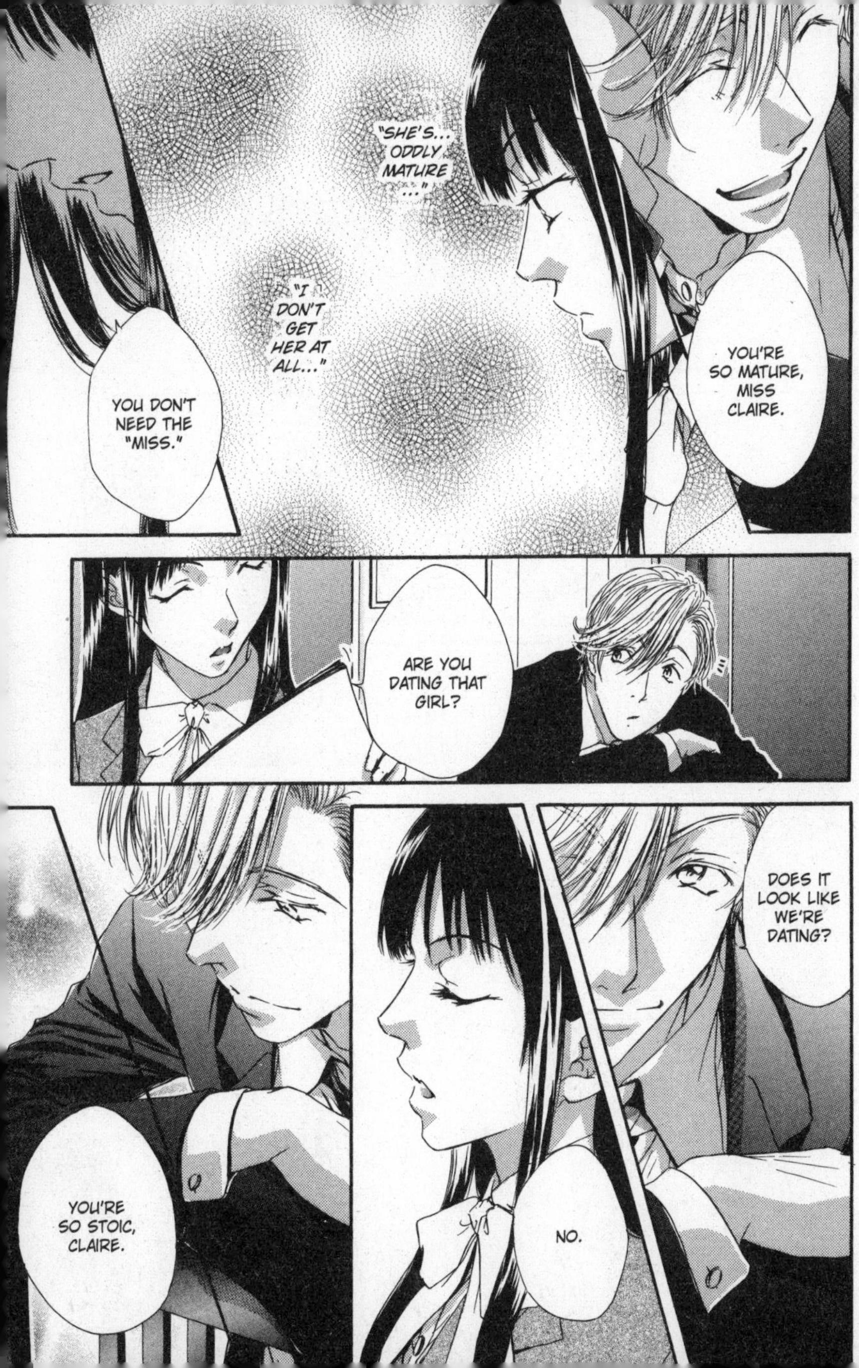
YOU'RE SO MATURE, MISS CLAIRE.
"SHE'S... ODDLY MATURE ..."
"I DON'T GET HER AT ALL..."
YOU DON'T NEED THE "MISS."
ARE YOU DATING THAT GIRL?
DOES IT LOOK LIKE WE'RE DATING?
NO.
YOU'RE SO STOIC, CLAIRE.

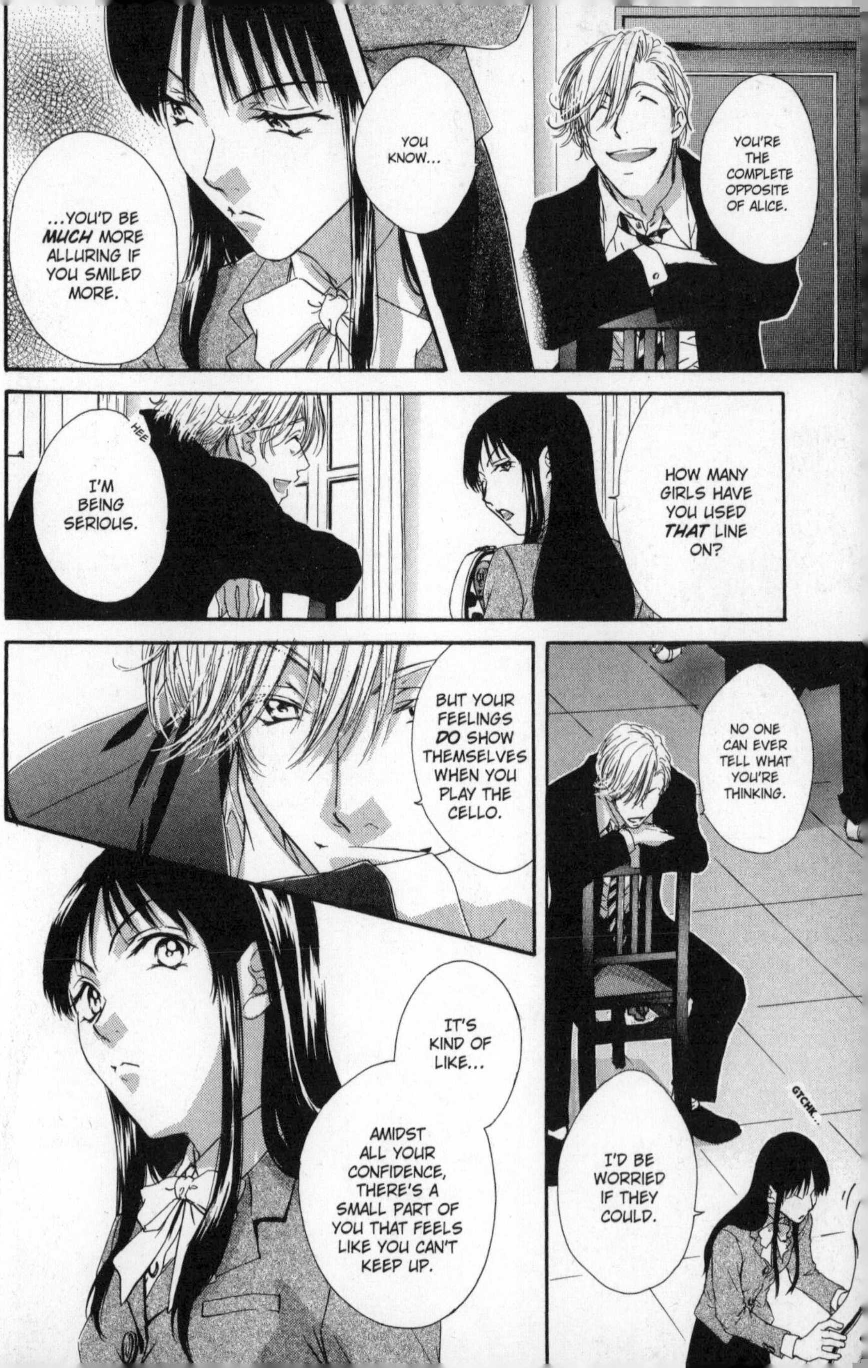
YOU'RE THE COMPLETE OPPOSITE OF ALICE.
YOU KNOW...
...YOU'D BE *MUCH* MORE ALLURING IF YOU SMILED MORE.
HOW MANY GIRLS HAVE YOU USED *THAT* LINE ON?
HEE
I'M BEING SERIOUS.
NO ONE CAN EVER TELL WHAT YOU'RE THINKING.
GTCHK...
I'D BE WORRIED IF THEY COULD.
BUT YOUR FEELINGS *DO* SHOW THEMSELVES WHEN YOU PLAY THE CELLO.
IT'S KIND OF LIKE...
AMIDST ALL YOUR CONFIDENCE, THERE'S A SMALL PART OF YOU THAT FEELS LIKE YOU CAN'T KEEP UP.

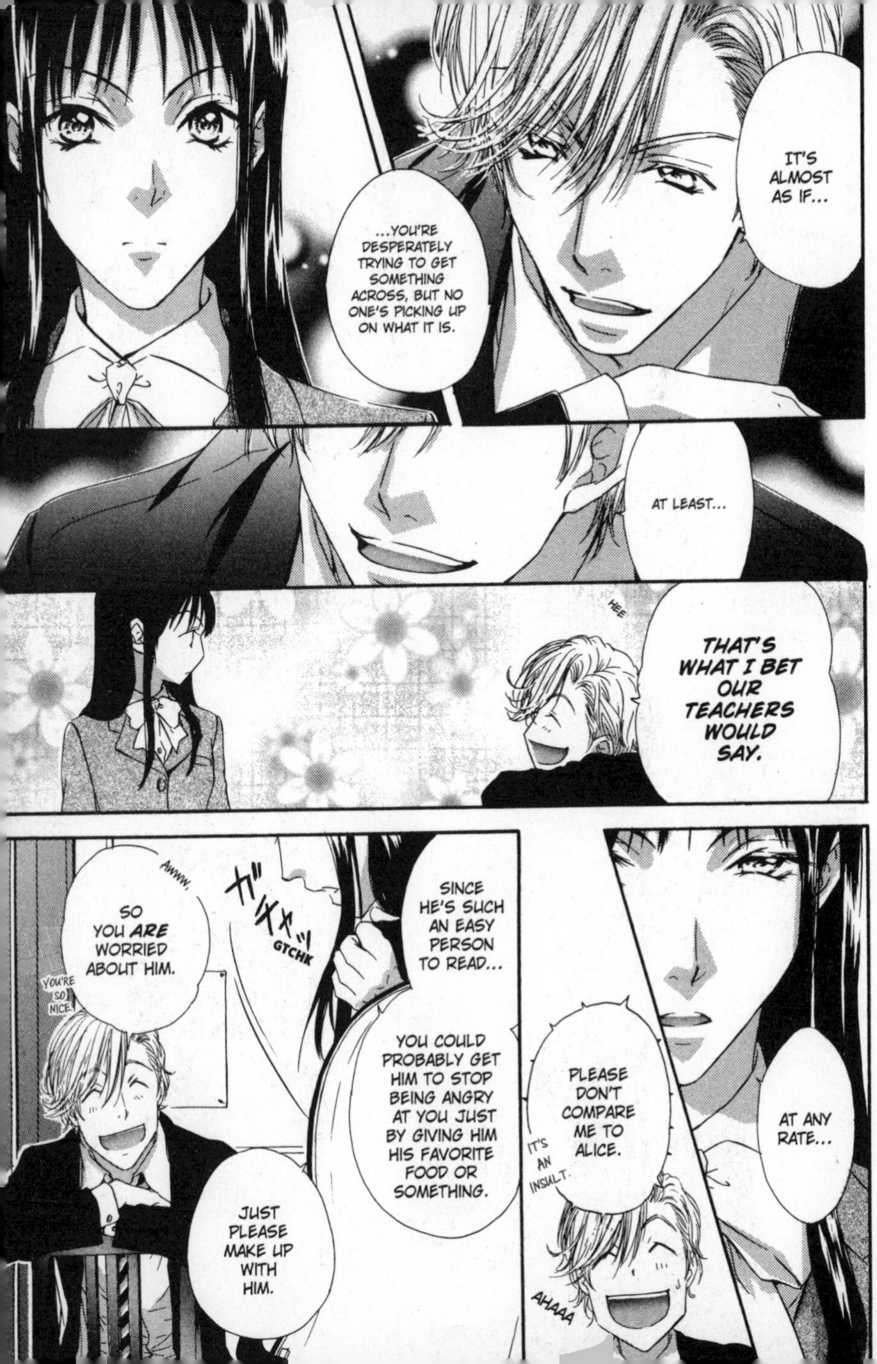
IT'S ALMOST AS IF...
...YOU'RE DESPERATELY TRYING TO GET SOMETHING ACROSS, BUT NO ONE'S PICKING UP ON WHAT IT IS.
AT LEAST...
HEE
THAT'S WHAT I BET OUR TEACHERS WOULD SAY.
AT ANY RATE...
SINCE HE'S SUCH AN EASY PERSON TO READ...
YOU COULD PROBABLY GET HIM TO STOP BEING ANGRY AT YOU JUST BY GIVING HIM HIS FAVORITE FOOD OR SOMETHING.
PLEASE DON'T COMPARE ME TO ALICE.
IT'S AN INSULT.
AHAAA
GTCHK
AWWW,
SO YOU ***ARE*** WORRIED ABOUT HIM.
YOU'RE SO NICE.
JUST PLEASE MAKE UP WITH HIM.

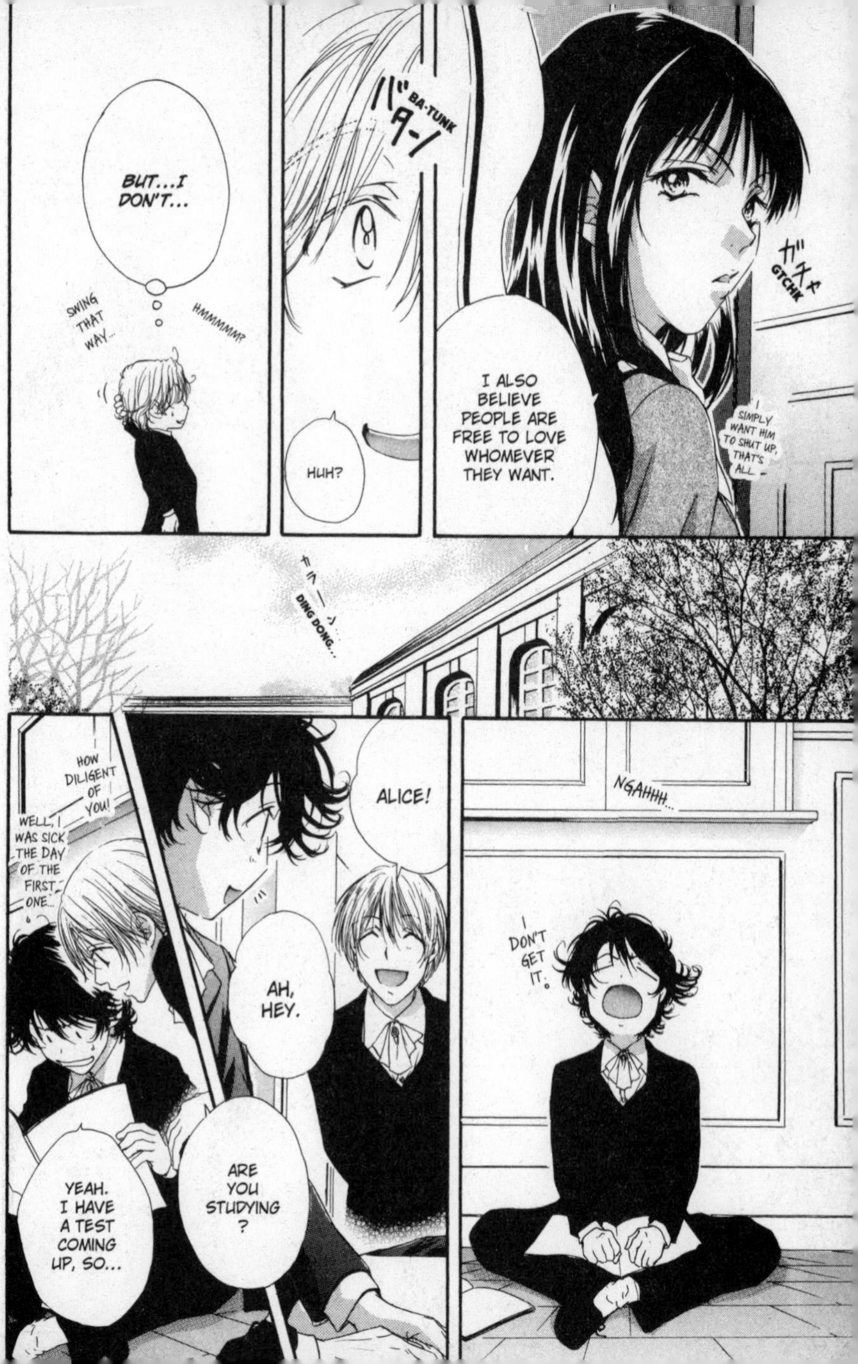
ガチャ
GTCHK
I ALSO BELIEVE PEOPLE ARE FREE TO LOVE WHOMEVER THEY WANT.
I SIMPLY WANT HIM TO SHUT UP, THAT'S ALL.
バターン
BA-TUNK
HUH?
BUT...I DON'T...
HMMMMMM?
SWING THAT WAY...
DING DONG...
NGAHHH...
I DON'T GET IT.
ALICE!
AH, HEY.
ARE YOU STUDYING?
YEAH. I HAVE A TEST COMING UP, SO...
HOW DILIGENT OF YOU!
WELL, I WAS SICK THE DAY OF THE FIRST ONE...

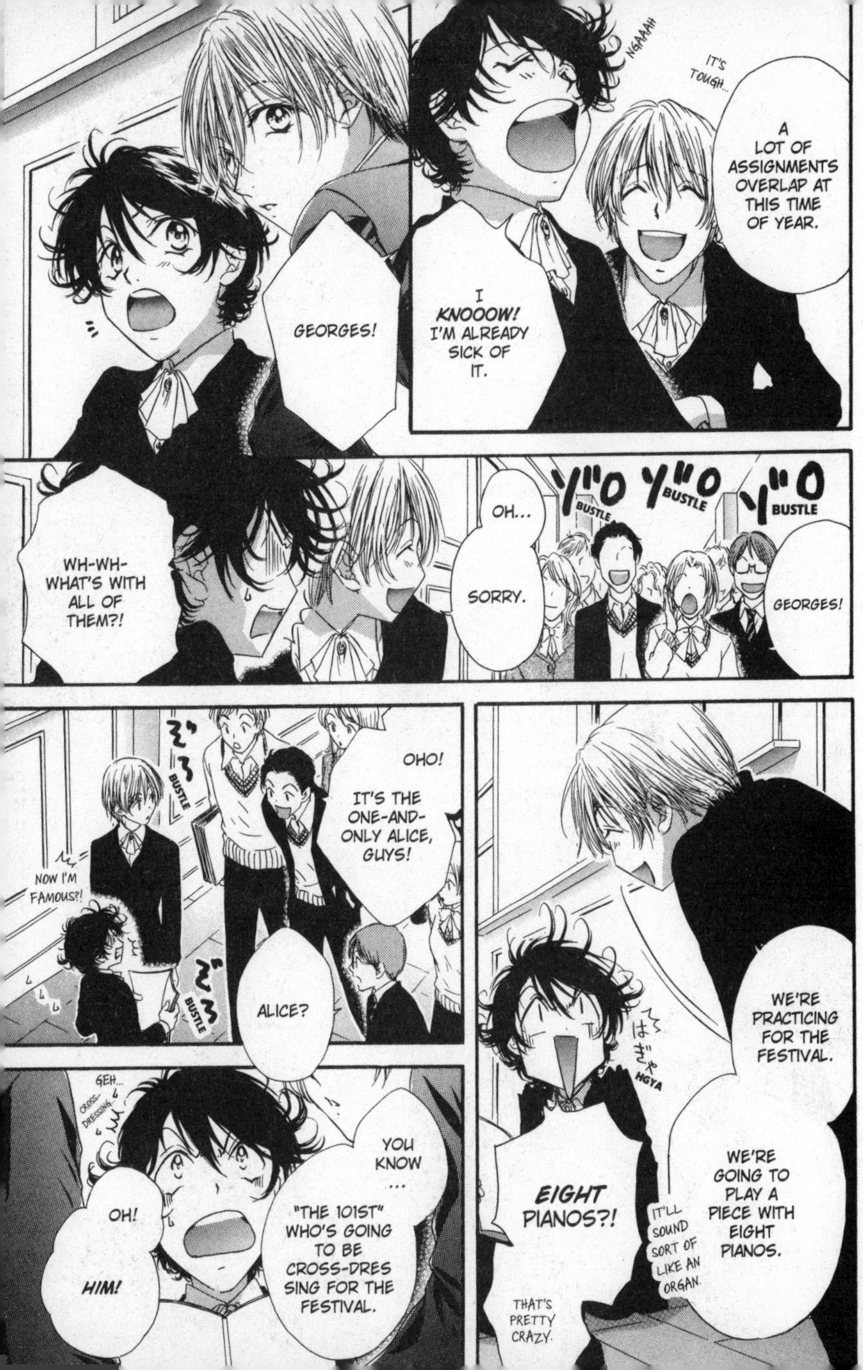
NGAAAH
IT'S TOUGH...
A LOT OF ASSIGNMENTS OVERLAP AT THIS TIME OF YEAR.
I KNOOOW! I'M ALREADY SICK OF IT.
GEORGES!
GEORGES!
BUSTLE
BUSTLE
BUSTLE
OH...
SORRY.
WH-WH-WHAT'S WITH ALL OF THEM?!
WE'RE PRACTICING FOR THE FESTIVAL.
HGYA
WE'RE GOING TO PLAY A PIECE WITH EIGHT PIANOS.
IT'LL SOUND SORT OF LIKE AN ORGAN.
EIGHT PIANOS?!
THAT'S PRETTY CRAZY.
OHO!
IT'S THE ONE-AND-ONLY ALICE, GUYS!
BUSTLE
NOW I'M FAMOUS?!
BUSTLE
ALICE?
YOU KNOW ...
"THE 101ST" WHO'S GOING TO BE CROSS-DRES SING FOR THE FESTIVAL.
GEH... CROSS-DRESSING
OH!
HIM!

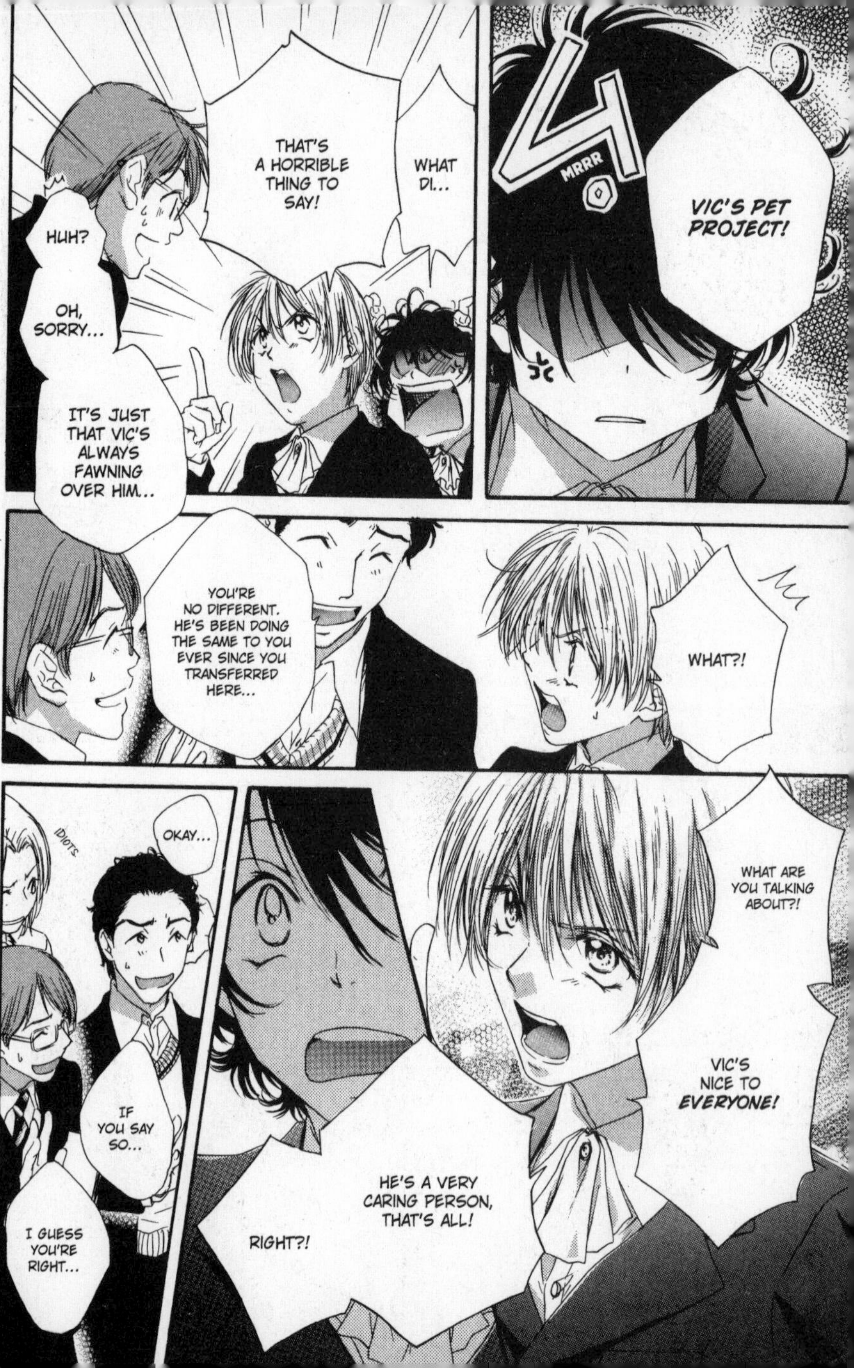
MRRR
VIC'S PET PROJECT!
WHAT DI...
THAT'S A HORRIBLE THING TO SAY!
HUH?
OH, SORRY...
IT'S JUST THAT VIC'S ALWAYS FAWNING OVER HIM...
WHAT?!
YOU'RE NO DIFFERENT. HE'S BEEN DOING THE SAME TO YOU EVER SINCE YOU TRANSFERRED HERE...
WHAT ARE YOU TALKING ABOUT?!
VIC'S NICE TO EVERYONE!
HE'S A VERY CARING PERSON, THAT'S ALL!
RIGHT?!
OKAY...
IDIOTS
IF YOU SAY SO...
I GUESS YOU'RE RIGHT...

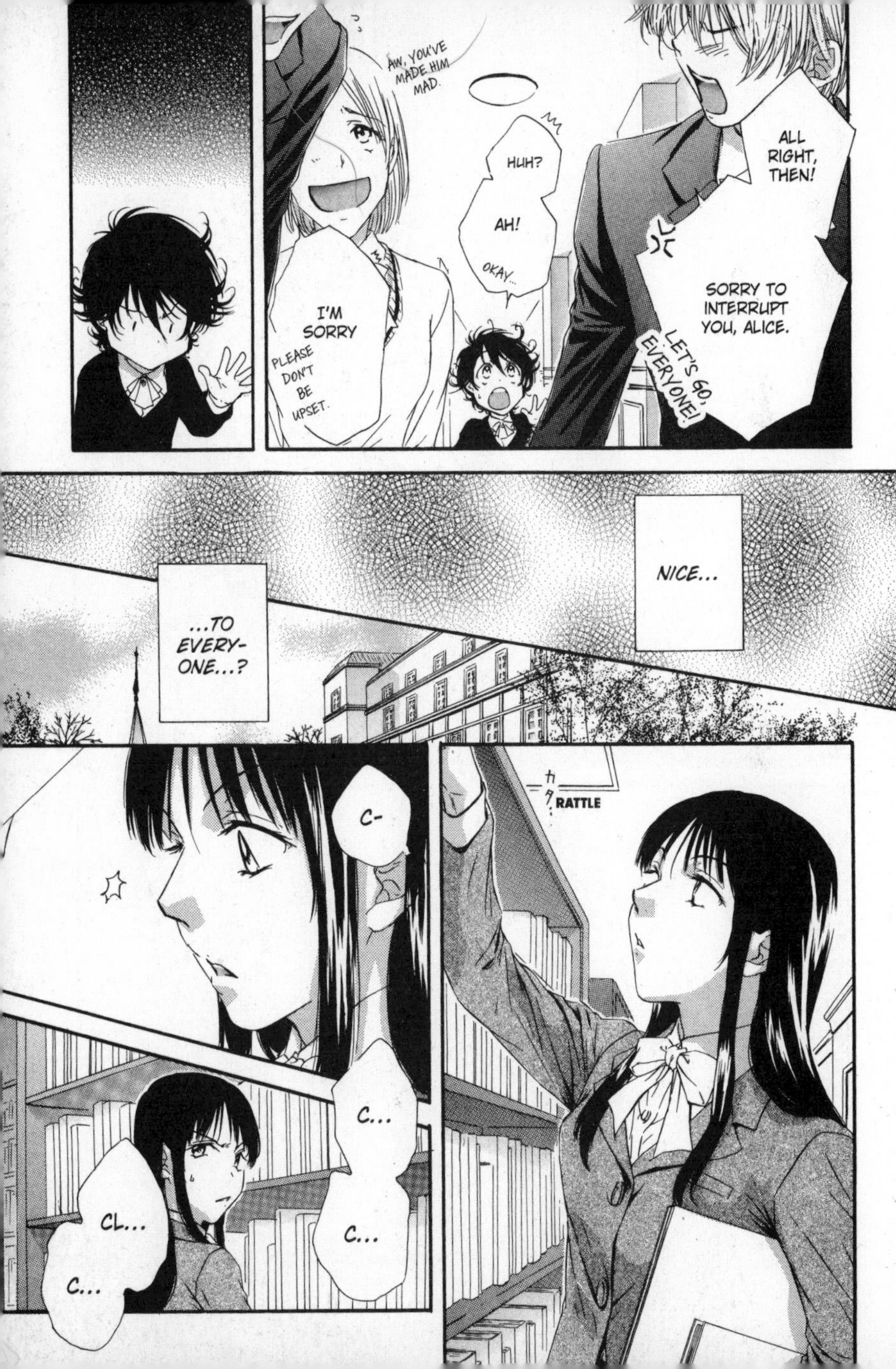

ALL RIGHT, THEN!
SORRY TO INTERRUPT YOU, ALICE.
LET'S GO, EVERYONE!
HUH?
AH!
OKAY...
AW, YOU'VE MADE HIM MAD.
I'M SORRY
PLEASE DON'T BE UPSET.
NICE...
...TO EVERY-ONE...?
カタ RATTLE
C-
C...
C...
CL...
C...

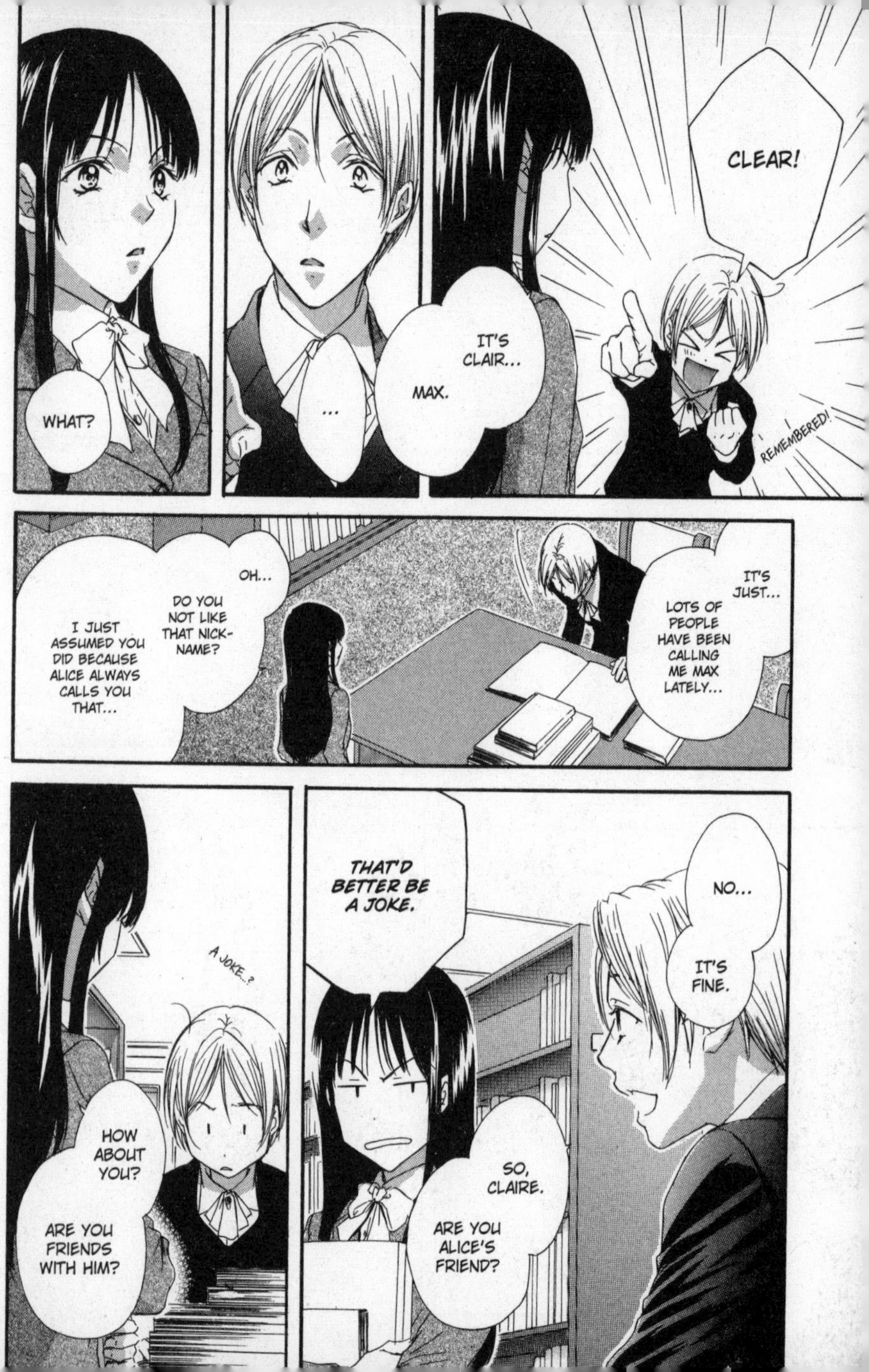
CLEAR!
REMEMBERED!
IT'S CLAIR...
MAX.
...
WHAT?
IT'S JUST...
LOTS OF PEOPLE HAVE BEEN CALLING ME MAX LATELY...
OH...
DO YOU NOT LIKE THAT NICK-NAME?
I JUST ASSUMED YOU DID BECAUSE ALICE ALWAYS CALLS YOU THAT...
NO...
IT'S FINE.
THAT'D BETTER BE A JOKE.
SO, CLAIRE.
ARE YOU ALICE'S FRIEND?
A JOKE...?
HOW ABOUT YOU?
ARE YOU FRIENDS WITH HIM?

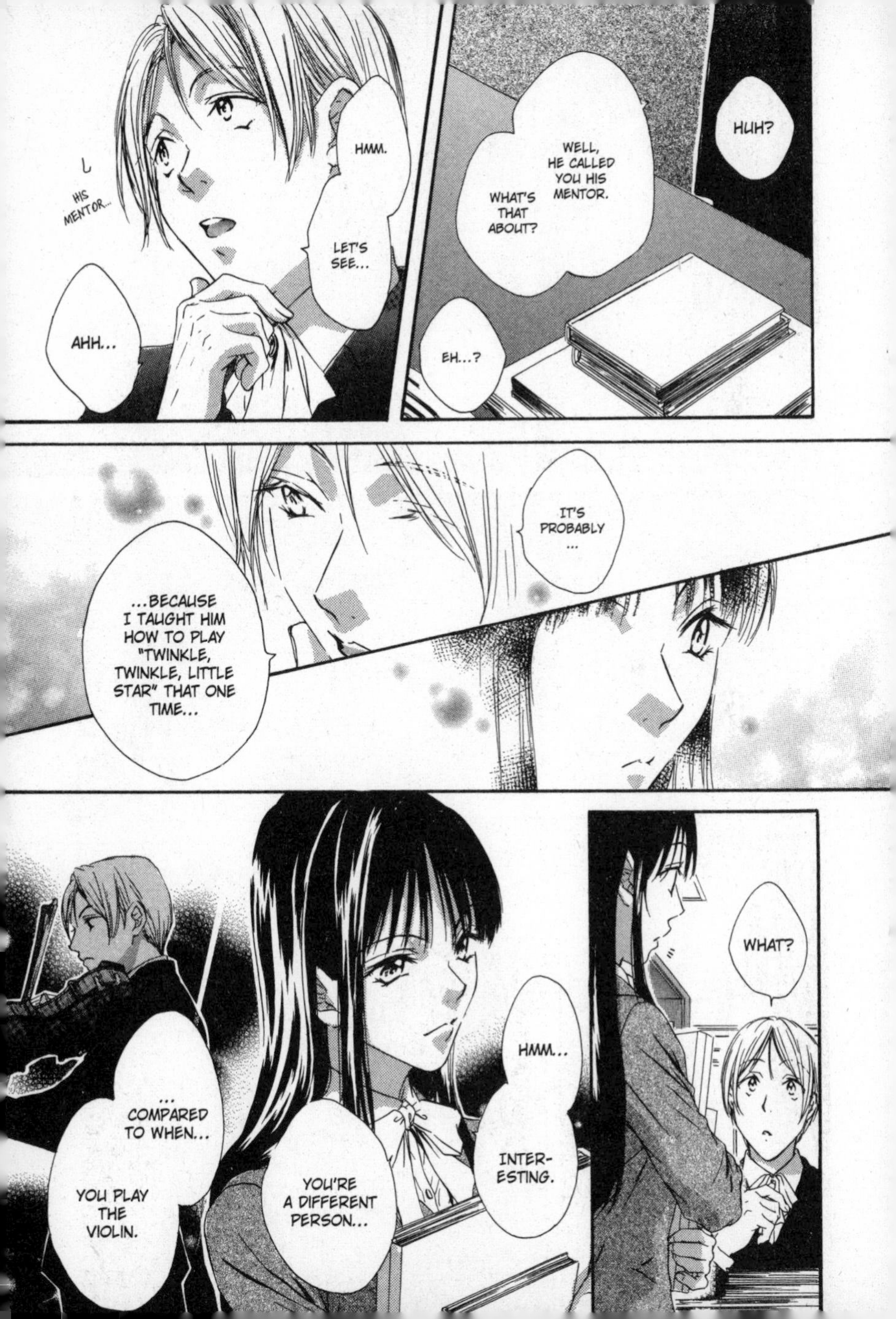
HUH?
WELL, HE CALLED YOU HIS MENTOR. WHAT'S THAT ABOUT?
EH...?
HMM.
LET'S SEE...
HIS MENTOR...
AHH...
IT'S PROBABLY...
...BECAUSE I TAUGHT HIM HOW TO PLAY "TWINKLE, TWINKLE, LITTLE STAR" THAT ONE TIME...
WHAT?
HMM... INTERESTING.
YOU'RE A DIFFERENT PERSON...
...COMPARED TO WHEN...
YOU PLAY THE VIOLIN.

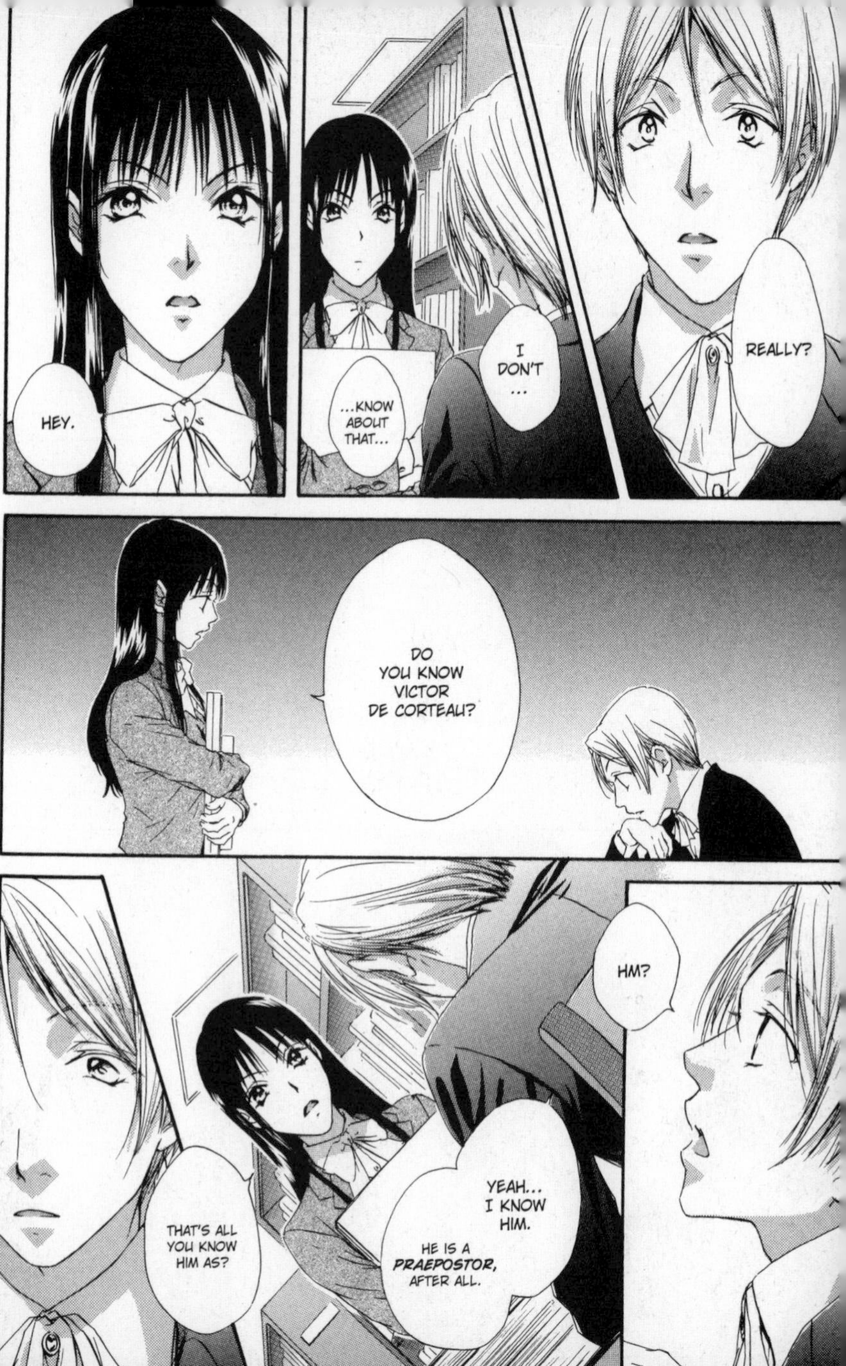
REALLY?
I DON'T ...
...KNOW ABOUT THAT...
HEY.
DO YOU KNOW VICTOR DE CORTEAU?
HM?
YEAH... I KNOW HIM.
HE IS A PRAEPOSTOR, AFTER ALL.
THAT'S ALL YOU KNOW HIM AS?

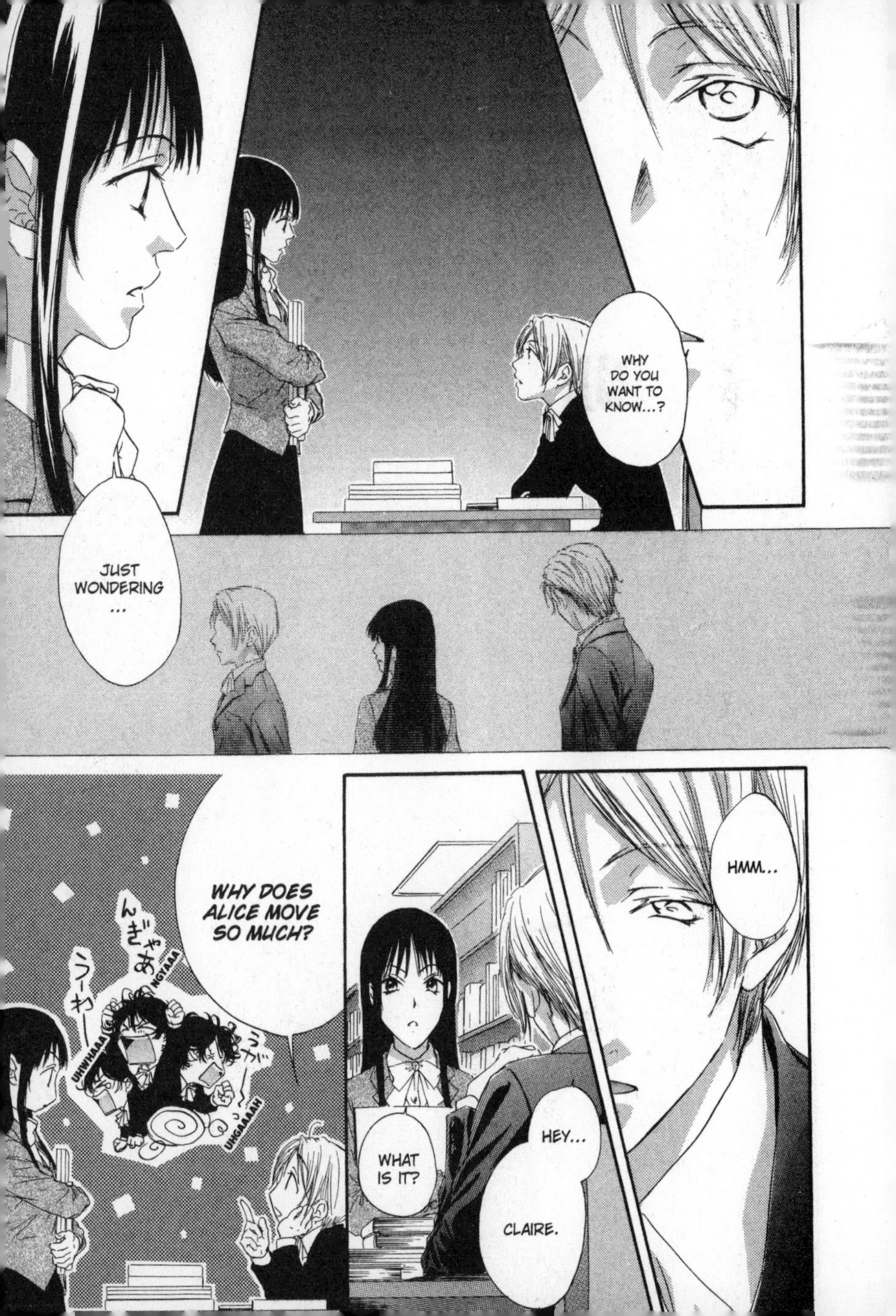
WHY DO YOU WANT TO KNOW...?
JUST WONDERING ...
HMM...
HEY...
CLAIRE.
WHAT IS IT?
WHY DOES ALICE MOVE SO MUCH?
んぎゃあ
NGYAAA
うーわー
UWHAAA
うがー
UHGAAAAH

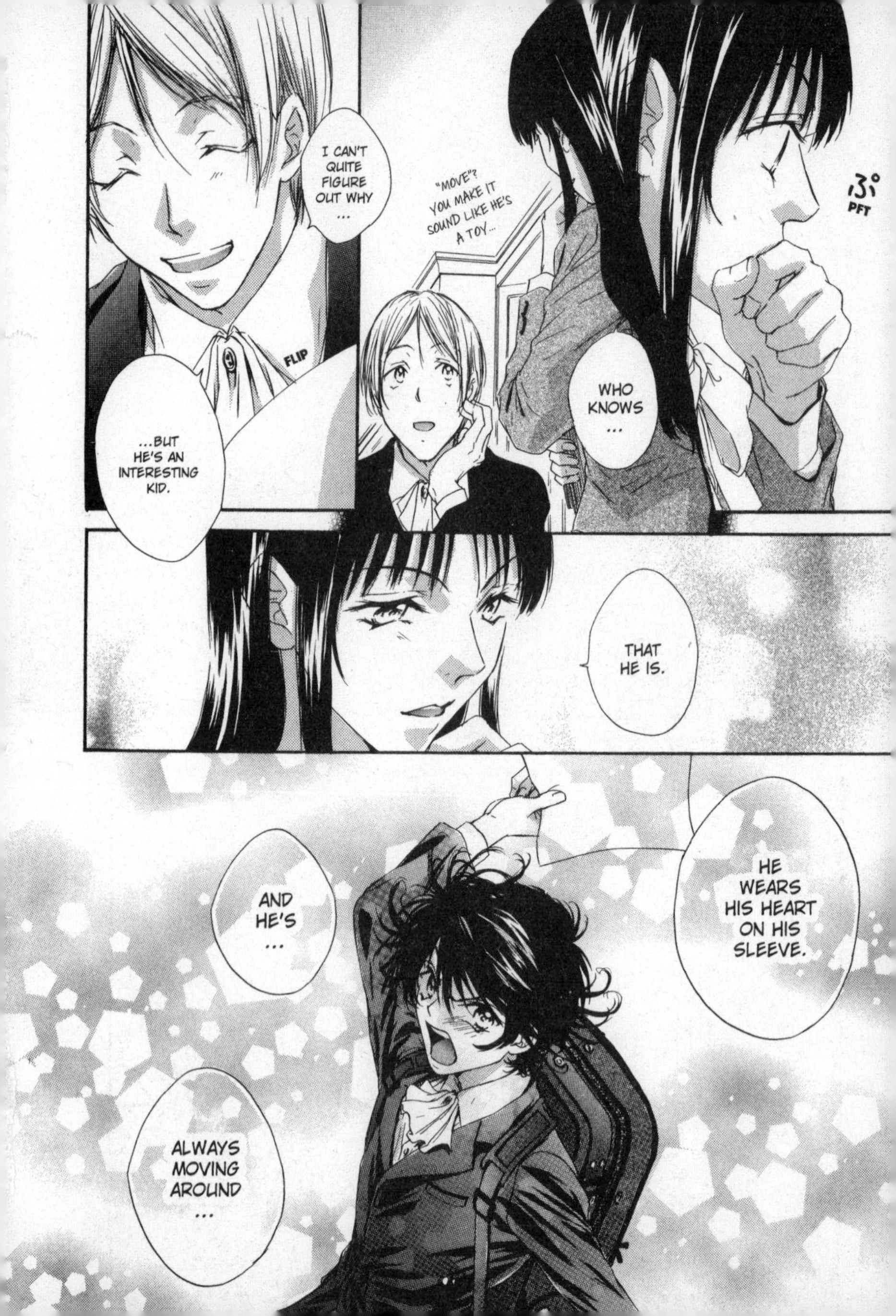
ぷ
PFT
"MOVE"? YOU MAKE IT SOUND LIKE HE'S A TOY...
WHO KNOWS ...
I CAN'T QUITE FIGURE OUT WHY ...
FLIP
...BUT HE'S AN INTERESTING KID.
THAT HE IS.
HE WEARS HIS HEART ON HIS SLEEVE.
AND HE'S ...
ALWAYS MOVING AROUND ...

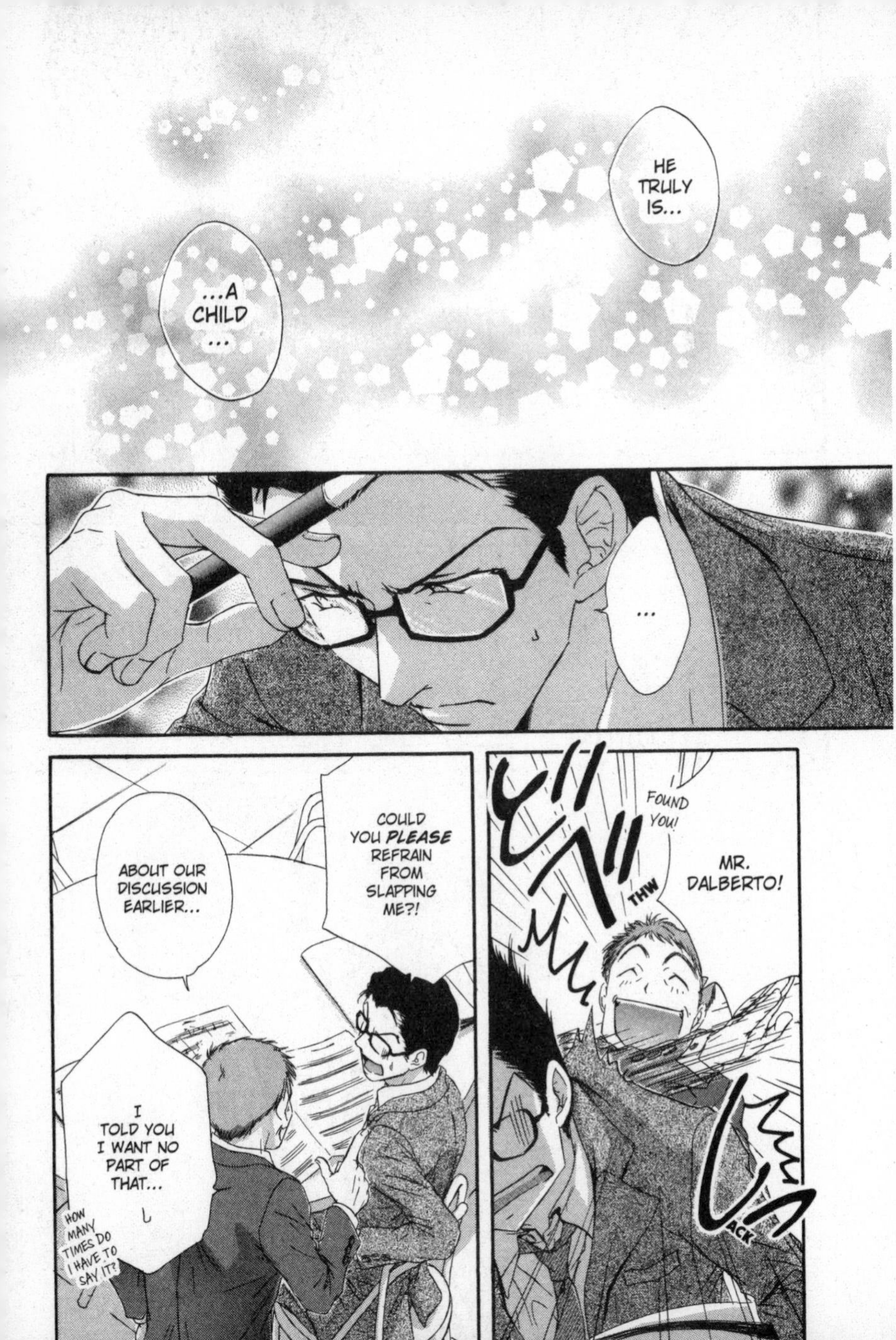
HE TRULY IS...
...A CHILD ...
...
FOUND YOU!
MR. DALBERTO!
THW
ACK
COULD YOU *PLEASE* REFRAIN FROM SLAPPING ME?!
ABOUT OUR DISCUSSION EARLIER...
I TOLD YOU I WANT NO PART OF THAT...
HOW MANY TIMES DO I HAVE TO SAY IT?

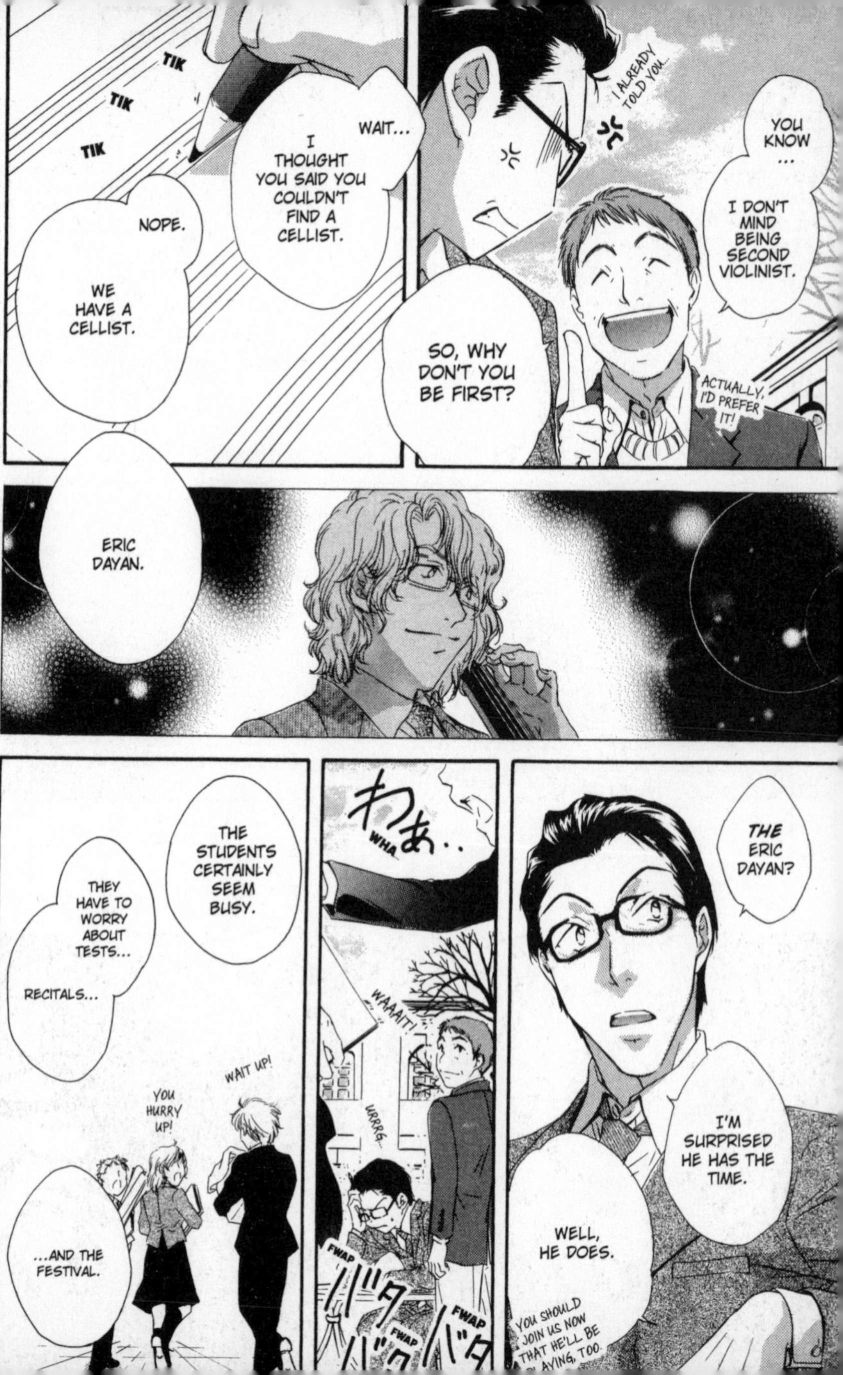
YOU KNOW ...
I DON'T MIND BEING SECOND VIOLINIST.
I ALREADY TOLD YOU...
ACTUALLY, I'D PREFER IT!
SO, WHY DON'T YOU BE FIRST?
TIK
TIK
TIK
WAIT...
I THOUGHT YOU SAID YOU COULDN'T FIND A CELLIST.
NOPE.
WE HAVE A CELLIST.
ERIC DAYAN.
THE ERIC DAYAN?
I'M SURPRISED HE HAS THE TIME.
WELL, HE DOES.
YOU SHOULD JOIN US NOW THAT HE'LL BE
LAYING, TOO.
わあ..
WHA
WAAAIT!
URRRG...
FWAP
バタ
FWAP
バタ
FWAP
THE STUDENTS CERTAINLY SEEM BUSY.
THEY HAVE TO WORRY ABOUT TESTS...
RECITALS...
WAIT UP!
YOU HURRY UP!
...AND THE FESTIVAL.

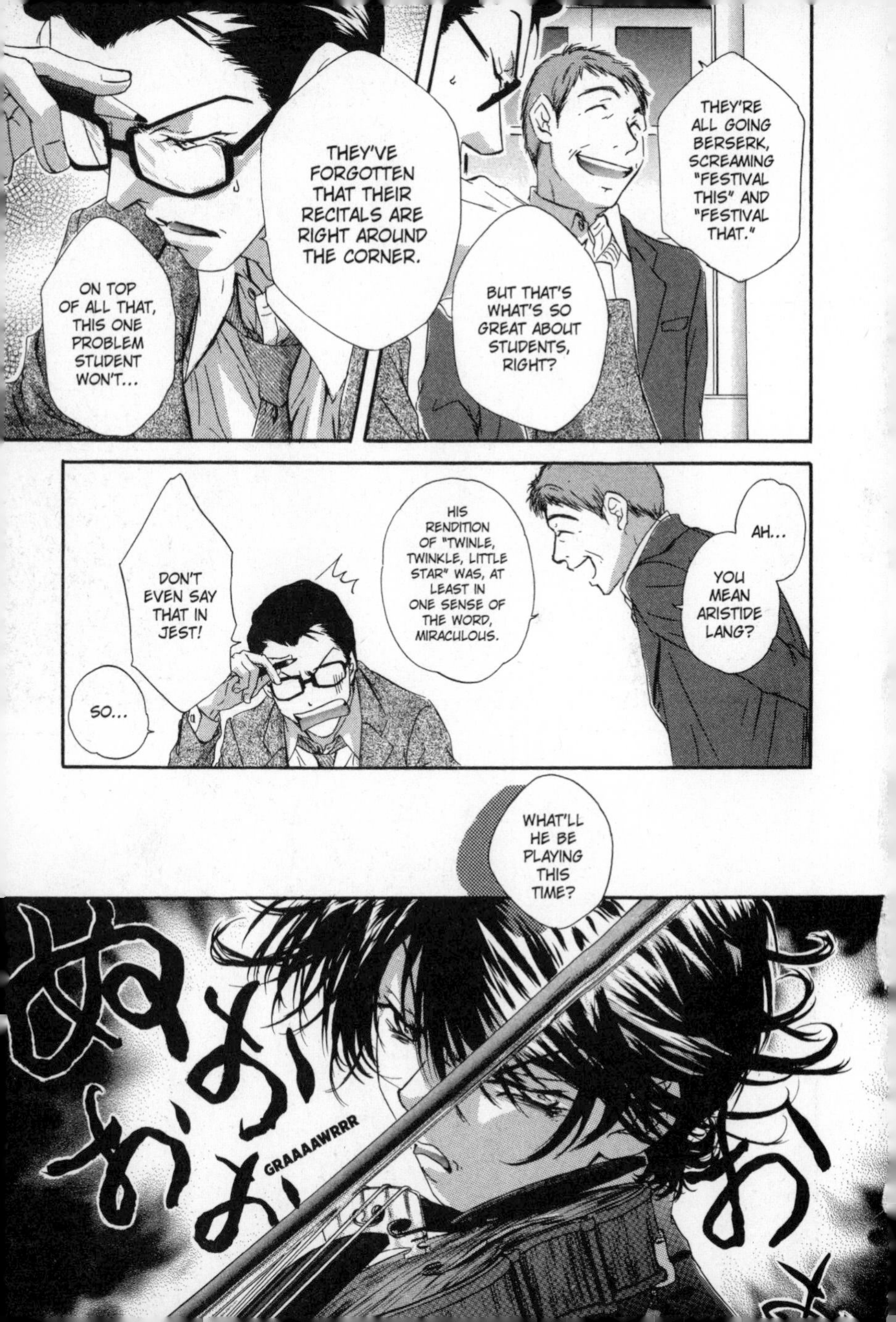
THEY'RE ALL GOING BERSERK, SCREAMING "FESTIVAL THIS" AND "FESTIVAL THAT."
THEY'VE FORGOTTEN THAT THEIR RECITALS ARE RIGHT AROUND THE CORNER.
BUT THAT'S WHAT'S SO GREAT ABOUT STUDENTS, RIGHT?
ON TOP OF ALL THAT, THIS ONE PROBLEM STUDENT WON'T...
AH...
YOU MEAN ARISTIDE LANG?
HIS RENDITION OF "TWINLE, TWINKLE, LITTLE STAR" WAS, AT LEAST IN ONE SENSE OF THE WORD, MIRACULOUS.
DON'T EVEN SAY THAT IN JEST!
SO...
WHAT'LL HE BE PLAYING THIS TIME?
GRAAAAWRRR

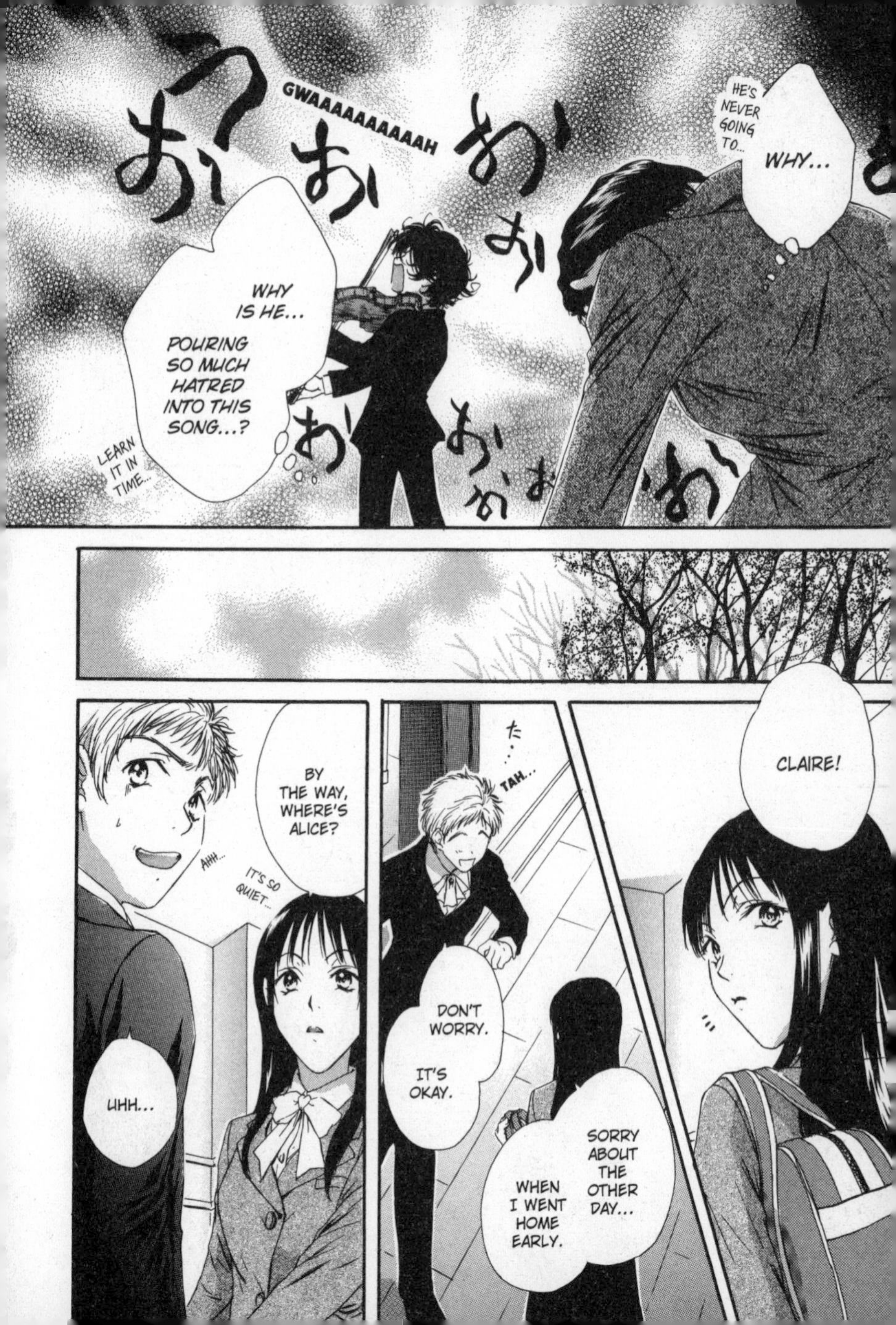

HE'S NEVER GOING TO...
WHY...
GWAAAAAAAAAAH
WHY IS HE... POURING SO MUCH HATRED INTO THIS SONG...?
LEARN IT IN TIME...
CLAIRE!
た...
TAH...
SORRY ABOUT THE OTHER DAY... WHEN I WENT HOME EARLY.
DON'T WORRY. IT'S OKAY.
BY THE WAY, WHERE'S ALICE?
AHH... IT'S SO QUIET...
UHH...

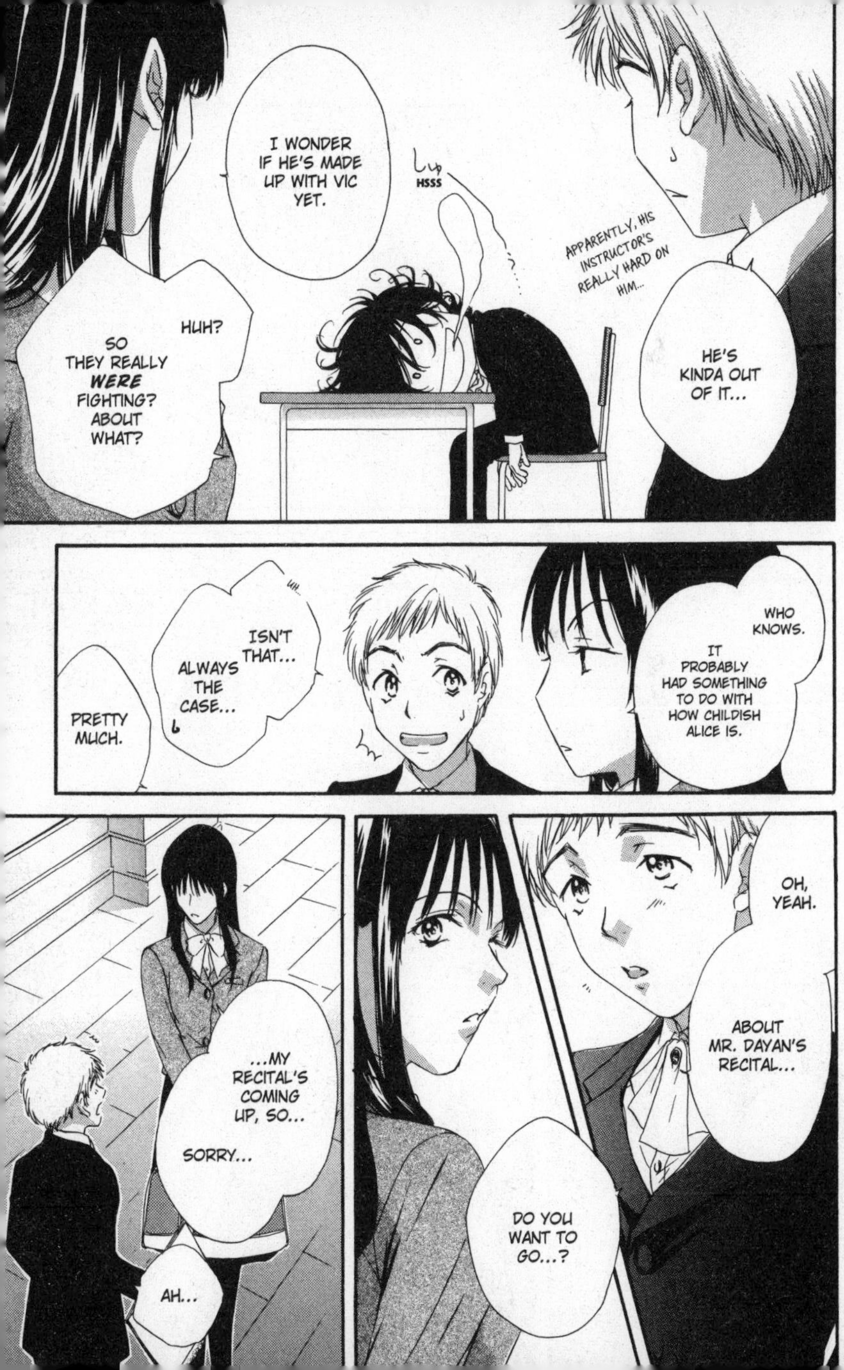
APPARENTLY, HIS INSTRUCTOR'S REALLY HARD ON HIM...
HE'S KINDA OUT OF IT...
HSSS
I WONDER IF HE'S MADE UP WITH VIC YET.
HUH?
SO THEY REALLY ***WERE*** FIGHTING? ABOUT WHAT?
WHO KNOWS.
IT PROBABLY HAD SOMETHING TO DO WITH HOW CHILDISH ALICE IS.
UH...
ISN'T THAT... ALWAYS THE CASE...
PRETTY MUCH.
OH, YEAH.
ABOUT MR. DAYAN'S RECITAL...
DO YOU WANT TO GO...?
...MY RECITAL'S COMING UP, SO...
SORRY...
AH...

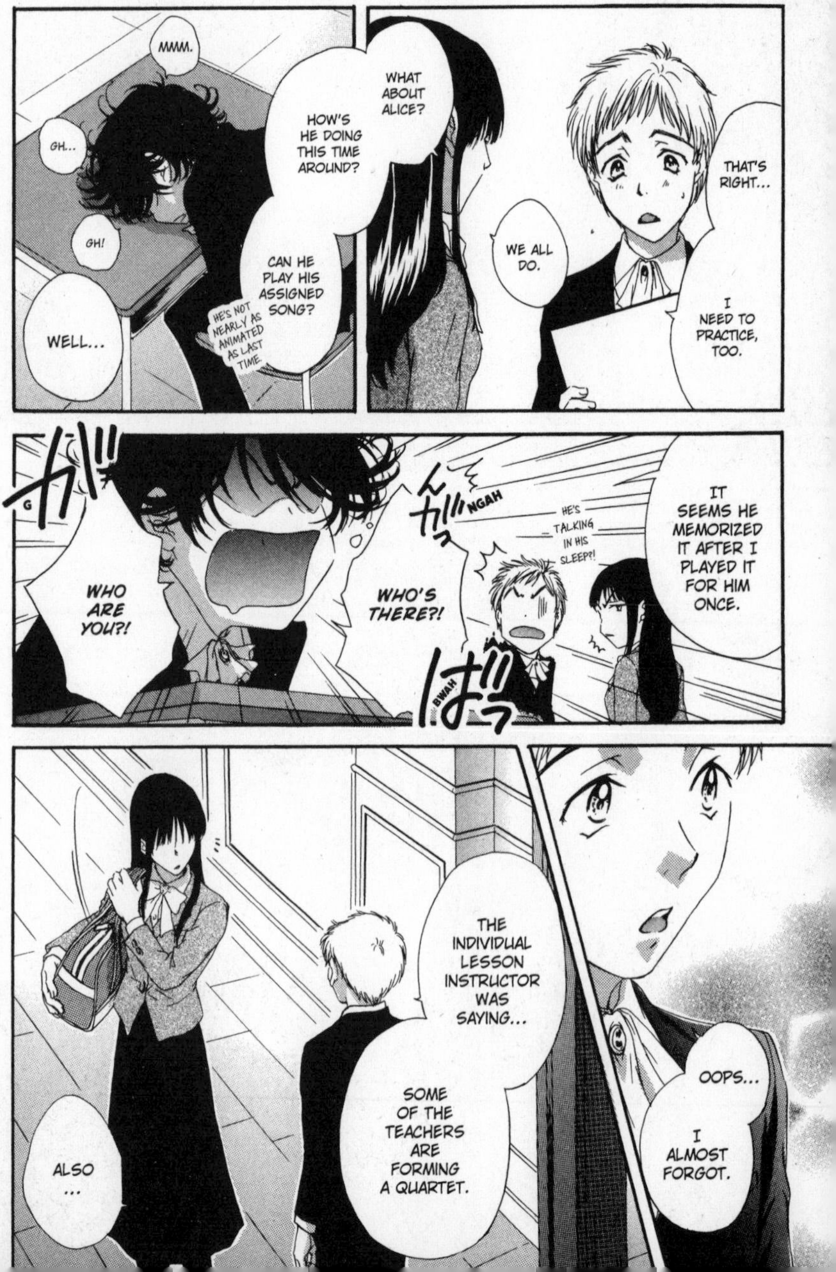
THAT'S RIGHT...
WE ALL DO.
I NEED TO PRACTICE, TOO.
WHAT ABOUT ALICE?
HOW'S HE DOING THIS TIME AROUND?
CAN HE PLAY HIS ASSIGNED SONG?
HE'S NOT NEARLY AS ANIMATED AS LAST TIME.
MMM.
GH...
GH!
WELL...
IT SEEMS HE MEMORIZED IT AFTER I PLAYED IT FOR HIM ONCE.
HE'S TALKING IN HIS SLEEP?!
NGAH
BWAH
WHO'S THERE?!
G
WHO ARE YOU?!
OOPS...
I ALMOST FORGOT.
THE INDIVIDUAL LESSON INSTRUCTOR WAS SAYING...
SOME OF THE TEACHERS ARE FORMING A QUARTET.
ALSO ...

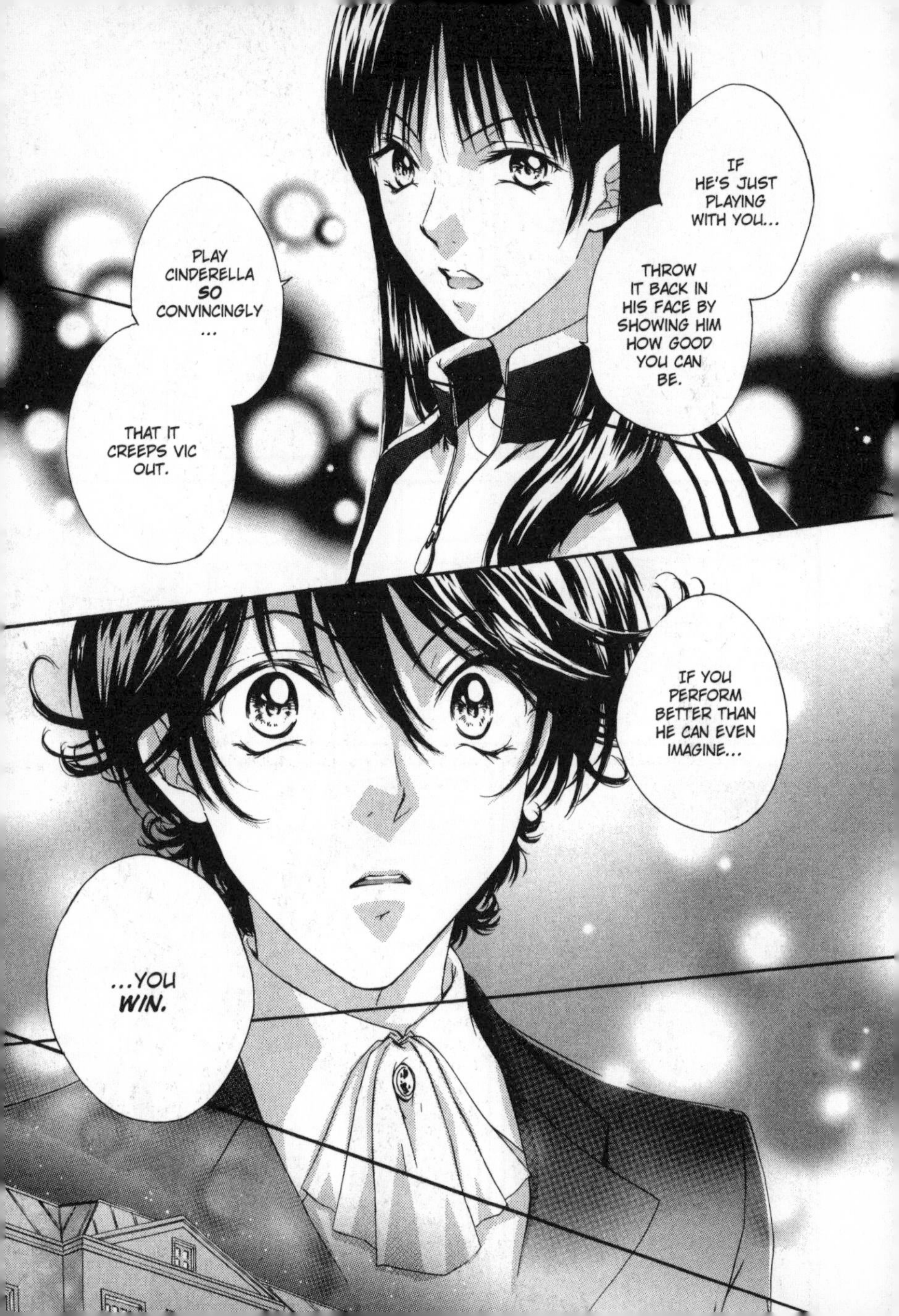
IF HE'S JUST PLAYING WITH YOU...
THROW IT BACK IN HIS FACE BY SHOWING HIM HOW GOOD YOU CAN BE.
PLAY CINDERELLA **SO** CONVINCINGLY ...
THAT IT CREEPS VIC OUT.
IF YOU PERFORM BETTER THAN HE CAN EVEN IMAGINE...
...YOU ***WIN.***

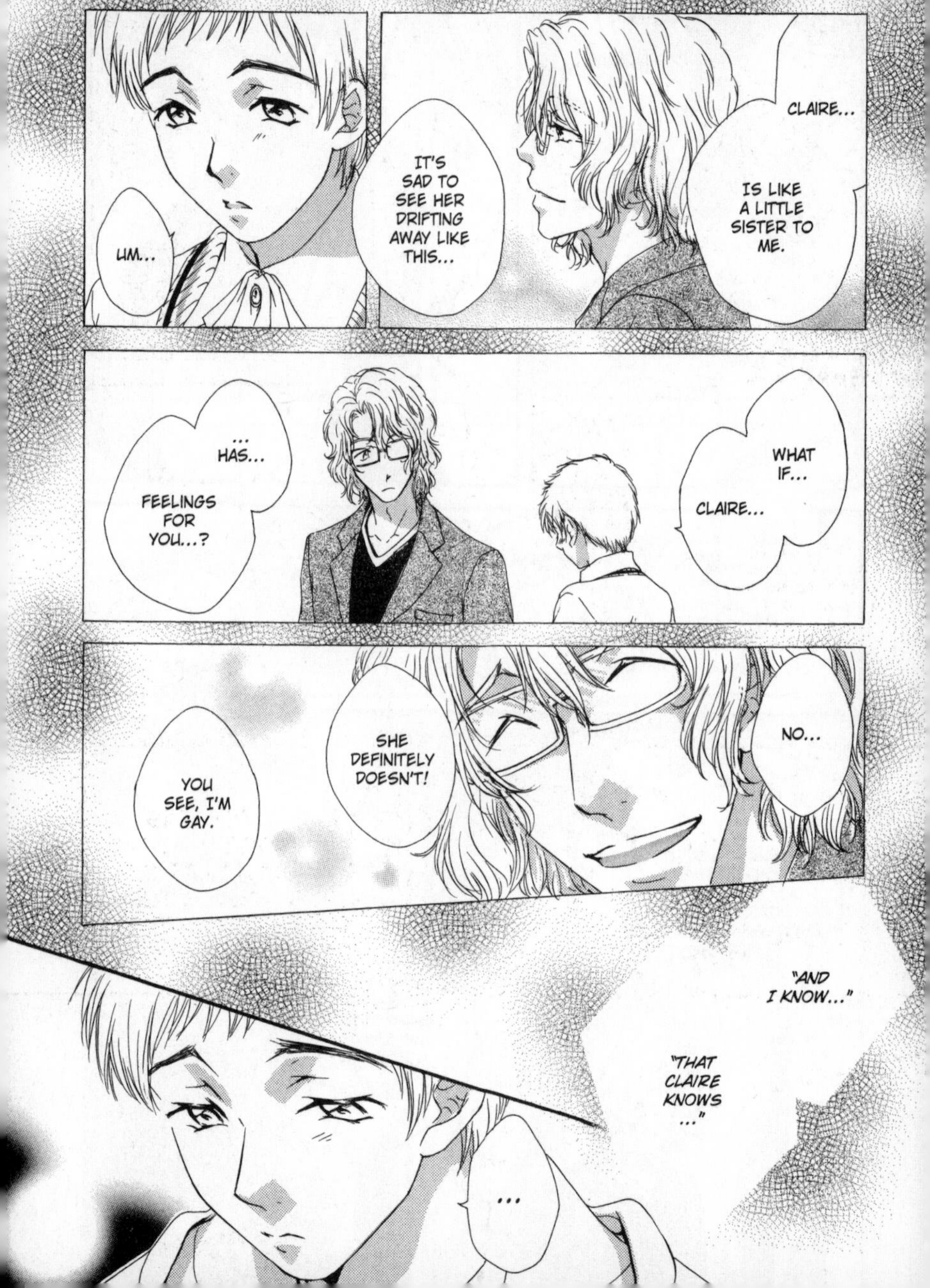
CLAIRE...
IS LIKE A LITTLE SISTER TO ME.
IT'S SAD TO SEE HER DRIFTING AWAY LIKE THIS...
UM...
WHAT IF... CLAIRE...
... HAS... FEELINGS FOR YOU...?
NO...
SHE DEFINITELY DOESN'T!
YOU SEE, I'M GAY.
"AND I KNOW..."
"THAT CLAIRE KNOWS ..."
...

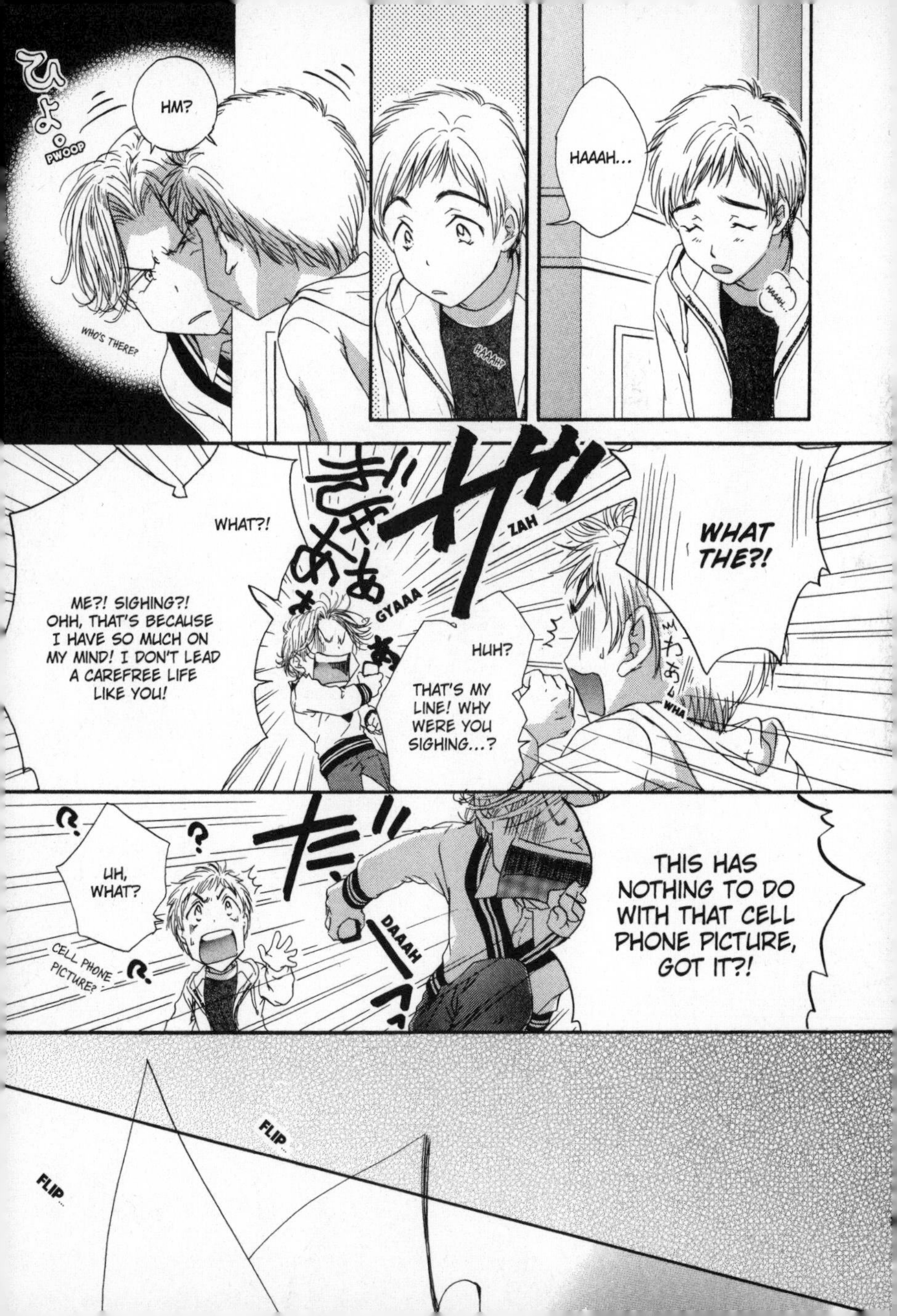
HAAAH...
HAAAH...
HAAAH?
HM?
PWOOP
WHO'S THERE?
WHAT THE?!
WHA
HUH?
THAT'S MY LINE! WHY WERE YOU SIGHING...?
ZAH
GYAAA
WHAT?!
ME?! SIGHING?! OHH, THAT'S BECAUSE I HAVE SO MUCH ON MY MIND! I DON'T LEAD A CAREFREE LIFE LIKE YOU!
THIS HAS NOTHING TO DO WITH THAT CELL PHONE PICTURE, GOT IT?!
DAAAH
UH, WHAT?
CELL PHONE PICTURE?
FLIP...
FLIP...

"I WANT HIM..."
"...TO NOTICE ME..."
"IF YOU PERFORM BETTER THAN HE CAN EVEN IMAGINE..."
FLIP...
"...YOU WIN."

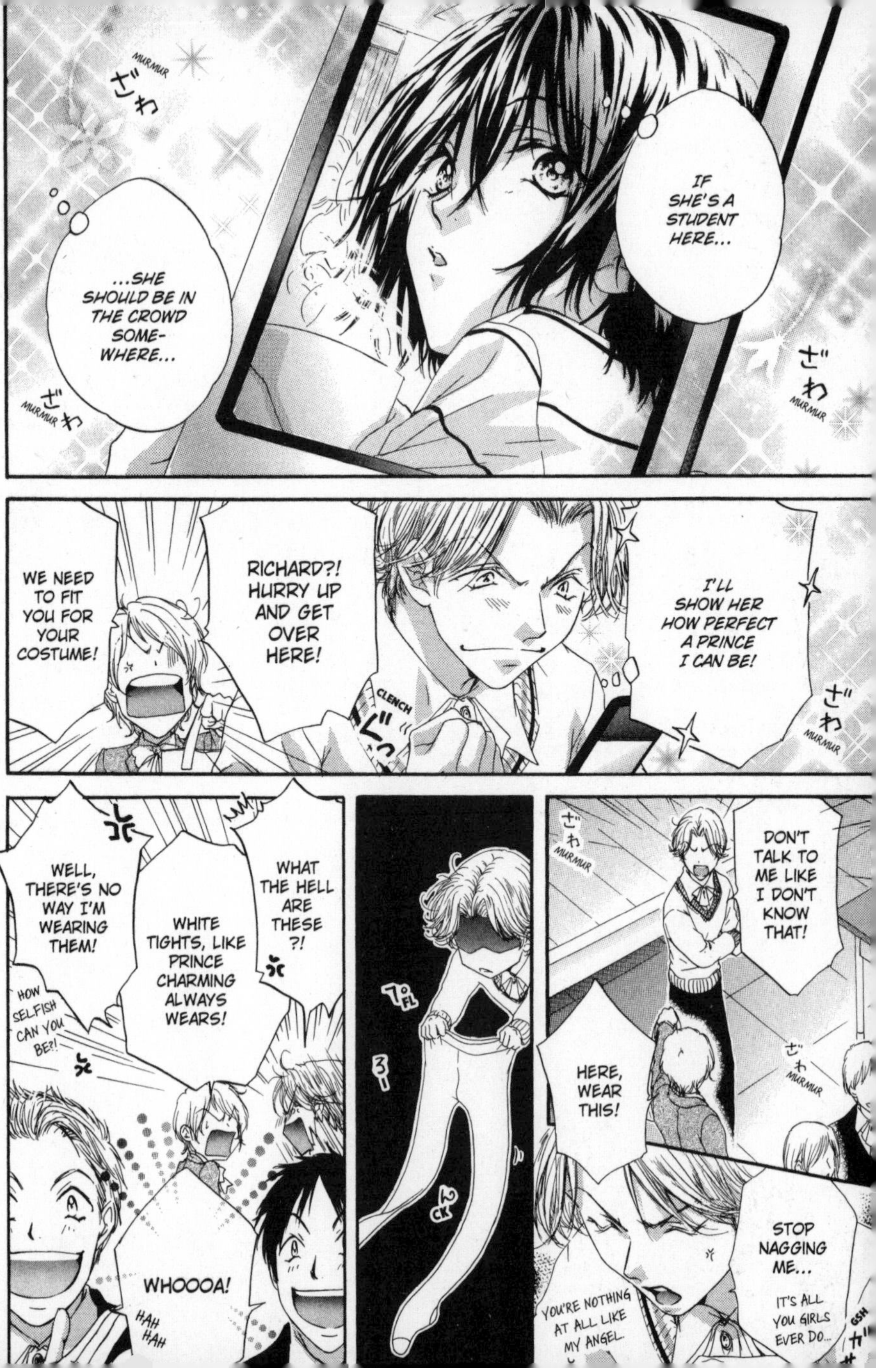
IF SHE'S A STUDENT HERE...
...SHE SHOULD BE IN THE CROWD SOME-WHERE...
ざわ MURMUR
ざわ MURMUR
ざわ MURMUR
I'LL SHOW HER HOW PERFECT A PRINCE I CAN BE!
ざわ MURMUR
CLENCH
RICHARD?! HURRY UP AND GET OVER HERE!
WE NEED TO FIT YOU FOR YOUR COSTUME!
ざわ MURMUR
DON'T TALK TO ME LIKE I DON'T KNOW THAT!
HERE, WEAR THIS!
ざわ MURMUR
STOP NAGGING ME...
IT'S ALL YOU GIRLS EVER DO...
GSH
YOU'RE NOTHING AT ALL LIKE MY ANGEL
FL
CK
WHAT THE HELL ARE THESE?!
WHITE TIGHTS, LIKE PRINCE CHARMING ALWAYS WEARS!
WELL, THERE'S NO WAY I'M WEARING THEM!
HOW SELFISH CAN YOU BE?!
WHOOOA!
HAH HAH

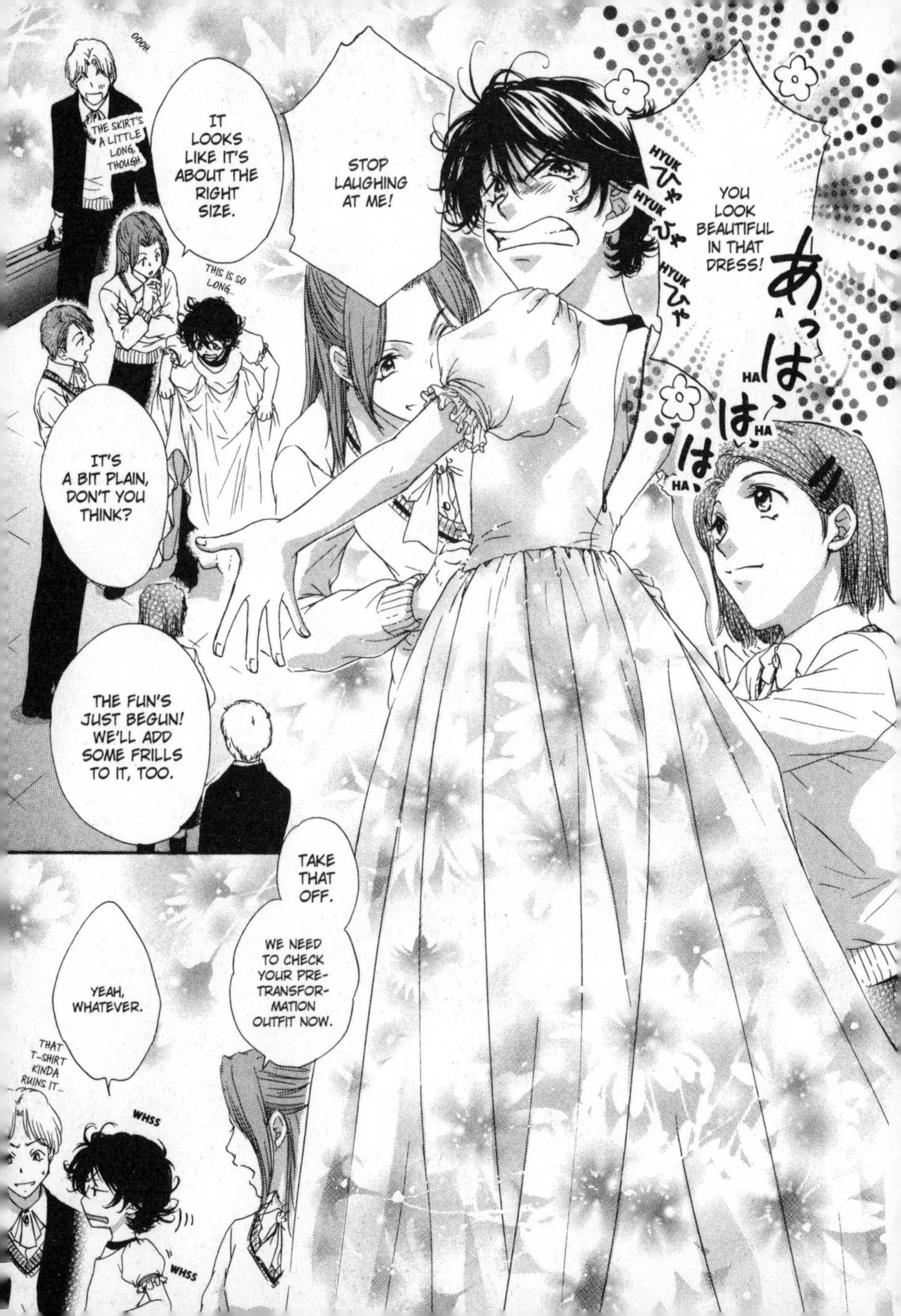
YOU LOOK BEAUTIFUL IN THAT DRESS!
あっははは
A HA HA HA
HYUK ひゃ HYUK ひゃ HYUK ひゃ
STOP LAUGHING AT ME!
IT LOOKS LIKE IT'S ABOUT THE RIGHT SIZE.
OOOH.
THE SKIRT'S A LITTLE LONG, THOUGH.
THIS IS SO LONG...
IT'S A BIT PLAIN, DON'T YOU THINK?
THE FUN'S JUST BEGUN! WE'LL ADD SOME FRILLS TO IT, TOO.
TAKE THAT OFF.
WE NEED TO CHECK YOUR PRE-TRANSFORMATION OUTFIT NOW.
YEAH, WHATEVER.
THAT T-SHIRT KINDA RUINS IT...
WHSS
WHSS

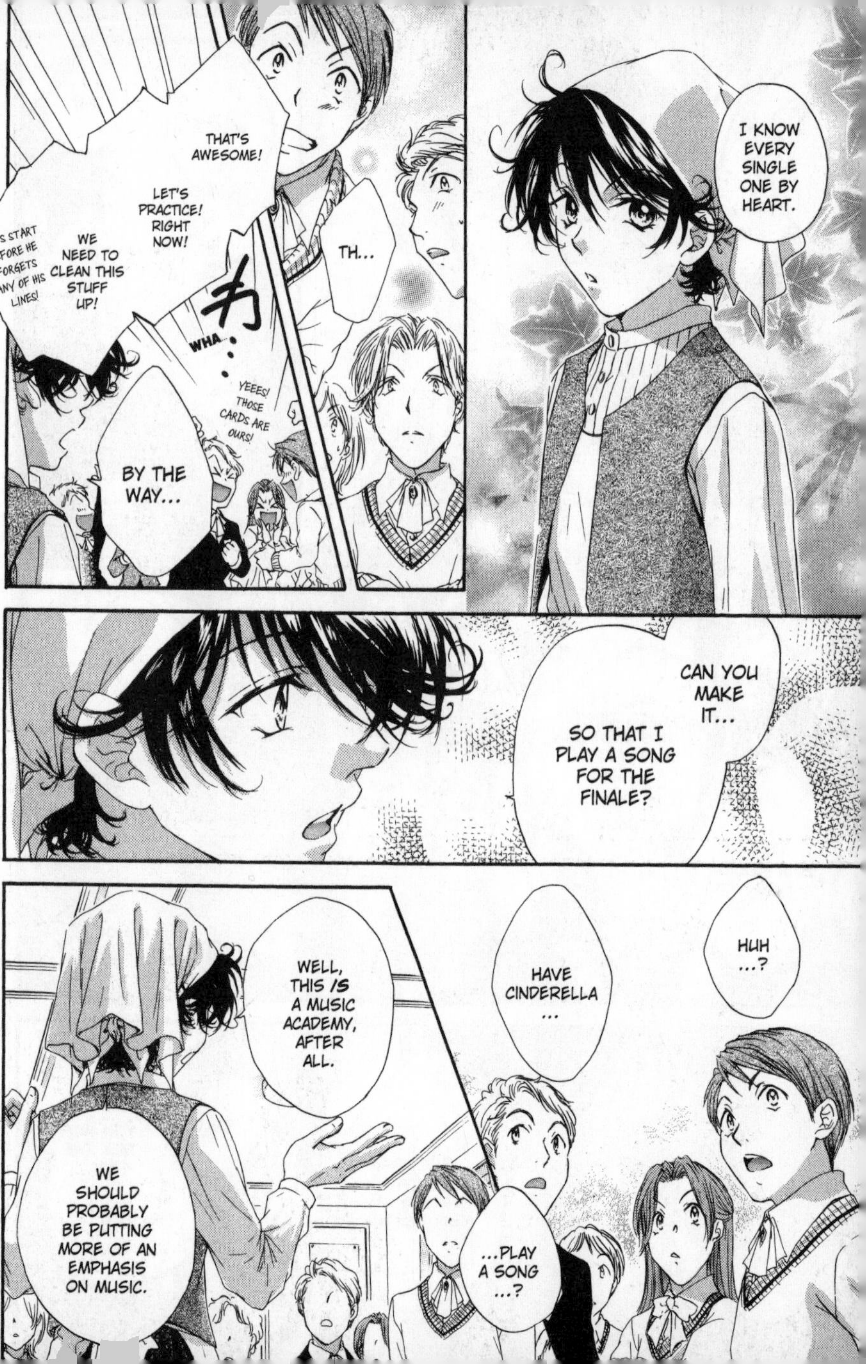
I KNOW EVERY SINGLE ONE BY HEART.
TH...
THAT'S AWESOME!
LET'S PRACTICE! RIGHT NOW!
WE NEED TO CLEAN THIS STUFF UP!
LET'S START BEFORE HE FORGETS ANY OF HIS LINES!
WHA...
YEEES! THOSE CARDS ARE OURS!
BY THE WAY...
CAN YOU MAKE IT...
SO THAT I PLAY A SONG FOR THE FINALE?
HUH ...?
HAVE CINDERELLA ...
...PLAY A SONG ...?
WELL, THIS *IS* A MUSIC ACADEMY, AFTER ALL.
WE SHOULD PROBABLY BE PUTTING MORE OF AN EMPHASIS ON MUSIC.

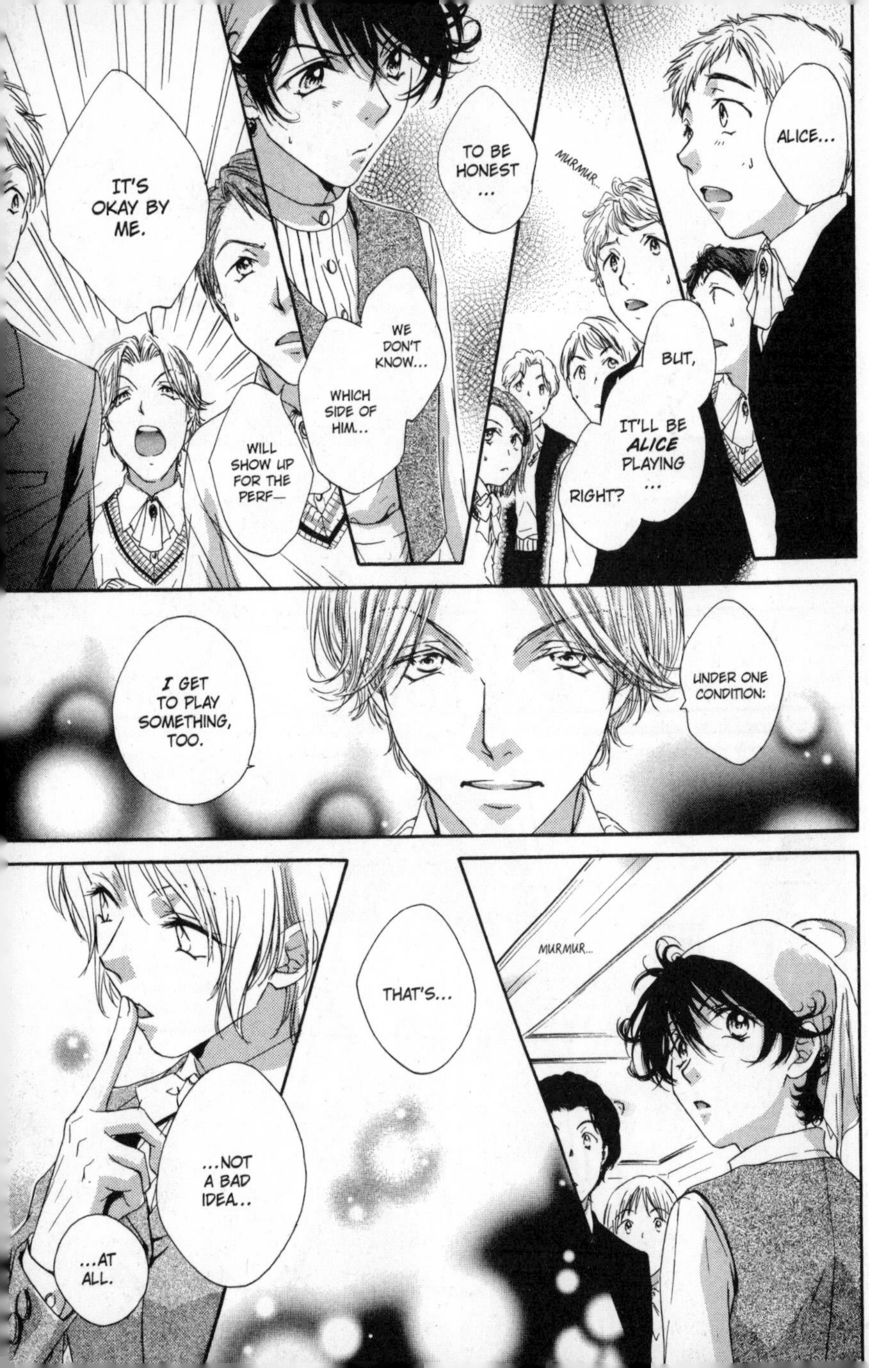
ALICE...
MURMUR...
BUT,
IT'LL BE ALICE PLAYING ...
RIGHT?
TO BE HONEST ...
WE DON'T KNOW...
WHICH SIDE OF HIM...
WILL SHOW UP FOR THE PERF—
IT'S OKAY BY ME.
UNDER ONE CONDITION:
I GET TO PLAY SOMETHING, TOO.
MURMUR...
THAT'S...
...NOT A BAD IDEA...
...AT ALL.

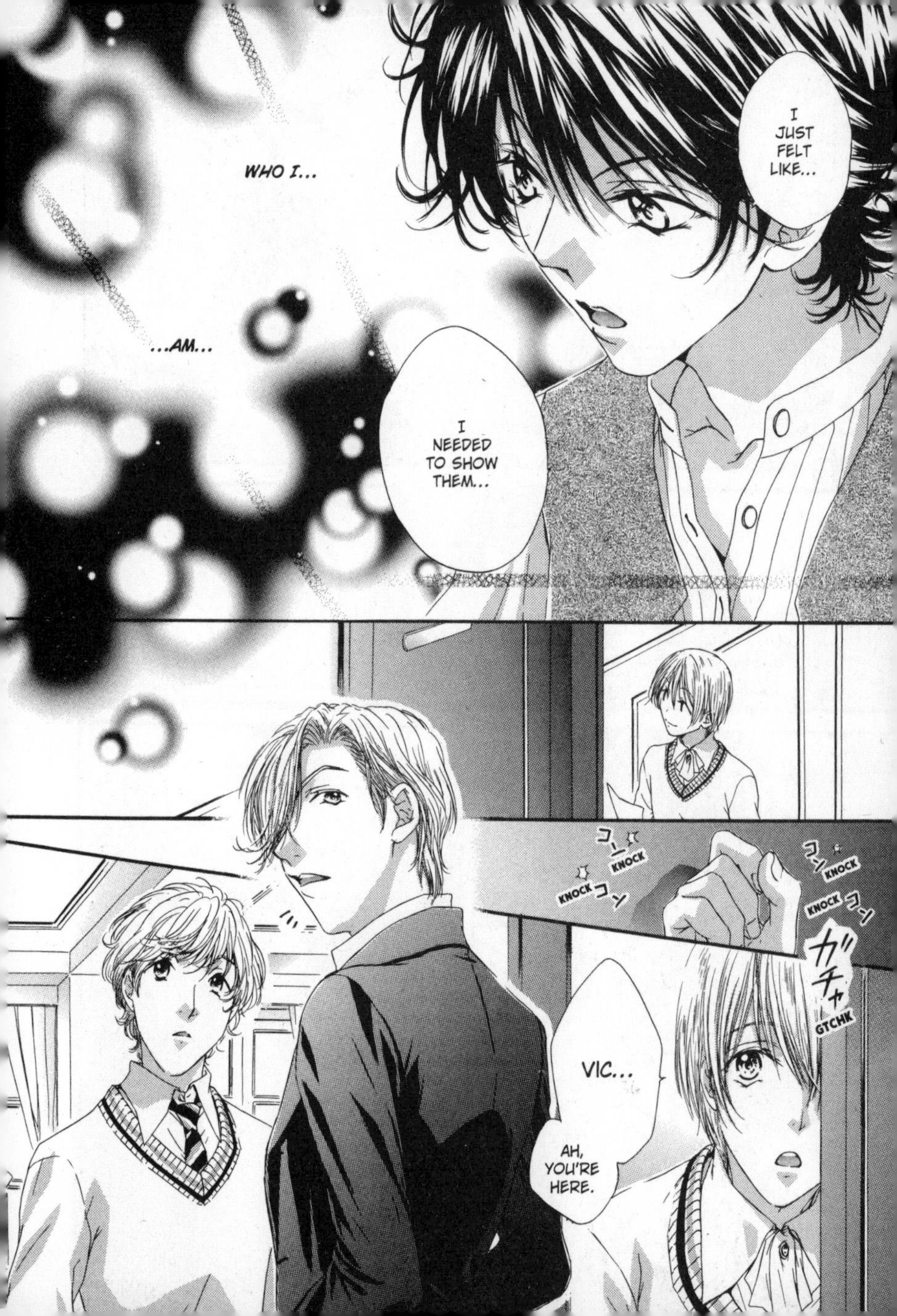
I JUST FELT LIKE...
I NEEDED TO SHOW THEM...
WHO I...
...AM...
KNOCK
KNOCK
KNOCK
KNOCK
ガチャ
GTCHK
VIC...
AH, YOU'RE HERE.